# The Sixth Market

## THE ELECTRONIC INVESTOR REVOLUTION

HOWARD ABELL | ROBERT KOPPEL | KEN JOHNSON

**DEARBORN**™
**TRADE**
A **Kaplan Professional** Company

This publication is designed to provide accurate and authoritative information in regard to the subject matter covered. It is sold with the understanding that the publisher is not engaged in rendering legal, accounting, or other professional service. If legal advice or other expert assistance is required, the services of a competent professional should be sought.

Associate Publisher: Cynthia A. Zigmund
Managing Editor: Jack Kiburz
Project Editor: Trey Thoelcke
Interior Design: Lucy Jenkins
Cover Design: Rattray Design
Typesetting: the dotted i

© 2000 by Howard Abell, Robert Koppel, and Ken Johnson

Published by Dearborn Trade
A Kaplan Professional Company

All rights reserved. The text of this publication, or any part thereof, may not be reproduced in any manner whatsoever without written permission from the publisher.

Printed in the United States of America

00 01 02 10 9 8 7 6 5 4 3 2 1

**Library of Congress Cataloging-in-Publication Data**

Abell, Howard.
    The sixth market : the electronic investor revolution / Howard Abell, Robert Koppel, Ken Johnson.
        p.      cm.
    Includes index.
    ISBN 0-7931-3913-9
    1. Electronic trading of securities.   2. Investments—Computer network resources.   I. Koppel, Robert.   II. Johnson, Ken, 1946–   III. Title.
HG4515.95 .A233 2000
332.64'0285'4678—dc21
                                                                    00-010808

Dearborn books are available at special quantity discounts to use as premiums and sales promotions, or for use in corporate training programs. For more information, please call the Special Sales Manager at 800-621-9621, ext. 4514, or write to Dearborn Financial Publishing, Inc., 155 N. Wacker Drive, Chicago, IL 60606-1719.

## Dedication

The securities markets have been forever dramatically changed. Millions of individual traders have abandoned the use of brokers, traders, banks, and other intermediaries to take control of their investments through the use of the Internet. The number of these investors will increase by many millions the next few years.

There's only one problem: most of these self-directed traders are not making consistent profits in the market. This book is written to give *you* a clear, comprehensive, and easy-to-use approach to prospering in the markets.

*The Sixth Market* is dedicated to all who have the courage and knowledge to pursue their visions of free enterprise and the promise of profits the Sixth Market can bring.

# Contents

*Acknowledgments* vii
*Foreword* ix
*Why You Need This Book* Now xiii

**PART I   Here Comes the Sixth Market**
1. A Brief and Clever History of the Securities Markets  3
2. It's a Miracle! Look What Had to Happen to Create the Sixth Market  15
3. Where Is All of This Change Heading?  25

**PART II   Getting Ready to Jump into the Sixth Market**
4. The Prepared Trader  35
5. I Just Spent a Fortune, and All My Stuff Is Obsolete  39
6. Is One Broker Better than Another?  47

**PART III   Winning in the Sixth Market through Education**
7. Aw, Mom. Do I Really Have to Go to School Today?  71
8. OK, I'm Ready to Learn. Now What?  75

**PART IV   The Six Steps™**
9. Step One: Building Self-Awareness  83
10. Step Two: Learning Market Fundamentals  105
11. More Step Two: Nasdaq Level II  125
12. Step Three: Understanding Price Movements and Charting  137
13. Step Four: Using Reliable Chart Setups  159
14. More Step Four: This Education Is Fine, but I Really Want the Answer  179
15. Step Five: Mastering Your Trading Plan  183
16. Step Six: I Don't Have the Willpower to Be Disciplined  193

*Recommended Reading* 199
*Glossary* 201
*Index* 215
*About the Authors* 223

# Acknowledgments

The authors would like to acknowledge their families for being patient, understanding, and supportive during the writing of this book. We would also like to thank Rick Engel, the cofounder of SixthMarket.com, for his inestimable contribution in offering editorial comments, all of which were taken. Rick's commitment to the development of the very best tools, processes, and infrastructure available to the self-directed investor has made the Sixth Market a reality from which all suitable investors can profit. Finally, thanks are due, as always, to Cindy Zigmund and the entire Dearborn staff for their excellent assistance.

# Foreword

Everything in life works it's way towards greater and greater efficiency. It has been observed that, in the whole history of the human race, not once have we ever opted for "slower." Nowhere is this more evident than when looking at the wholesale changes in the stock markets over the last four years.

My firm, TradeCast, was started back in 1995 with the idea that there must be a faster, more efficient way to trade stocks—and we were right.

TradeCast has been a true pioneer in electronic trading. For example, we were the first Windows-based system to directly access the markets. We have been a driving force for the elimination of the broker from the execution of stock orders simply because computers can do the job faster, with fewer mistakes, at a lower cost. Our Direct Access model changed the markets permanently, making faster, more equal market access possible. Now this model has been adopted and legitimized by some of the largest brokerages, including Schwab and Goldman Sachs.

Beyond Direct Access, we also pioneered powerful new trading tools to help the emerging electronic trader make better decisions, get better executions, and hopefully make more money.

With pride, we acknowledge the observation that it was the work of firms like TradeCast, and others, that made electronic trading possible.

During this same time, the active day trader was another important catalyst for change, demanding faster quotes, more information and equal treatment under the regulations. The result was more and better service vendors, the rise of the ECNs, and the SEC-mandated order handling rules. With these powerful new resources, the day trader has proven to be the equal of any trader anywhere. The day trader has shown us that the self-directed investor can learn the skills and the discipline to earn consistent profits from the markets.

So where are we today? I believe we are still at the dawn of the Sixth Market. The full potential of the electronic trading of securities by the self-directed investor has only been glimpsed.

We are no longer fighting for equal market access or for the legitimacy of the individual trader. We are now fighting to extend the markets to more and more people. This next generation of successful traders will come from a whole new group of smart people: doctors, lawyers, dentists, retired people, housewives, etc. Many are already trading online but have not used the next generation of tools. Few have the skills needed to compete and to prosper in the markets.

Clearly, the key to trading success in the future will be in training and education.

That is why I am so delighted to be writing this foreword to *The Sixth Market: The Electronic Trading Revolution.*

This book is written by three close and trusted associates:

- **Ken Johnson** is a true pioneer of the electronic trading world. One of the earliest day traders, Ken embraced the movement from verbal to electronic trading; in fact, the brokerage firm he founded was TradeCast's first licensee. He began training professional traders in 1996 and has developed a well-earned reputation as an innovative and effective educator.
- **Howard Abell** has been a successful trader of equities, futures and options for more than 30 years. He is the author of: *Digital Day Trading, The Day Trader's Advantage, Risk Reward, The Market Savvy Investor,* and *The Electronic Trading of Options.*
- **Bob Koppel** is the author of five books on the psychology of trading: *The Innergame of Trading; The Outer Game of Trading; Bulls, Bears, and Millionaires; The Intuitive Trader;* and *The Tao of Trading.* He writes on investment for Onmoney.com.

The strength of this book is in its direct approach: to how we got here, to where we are going, and most importantly to what you can do to find success in the Sixth Market.

The victors in the Sixth Market will be those that are the best prepared. This book is a must for anyone who seeks that preparation.

Bobby Earthman

Cofounder and President
TradeCast Ltd.

# Why You Need This Book *Now*

*"Money isn't everything . . . but it ranks right up there with oxygen."*

RITA DAVENPORT

The Sixth Market is the electronic trading of securities by the self-directed individual. In other words, the Sixth Market is *you,* and you are changing the securities markets more profoundly than any force before you.

The emergence of the self-directed, electronic trader brings with it an overwhelming need for training. Despite their enthusiasm, most people entering the markets today simply do not have the skills and experience to trade effectively. Put another way, if they don't learn to trade, they are broke!

The authors have been involved in trading, and training, for years. We often have wondered why so many of the "educational experts" have insisted on making learning to trade so hard. Learning to trade does not have to be difficult, or intimidating, or complicated, or boring.

As authors, we have taken a different approach—we make learning fun. We also keep everything simple and cover only the things you need to know to start making money *right now.*

In Part One, we explore the origins and the ongoing metamorphosis of securities trading. *To know where you're going, you first must know where you've been.* The first five markets are entertainingly explained.

The most unlikely story of all is the one about the Sixth Market; how the following collection of events came together to make modern individual trading possible:

- The increasing availability of information
- The changing of key regulations
- The availability of abundant, cheap bandwidth
- The irrelevance of the traditional stockbroker
- The emergence of a new kind of trader

The story of the Sixth Market is really only beginning, because even more change is coming. We get you ready for the future by examining:

- *ECNs,* and their impact on liquidity, executions, and existing exchanges
- *NASD,* and how regulation will shape trading
- *Technology,* and the move toward more automated trading
- *Training,* and how education will be your source of competitive advantage

Part Two describes what you need to do to be prepared to trade in the markets. Training yourself to know the technology, markets, personalities, and legalities of trading will strengthen your chances of success.

How do you keep up with technology when it changes so fast? Trading drives technology, and technology drives trading; it is an endless chase. The authors bring much-needed clarity to these issues, and suggest practical and affordable ways for you to stay technologically competitive.

How do you choose the right broker? It's not a matter of which broker has the funniest ad; this is serious stuff. We give you specific guidelines for choosing the broker with the resources to help you gain an edge in the markets.

In Part Three, we face the heart of the matter: profiting in the Sixth Market.

For years, the brokerage industry encouraged the myth that trading was hard, that it was complicated, that it was beyond the abilities of mere mortal people. The good news for you is that you can do it. Trading is a skill that can be learned, and the concepts for success are easy to understand.

In the past, learning to trade successfully meant you had to learn about trading psychology from one authority, technical analysis from another expert, and money management from still a third. In *The Sixth Market,* we offer the first comprehensive approach to learning how to trade, which we call The Six Steps™. We teach trading as a *process,* training you to integrate a set of specific skills to produce the results you want from the market.

In Part Four, we teach you a specific trading strategy, one that is appropriate for the absolute beginner or the seasoned professional. This strategy can be easily learned and mastered, even if you have no experience in the markets. Yet it is so powerful that it is used by some of the best professional traders in the country.

Following Part Four is a glossary. Whenever you are uncertain, use the glossary to be sure you understand these instructions and explanations.

Once you have learned *how* to trade, you must learn *what* to trade each day.

How can you have a 9-to-5 job, raise kids, and watch almost 10,000 symbols each night to find the right opportunities for each trading day? We show you how to choose, and how to use, Digital Discipline ™ to help you spot good opportunities each day, and to maximize your effectiveness in the market. While lack of discipline has probably been at the root of more trading losses than any other single cause, we believe that personal discipline is not a matter of willpower. Instead, we show you the secret to making discipline the easiest part of your trading equation.

With a commitment to education, and discipline to a proven trading plan, your potential for market success is real!

Success in Trading!

# PART I

# Here Comes the Sixth Market

CHAPTER 1

# A Brief and Clever History of the Securities Markets

*"Progress might have been all right once . . . but it has gone on too long."*

OGDEN NASH

*Imagine what it must feel like to be a 60-year-old stockbroker today. How can you possibly digest and cope with the changes that have taken place in your business and in your life?*

*The securities markets have been dramatically changed forever. Millions of individual traders have taken control of their investments through the use of the unprecedented power of the Internet, and that number will increase by many millions more in the next few years.*

*These are the electronic, self-directed investors . . . and they don't need you any more. Not even Ogden Nash can save you now . . .*

    **C**hange is the only constant in our lives. Nowhere has change been more tumultuous than in the securities markets over the past six years. Much of that change has been driven by the emergence of a new kind of investor, the individual who is determined to take control of his financial future—the electronic, self-directed investor.

The phenomenon surrounding this new kind of investor has been called by many names: online investing, electronic trading, day trading, SOES trading, and plain, old gambling, just to name a few. More often than not, these epithets have been meant to be less than flattering.

The old-line brokerage firms, market making firms, mutual fund managers, financial advisors, business press, and a wide range of regulators, have all had their say about this explosion of electronic traders, and what they say has largely been negative.

But the deprecations, and the deprecators, totally miss the point.

The self-directed electronic investor is here to stay. This genie is out of the bottle and there is no way to get it back inside. Millions of people have felt the power of the Internet, and have tasted the exhilaration of being in control of their investments.

Some have lost money in their trading experiments, but many more are learning that successful trading is neither difficult to learn nor impossible to achieve. Even without prior skill or training in how to trade, many individuals intuitively sense what market professionals already know: trading is a skill that can be learned.

Figure 1.1 shows the steps to building a base of trading knowledge that will put you on the trading success cycle: knowledge breeds confidence; confidence breeds focus; focus breeds discipline; discipline produces great results; and, great results breed more confidence . . . and on and on.

This market force—the force of self-directed, electronic trading—is becoming more powerful in the markets each day, with the promise of becoming perhaps the most powerful market force in the history of securities trading.

Like the five great market forces which preceded this one, the emergence of the electronic, self-directed investor deserves to be called by a name that recognizes its uniqueness, appreciates its importance, and which respects its power to shape the future.

Because this is the sixth great market force, we propose to call it: the Sixth Market—the electronic trading of securities by the self-directed individual.

Think about it . . . the Sixth Market is *you!*

At this point, you are asking a great question: If this is going to be called the Sixth Market, what are the other five markets?

Let's begin at the beginning. On May 17, 1792, twenty-four stock brokers signed the *Buttonwood Agreement* to trade with one another beneath that famous tree, at what is now 68 Wall Street.

**FIGURE 1.1** The Trading Success Cycle

Knowledge → Confidence → Focus → Discipline → Great Results → (Confidence)

From that very humble beginning has grown an almost unimaginable financial powerhouse that has long been the envy of the world, and that is becoming more global each day. The trillions and trillions of dollars that have flowed through our securities markets . . . have financed world wars, built cities, launched awe-inspiring public works, and given rise to great business empires. And, countless millions of individuals have enjoyed the growth of their financial assets.

How did this all happen? From a loose collection of brokers under a single tree grew an amazingly productive, yet complicated, financial world. There are equity markets, bond markets, option markets, commodity markets, currency markets, and on and on.

Each market is driven by its own unique specialists, working in highly specialized firms, who effect the trading of a specialized group of securities, following specialized rules and customs, and even speaking their own specialized business language. It is this very ability to specialize that makes this growth all possible, and within the equity markets, it is specialization that has been at the root of the creation of the first five markets.

## THE PRIMARY MARKET

In the beginning was the Primary Market. Securities trading starts when an issuer decides to sell its security to the public market. This is called the initial public offering, or IPO. This initial offering, the sale of a security from issuer to public buyer, is done in the Primary Market. The Primary Market is the first great market force; without it, there would be no securities trading.

The Primary Market is so different from all other securities trading that it is easy to see why it is considered a separate market. Bringing a security issue to the public market involves a world of complicated legal work, meticulous regulatory filings, sensitive syndicate negotiations, considerable selling effort, and the exhausting and frightening task of underwriting and pricing the issue. All of these activities continue right up to the moment of the first sale. These tasks only occur in the Primary Market.

For the Primary Market specialists, it's on to the next IPO.

## THE SECONDARY MARKET

After that first sale, the security is now owned by the "public," and subsequent trades of that particular security will occur in the Secondary Market, which is where securities are traded from public seller to public buyer.

The Secondary Market is what most people think of as "the stock market." This is also a specialized and unique market, with its own set of specialized experts. The Secondary Market is the world of stock exchanges, brokers, specialists, market makers, price quotes, new highs, new lows, earnings announcements, analyst pronouncements, CNBC and CNNFN telecasts, institutional investors, and individual investors. This is where the action is!

Today we regularly see *billion* share days in the Secondary Market. The NYSE set a record with 1,349,711 shares traded on December 17, 1999; a record that is sure to be broken soon. We take this incredible ability of our markets to facilitate trading for granted, but it was a painful and slow climb to these heights.

Our younger readers cannot imagine a world without the ubiquitous power of the computer, but until very recently much of the transaction processing in the securities markets was done by hand! Take a look at this chart, which shows some NYSE share volume milestones. Between

1982 and 1987, computer-based processing began to make a huge difference in the number of shares that could be handled each day.

| Share Volume | First Day Over |
|---|---|
| 1 million | 1886 |
| 5 million | 1928 |
| 20 million | 1968 |
| 50 million | 1978 |
| 100 million | 1982 |
| 500 million | 1987 |
| 700 million | 1997 |
| 1 billion | 1997 |

Let's look at the Dow Jones Industrial Average, the benchmark for the financial health of our equities markets. It was first published in 1896, and reached the value milestones shown below:

| Price Level | Date |
|---|---|
| 100 | January 12, 1906 |
| 500 | March 12, 1956 |
| 1,000 | November 14, 1972 |
| 1,500 | December 11, 1985 |
| 2,000 | January 8, 1987 |
| 3,000 | April 17, 1991 |
| 4,000 | February 23, 1995 |
| 5,000 | November 21, 1995 |
| 6,000 | October 14, 1996 |
| 7,000 | February 13, 1997 |
| 8,000 | July 16, 1997 |
| 9,000 | April 6, 1998 |
| 10,000 | March 29, 1999 |
| 11,000 | July 16, 1999 |

Isn't it interesting that share volumes and share value both experienced their most explosive increases since the mid-1980s? Is it possible to draw a meaningful correlation between the ability of the exchange to handle larger share volumes and these increased price levels? Does the ability to handle larger volumes bring more capital to the markets, thereby driving prices higher? Does increased liquidity foster more confidence in market participants?

Over the years, the basic Secondary Market became unable to meet the needs of all of its customers. Within the Secondary Market were many groups that had special requirements or goals, and new market forces went to work creating further specialization within the Secondary Market to meet those needs.

New markets emerged from the Secondary Market to serve these customers and to fuel the growth in trading. Each of these market developments has earned the distinction to be termed a unique market because each has evolved its own specialized firms, customers, rules, procedures, and systems. More important, each of these markets offers its customers distinct advantages over the others.

## THE THIRD MARKET

NYSE Rule 390 requires that all exchange-listed shares must be traded on the floor of the exchange by an exchange member. An exception to Rule 390 was granted many years ago to allow for the trading of securities that are listed on a stock exchange (such as the NYSE) to be traded in the over-the-counter market through Third Market firms. Trades in the Third Market are among institutional investors and broker/dealers for their own accounts (not as agents for other buyers and sellers).

The Third Market filled a very specific group of needs for its traders' customers. Traders of large blocks of stock found that news of their trading activity created a very unsettling effect on the market, which cost them money because of exaggerated price swings. The earliest Third Market firms handled these large blocks "off the floor" to minimize these effects.

Soon, these traders realized that trading through Third Market firms was a way to avoid paying the high exchange-regulated commissions on large transactions.

As the Third Market firms developed their abilities further, they built a reputation for often providing faster executions than the floor of the exchange. Time truly became money for these Third Market customers.

## THE FOURTH MARKET

The evolution of the Fourth Market was inevitable. It is the direct trading of large blocks of Nasdaq securities between institutional investors.

The institutional investment community realized that they did not need many of the services of the traditional brokerage houses, and they certainly did not need to pay the high brokerage commissions for their trades.

The Third Market firms were providing anonymity for exchange-based trades and these institutions needed a way to preserve their anonymity in Nasdaq trades as well. Imagine the effect on the market if it was known that a major trader such as Peter Lynch or Warren Buffet was selling a particular stock.

To fill these needs, a new market—soon called the Fourth Market—arose. It was pioneered in 1969 by a firm named Instinet. Instinet offered a computerized service for Nasdaq trades that displayed subscriber's bid and ask quotes, executed matches, and ensured anonymity in the transaction.

The Fourth Market has grown to become an important segment of the Nasdaq market; published estimates indicate that Instinet executes in excess of 25 percent of the entire Nasdaq share volume.

Let's get to the heart of the matter: the Third Market and the Fourth Market transformed the markets for the institutions. They gave the institutions lower transaction costs and the ability to remain anonymous as they carried out large market transactions. The result was what every trader dreams of—better returns.

This was the start of a powerful cycle. Better returns attracted more capital to the institutional players, which fed more liquidity into the markets, which supported and enhanced share prices, which increased the wealth of our nation, which created more funds to invest, which fed back into the institutions. The cycle has repeated endlessly for years.

Although most Americans have not even heard of the Third Market or the Fourth Market, they have had an important role in the creation of much of America's enduring wealth.

## THE FIFTH MARKET

The Fifth Market is the first to bring important market changes for the benefit of the individual investor. The Fifth Market is a much more recent development, with the arrival of the first Electronic Communication Network (ECN) in 1996.

An ECN is defined by the NASD to be "any electronic system that widely disseminates to third parties orders entered . . . and permits such orders to be executed against in whole or in part."

The ECNs arose to provide their customers better liquidity and better price execution for Nasdaq stocks. In effect, they were offering the active individual trader many of the same advantages that the Third Market and Fourth Market brought to the institutional trader.

## 10  THE SIXTH MARKET

The need for the Fifth Market was a direct result of NASD rules changes to SOES (the Small Order Execution System). SOES was created in 1984 to automatically execute small orders in Nasdaq stocks against the best available quotations.

After the crash in October 1987, when the small investor was unable to exit his plummeting shares at any price, the regulators strengthened the requirements for market makers in SOES. The intention was for the market makers to be a ready supply of liquidity for the market at all times.

Several years later, Harvey Houtkin and a small group of enterprising traders realized the execution advantages of trading against SOES market makers who were slow in adjusting their prices, and the "SOES bandits" were born. Executions against SOES grew rapidly.

By 1995, market makers on SOES were required to fill two orders for 1,000 shares each at their posted price. A typical level II screen in 1995 for Microsoft (MSFT) might have looked like the one in Figure 1.2.

**FIGURE 1.2**  1995 Level II Screen

MarketMakers: MICROSOFT CORP

| MSFT | | 120 1/2 | | +1/2 | down | |
|------|---|---------|---|------|------|---|
| Hi   | 121 3/4 | | Lo | 119 3/4 | Vl | 2356000 |

| ID | Bid | Size | ID | Ask | Size |
|------|--------|----|------|--------|----|
| GSCO | 120 3/8 | 10 | ABSB | 120 1/2 | 10 |
| MSCO | 120 3/8 | 10 | LEHM | 120 1/2 | 10 |
| FBCO | 120 3/8 | 10 | SALB | 120 1/2 | 10 |
| DMGL | 120 3/8 | 10 | DLJP | 120 1/2 | 10 |
| CANT | 120 3/8 | 10 | MONT | 120 1/2 | 10 |
| RPSC | 120 3/8 | 10 | COWN | 120 1/2 | 10 |
| RSSF | 120 3/8 | 10 | PWJC | 120 1/2 | 10 |
| PRUS | 120 1/4 | 10 | TSCO | 120 1/2 | 10 |
| OLDE | 120 1/4 | 10 | DEAN | 120 1/2 | 10 |
| WEED | 120 1/4 | 10 | NITE | 120 5/8 | 10 |
| MASH | 120 1/8 | 10 | SBSH | 120 5/8 | 10 |

If you have not worked with level II screens before, they contain a considerable amount of valuable information.

This is a screen for Microsoft (MSFT) that shows the "inside market," which is the best bid (120⅜) and the best offer (120½). These are the best prices available in the market at this instant.

The size column shows "10," which is shorthand for 1,000 shares. (Remember that the market maker had to take two hits at 1,000 shares each. So, you can see that these prices are well supported by seven market makers on the bid and by nine on the offer. At 2,000 shares per market maker, there was a considerable amount of liquidity to trade against.

The spread, which is the difference between best bid and best offer is a comfortable ⅛ of a point. The astute trader could, at a glance of the Level II screen, discern *price support* and *spread risk*.

Then, a much debated rule change, the Actual Size Rule, became effective in January 1997 which had significant, practical affects on trading. The major change in this rule was that the market maker only had to honor one 100 share execution at this posted price. This reduction, from 2,000 shares to 100 shares, represented a 95 percent reduction in liquidity. In early 1997, a typical level II screen might have looked like the one in Figure 1.3.

Now, the inside market shows just two market makers' bid at 120⅜ and just one on the ask at 120½.

Worse, the size now shows "1," which is short for 100 shares, and the market maker is now responsible for only one "hit."

Although the spread still looks to be ⅛, the "effective spread" is actually much wider because of the reduced liquidity at the best bid and best offer. A trader can only buy 100 shares at 120½; any other shares the trader wants will cost more, effectively widening the trader's spread.

Traders quickly learned that they could not count on getting orders filled quickly, or at a satisfactory price, through SOES. A better alternative was needed.

Led by the Island and Archipelago ECNs, traders soon were given excellent alternatives to SOES. The ECNs brought fast, electronic matching capabilities to the market, along with a considerable increase in liquidity.

Figure 1.4 shows what a typical level II screen looks like now that the ECNs of the Fifth Market have become active.

The first thing you will see is that the ECNs brought liquidity back to the markets; they are showing substantial size behind their bids and offers. For example:

**FIGURE 1.3** 1997 Level II Screen

| MarketMakers: MICROSOFT CORP | | | | | | |
|---|---|---|---|---|---|---|
| MSFT | 120 1/2 | | +1/2 | down | | |
| Hi | 121 3/4 | Lo | 119 3/4 | VI | 2356000 | |
| ID | Bid | Size | ID | Ask | | Size |
| GSCO | 120 3/8 | 1 | ABSB | 120 1/2 | | 1 |
| MSCO | 120 3/8 | 1 | LEHM | 120 9/16 | | 1 |
| FBCO | 120 5/16 | 1 | SALB | 120 9/16 | | 1 |
| DMGL | 120 5/16 | 1 | DLJP | 120 5/8 | | 1 |
| CANT | 120 1/4 | 1 | MONT | 120 11/16 | | 1 |
| RPSC | 120 3/16 | 1 | NITE | 120 11/16 | | 1 |
| RSSF | 120 3/16 | 1 | PWJC | 120 11/16 | | 1 |
| PRUS | 120 1/8 | 1 | TSCO | 120 3/4 | | 1 |
| OLDE | 120 1/8 | 1 | DEAN | 120 3/4 | | 1 |
| WEED | 120 1/8 | 1 | HRZG | 120 13/16 | | 1 |
| MASH | 120 | 1 | SBSH | 120 13/16 | | 1 |

- ISLD is bidding 800 shares and INCA is bidding 2,500 shares at 120⅜.
- BTRD is offering 11,000 shares at 120½.
- REDI and ISLD are offering a total of 6,500 shares at 120⁹⁄₁₆.

There is real depth to this market.

Where did this liquidity come from? It came from the broad universe of traders themselves, who were now able to display their bids and offers through the ECNs.

Both this market and this liquidity were there all along. But, until the ECNs came along, it was hidden from view, and only the market makers could really see the depth of the market. That gave them considerable advantage against the individual trader.

The ECNs brought the real market—with its liquidity and price—out into the open for all traders to see. Clearly, the ECNs had provided

**FIGURE 1.4** ECN Level II Screen

| MarketMakers: MICROSOFT CORP | | | | | |
|---|---|---|---|---|---|
| MSFT | 120 1/2 | | + 1/2 | down | |
| Hi | 121 3/4 | Lo | 119 3/4 | Vl | 2356000 |

| ID | Bid | Size | ID | Ask | Size |
|---|---|---|---|---|---|
| ISLD | 120 3/8 | 8 | BTRD | 120 1/2 | 110 |
| INCA | 120 3/8 | 25 | REDI | 120 9/16 | 40 |
| GSCO | 120 5/16 | 3 | ISLD | 120 9/16 | 25 |
| NITE | 120 5/16 | 5 | INCA | 120 5/8 | 13 |
| ARCA | 120 1/4 | 10 | MONT | 120 11/16 | 2 |
| ATTN | 120 3/16 | 15 | COWN | 120 11/16 | 1 |
| LEHM | 120 3/16 | 1 | PWJC | 120 11/16 | 4 |
| PRUS | 120 1/8 | 1 | TSCO | 120 3/4 | 1 |
| DEAN | 120 1/8 | 1 | DEAN | 120 3/4 | 1 |
| WEED | 120 1/8 | 1 | HRZG | 120 13/16 | 1 |
| MASH | 120 | 1 | SBSH | 120 13/16 | 1 |

their customers with pricing and liquidity that was an improvement on the traditional market.

As of April 2000, there are ten ECNs: Island, Instinet, Archipelago, B-Trade, Strike, Redi, Brut, Next, Attain, and Market XT.

Although active day traders were the original customers for the ECNs, a large and increasing number of online traders, using Level II capabilities, have embraced the Fifth Market as well.

Until now, the big advantage of the ECNs was largely confined to the Nasdaq. Recently, the NYSE has voted to repeal Rule 390. Pending approval by the Securities and Exchange Commission, this decision would allow NYSE member firms to trade NYSE-listed stocks away from an exchange, an unprecedented event. With the elimination of Rule 390, all NYSE-listed stocks could be traded through the ECNs in the Fifth Market as early as the second quarter of 2000.

The addition of NYSE shares is another important victory for the Fifth Market and for those traders' customers, the millions of traders in the Sixth Market.

Now, let's take a look at how the Sixth Market came into being . . .

CHAPTER 2

# It's a Miracle! Look What Had to Happen to Create the Sixth Market

*"We will either find a way or make one"*

HANNIBAL

*F*or hundreds of years, people all across the globe have invested in all types of securities. Although their individual reasons for investing were countless, the bottom line has always been to make money from their investments.

Great institutions arose that took control of the investing process and they have dominated the securities markets for generations. Information has been controlled by these institutions, and has often been withheld from the investing public. Market access has been controlled by these institutions, with the result that the individual investor lived in a world of high transaction costs and poor price executions. The individual had little or no control over his investment decisions or results. The institutions were king.

Now, this cozy and very profitable institutional world has been turned upside down by the power of the Sixth Market.

The individual has found a better way to invest. He or she now can obtain an almost unlimited array of market information, analysis, and *advice. The individual now can get market executions at the same speed as the most well-connected trading firm. The individual now has the use of electronic trading tools that rival the very best available to the institutional trading establishment. The institutions are no longer in control; their old style of business is threatened. In the Sixth Market, the individual is the new king. Long Live the King!*

Sounds great doesn't it? Well, don't make the mistake of taking any of this progress for granted; a bizarre and unprecedented collection of achievements came together at the right time to make the Sixth Market possible.

Let's look at the definition again: the Sixth Market is the electronic trading of securities by the self-directed individual.

Look at what had to come together to create the electronic trading of securities:

- Powerful processors
- Abundant and affordable bandwidth
- A reliable Internet
- Fast, reliable electronic trading platforms

And then, think about what had to come together to unleash the self-directed individual:

- Almost unlimited information
- New regulations
- A new kind of investor

Think about it—if even one of those things were missing, none of today's trading would be possible. It is an improbable story at best.

## POWERFUL PROCESSORS AND MOORE'S LAW

> *"Any sufficiently advanced technology is indistinguishable from magic."*
> Arthur C. Clarke

To understand the magic of technology—as with so much of the magic of the last 20 years—you must start with Gordon Moore and his startling *law*. In 1965, Gordon Moore, of Intel, was preparing a speech and made a memorable observation. When he started to graph data about the growth in memory chip performance, he realized there was a

## 2 / It's a Miracle! Look What Had to Happen to Create the Sixth Market

striking trend. Each new chip contained roughly twice as much capacity as its predecessor, and each chip was released within 18–24 months of the previous chip. If this trend continued, he reasoned, computing power would rise exponentially over relatively brief periods of time.

Moore's observation, now known as Moore's Law, described a trend that has continued and is still remarkably accurate. It is the basis for many planners' performance forecasts. In 26 years, the number of transistors on a chip has increased more than 3,200 times, from 2,300 on the 4004 in 1971, to 7.5 million on the Pentium® II processor.

This exponential growth in chip functionality is closely tied to the exponential growth in the chip market, which has been approximately doubling every five years. This dramatic climb has fueled the fortunes of several major companies that either make or utilize chips, and has also been a significant factor in the growth in the gross national product of several nations.

Exponential growth is one thing to talk about, it's quite another thing to really understand. For example, do you remember that old trick about starting with a penny on day one, and doubling the amount every day for a month? It seems laughable at first. After 10 days, you only have $5.12. After 20 days, you have still made little progress, only up to $5,242.88. By day 25, with only 6 days to go, you have only just cleared $100,000. Then the wonder of exponential growth kicks in, and by day 31, you have $10,737,418.20.

How does this growth relate to the Sixth Market? Well, what if Moore had been wrong? What if it had taken five years to double capacity instead of 18 months?

If that had happened, we would still be using an Intel 386 processor, the Internet would still be a fantasy, online trading would simply not be possible, and all of those stockbrokers at Merrill could go back to charging $300 and more for a 1,000 share trade. There would be no Sixth Market . . . yet.

But, Moore's Law is still chugging along, and the first requirement for the Sixth Market—powerful processors—is solidly in place.

## ABUNDANT AND AFFORDABLE BANDWIDTH

And then there's bandwidth. The Sixth Market takes lots and lots of bandwidth to move information and give you fast executions. George Gilder postulated his Law of the Telecosm: "The Law of the Telecosm ordains that the total bandwidth of communications systems will triple every year for the next 25 years."

Rich Karlgaard, publisher of *Forbes* magazine, tells us that new advances in fiber optics now make it possible to "zap—in one second—6 trillion bits of information down a fiber strand the width of a human hair."

Not to be out-thought, Bill Gates, in *PC Magazine* on October 11, 1994 said: "We'll have infinite bandwidth in a decade's time."

These are smart guys, so it is not surprising that the growth in bandwidth is proceeding nicely, just as they predicted. But what if they had been wrong?

If we were still tied to a 14.4k modem, dialed over an analog line, the Internet would be functionally useless. Quotes would never be "real time," and all of those stockbrokers at Merrill could go back to big lunches and even bigger bonus checks. There would be no Sixth Market . . . yet.

However, just as processors were getting fast enough to handle increased bandwidth, here it came! Could that have been a coincidence, or do these techno-geeks really know what they're doing?

The second requirement for the Sixth Market has been met.

## RELIABLE INTERNET

Think back just 24 months. Processors were too slow, bandwidth was too narrow, and the Internet was a real hassle of busy signals, lockups, and lost connections. Was it reasonable to expect millions of people to put their hard-earned money at risk by trading securities over the thing? No way!

So what has happened to turn it all around? Faster processors and direct, high-speed, broad bandwidth connections have made a huge difference. But the Internet has gotten more stable and more useful even for the person still using the 28.8k modem and the P-90 processor.

Give credit to the ISPs (Internet service providers). They have mastered many arts: redundancy, recovery, network reliability, and network security. Now they measure downtime in microseconds instead of in hours.

User surveys show a truly remarkable increase in consumer confidence, and it has been well earned. People are no longer afraid to use their credit cards on the Web, and they are no longer afraid to make a stock trade.

## 2 / It's a Miracle! Look What Had to Happen to Create the Sixth Market

If *these* improvements had not been made, there would be no Sixth Market. Period. But they did, and there is. *Yahoo!*

## FAST, RELIABLE ELECTRONIC TRADING PLATFORMS

Now we needed something to present quotes, display charts, spot trading opportunities, send orders to the exchanges electronically, receive confirmation messages, keep track of open trades, account for closed trades, and do it all quickly and without error.

We needed electronic trading platforms. One small problem was that, as recently as 1996, there just weren't any.

This is one of those points where you can thank your lucky stars you were born in a capitalist, free market country. Because a bunch of entrepreneurs got started doing just what they're supposed to do, they created products to fill those needs.

Companies like TradeCAST, CyBer Corporation, and Townsend Analytics were among the first on the scene. Their early "point and click" systems may seem a bit crude by today's standards, but how miraculous they were for those of us who were using them to make trades every day.

In just three or four short years, these software pioneers solved enormously complicated integration and communication problems, while retaining the ability to change direction on a dime as regulations and market conditions dictated. The story of their challenges and triumphs is the subject for another book. Let us simply say that the advanced trading systems available to you today are the work of some remarkably capable and determined people.

The Sixth Market could not exist without these advances.

OK, so Moore's Law and the Law of the Telecosm are right on track, and the Internet and the trading platforms are in place. All this means is that these new emerging traders could trade electronically. They still had to become self-directed, and that was no easy task!

## INFORMATION EVERYWHERE

Consider all of the information that someone might want before making a securities trade (this is a very abbreviated list):

Company information
   Financial information
   Market information
   Industry information
Analyst's reports
News reports and news bulletins
Stock performance information
   Historical data
   Back testing
   Analysis by dozens of different studies
Real-time information
   Level I quotes
   Level II quotes
   Exchange quotes
   Time and sales
   Tickers

Grand companies have been providing this kind of information for years, but only to a selected group of other grand companies in the industry. Now ask yourself, why would any of these companies want to upset this fairly easy—and very profitable—way of doing business? Why would they want to start making this information available to the poor, pitiful public and run the risk of angering their long-standing, good-paying customer base? Why indeed? Well, many of them didn't.

Company information was available, but generally the public received information after the securities industry giants. Analysts reports were proprietary and off-limits except to customers. The public was at a disadvantage to institutional traders. News reports and bulletins were filtered through the brokerage houses or the TV and radio and then to the public. Again, the public was at a disadvantage.

So, a bunch of enterprising analysts quit the old firms to start new firms like "Zacks" and "Fly on the Wall" to cater to the public's insatiable need for company information and analysis. So today dozens of firms provide "real-time" news at sites all over the Internet.

Stock performance analysis was generally in the hands of the large trading firms. Today, firms like *TradeStation* and *TC2000* bring those capabilities to the individual.

Quotes, time of sales data, and tickers were either very expensive or delayed fifteen minutes. The public was again at a disadvantage. Today, instant quotes and related trading data are readily available, often at no charge.

The old line brokerage houses traded on information, so they had every incentive to keep as much of that information to themselves as they could. Proprietary information gave them value. They knew something that you did not know, so you needed them. You couldn't live without them!

Now, all of that has changed because, for every kind of information need, a group of enterprising businesspeople took on the task of getting the information to the public. Without their efforts, and their successes, there would be no Sixth Market.

## NEW REGULATIONS

Securities trading in the United States is overseen by an extensive—and quite effective—collection of regulators. A brief, and not at all comprehensive, description of the regulatory system would be:

- The Securities Exchange Commission (SEC) is the ultimate power. It has been charged to carry out various laws passed by Congress.
- The NASD is an SRO (self regulating organization): that simply means that it creates the regulations that govern securities transactions. These regulations must comply with the laws, and are subject to SEC approval.
- The exchanges (NYSE, Nasdaq, et al) set specific regulations regarding trading on their specific exchanges.
- The State Securities Boards oversee securities trading in their respective states.

Once an individual had one's electronic capabilities in place, and had access to all necessary information, one was still not on a "level playing field" with the professional traders.

Until 1997, the professional trading firms still held very specific trading advantages over the individual. The most important of these was in the area of price disclosure. Market making firms were not required to disclose limit orders that were above the posted best bid or below the posted best offer. In other words, if the best bid on DELL was 48, but a market maker had an order to buy 10,000 shares of DELL at 48⅛, he could reasonably predict that the price for DELL was going up. The individual did not have that information, and consequently was at a disadvantage.

As part of the Actual Size Rule in 1997, these improved prices were required to be exposed to the public. The regulators also took firm action, including more than $100 million in fines and penalties, against a group of the largest market makers, to cure abusive trading practices, including collusion (another word for price fixing) and backing away (quoting a price, but not honoring it). The result of these regulatory actions has been to give the Sixth Market trader the opportunity to have equal access to valuable information.

## A NEW KIND OF INVESTOR

Until the mid-1990s, the active investor/trader community was quite small. The vast majority of Americans who owned stocks relied on a personal broker for advice, recommendations, and trade executions. A conventional belief system had developed that held that investing in stocks was a difficult and complicated process which was best left to the professionals. And there was just no way that any normal person could even think of being a *trader!*

It is truly amazing that, at the same time that all of these other profound developments we have been discussing were taking place, perhaps the most amazing development of all was happening. A new kind of investor was being created, one who was embracing *trading*.

This investor had a belief system that was radically different from preceding traders;

- One believed that there was a place in one's portfolio for long-term investments. This investor was comfortable with using a market professional (money manager, mutual fund, or pension fund) for that purpose.
- One believed that, in another part of one's portfolio, one could make more money trading one's own stocks than by investing on the advice of a stockbroker.
- One believed that trading was just another skill that could be learned, and one anticipated the challenge of mastering those techniques.
- One believed that one did not need someone else's advice, and that one was fully capable of gathering and interpreting the information one needed to make an informed trade.
- One believed that one could fit the trading of securities in among the other demands in one's life.
- One believed that the traditional stock broker did not provide a service that was worth the traditional commission charged.

- One believed that one would really enjoy trading, and have fun doing it.

This new kind of investor who embraced trading was the catalyst for all of the other changes. On the other hand, maybe the wide range of new capabilities made this new kind of trader inevitable?

This is one of those "chicken or egg" puzzles for which there is no final answer. No matter. There can be no doubt that without this new breed of trader, there could have been *no* Sixth Market.

The Sixth Market is here, so where is all of this change heading?

CHAPTER | 3

# Where Is All of This Change Heading?

*"The future will be better tomorrow."*

VICE PRESIDENT DAN QUAYLE

**G**eorge Jetson steps out of his Personal Preparation Module®, where he has been automatically scrubbed, polished, dressed, preened, and given his complete daily medical inspection—all in 15 seconds. His wife, Peg, has prepared his favorite breakfast, migas con chorizo, using her Thought-Driven Food Delivery System®. George eats breakfast while his Mental Transfer Unit® downloads the global news directly into his brain. Then he's off in his brand-new SUV (Spacetravel Utility Vehicle®), preprogrammed to fly him directly to his Productivity Output Station®.

On the journey, George reviews his upcoming day. His personal Robo-Mate® has long ago been programmed to do his entire job for him. Meetings are a thing of the past. He and his coworkers now communicate everything they need to know while they sleep, using their Universal Dream Communicator®. Happily, he realizes that he is free to do what he really loves to do—trade securities! And he can't wait to try out his new Think and Execute® trading platform. He is ready to conquer the day!

Is this where we're heading? Will everything in our trading world be faster, more efficient, easier, and more productive? In a word, *yes!*

This is not to seriously suggest that we are heading for a Jetson lifestyle. As you look at what the various players in the securities industry want to do over the next several years, however, a very positive and exciting picture emerges for the Sixth Market trader.

## REGULATORS

Do you know what the regulators really want? They want investors to have the highest possible chance to succeed. It's that simple. The regulators want a level playing field where price, order flow, and depth of market are known to all, so that an individual trades with the same knowledge and market access as the most well-connected professional. Regulators will continue to take regulatory and disciplinary actions to ensure that these things happen.

The regulators also want an informed trader. On January 27, 1999, Arthur Levitt, chairman of the SEC, commented that he is most concerned about the lack of education in most online traders:

> Over the past two years, particularly in recent months, the SEC has been hearing concerns about retail, online (Internet) investing. In fact, the number of complaints concerning online investing has increased by 330 percent in the last year. Some of the issues raised specifically relate to online trading, others are generic to all investing. The majority of them can be addressed through better education and investors ensuring that they have done their homework.

We will come back to this theme time and again in this book. Trading consists of skills that can be learned, and those skills are not that difficult to master. The professionals on Wall Street have those skills. The trader in the Sixth Market who does not have those skills is at a big disadvantage. The regulators will continue to push for an educated public.

The regulators want *suitability;* they want to ensure that, before someone makes a single trade, that individual has the education and the financial capacity to manage the risks of that trade. If the broker makes a trading recommendation of any kind, the burden of determining suitability rests squarely with that broker. The regulators will take serious action against those companies which flout the suitability regulations.

The result of these efforts by the regulators will be that the individual will have a better chance competing against the professional in the markets.

## THE EXECUTIONERS

Do you know what the NYSE, Nasdaq, and all of these ECNs really want? They want to survive in the coming restructuring of the world trading markets.

Restructuring of the world trading markets? You bet! Soon there will be a single, central, global, limit order book against which all orders will be matched and executed.

Because the "middleman" is becoming obsolete, the specialists and the market makers are especially threatened. Their spreads are shrinking, reducing their ability to make money in their business. Electronic "matching" networks can pair bids and offers to execute trades without their intervention. They just don't fit into this new world.

Here's a real-world example: In 1996 the German stock exchange added an electronic trading system to run alongside its traditional "open outcry" trading floor. Within two years, 90 percent of all trades were being done electronically.

A lot of this move started with the ECNs. They destroyed the old order. They set out to render the exchanges, specialists, and market makers obsolete; and they have done quite a good job of it. It has been reported that the NYSE averages 22 seconds to make a trade. The Island ECN can do it in a fraction of a second. These executioners use just a few workhorse servers, avoiding the overhead of a group of frenetic, highly-paid professional traders.

For all of these executioners, this is a frightening period. Who will lead these changes? Who will control this enormously powerful new system? Who will have a job tomorrow? Each executioner is exploring financial restructuring to raise capital. Each is engaged in megamerger discussions to increase its respective clout.

The only certainty at this time is that you—the Sixth Market trader—will think you have grabbed the golden ring. You will see improved information flows, reduced transaction costs, more and more liquidity, better and better price execution, smaller and smaller spreads, more robust 24-hour worldwide trading, and a wide array of customer service improvements.

No institution and no industry insider ever again will have a protected trading advantage over the average trader.

## THE INSTITUTIONS

What do the institutions really want? They all want to manage your money. Let's look at them by broad category.

- *Mutual funds* want to continue to provide value to the public for their long-term investing needs; they will continue to compete on return.
- *Money managers and financial consultants* want to be credible alternatives to the mutual funds.
- *Pension funds* want to keep a lock on their large corporate clients.
- *Retail brokerage firms* want to continue to add financial services to attract your long-term funds.

Because this book is about online trading in the Sixth Market, we are concerned only with the portion of your assets devoted to that purpose. But in addition to your online trading activities, you likely will place long-term investments. The institutions will continue to compete with one another to manage the dollars in that pile for you.

## ONLINE BROKERS

What do the online brokers really want? They want to survive.

First, they have a problem with competition. Today there are almost 200 online brokers; in five years there will be a dozen or fewer. To survive, they are mounting furious battles to win and to keep customers. Much of this battleground is being fought over financial services. Today, you can get a mortgage, purchase theater tickets, order take-out food, and who knows what else, all through your online financial services firm. Great, but what does this have to do with trading?

Go ahead and open an account with one of these "everything for everyone" behemoths and take full advantage of their expansive services. But also open your trading account with a firm that specializes in trading! The online broker you want will continue to give you the trading edge with innovations such as:

- *Look for transaction costs* to continue to decline. At some point, those with large accounts will see transaction costs reduced to zero, in recognition of their account balances.
- *Look for an increasing amount of information* to be delivered at no cost.
- *Look for increased portability* represented by truly effective alerts and trading capabilities delivered to your portable or wireless device.
- *Look for an expanding array of trading tools* that help you spot and capture good trading opportunities. Isn't that what you're here for?
- *Look for a strong move toward automated trading*—a "set it and forget it" capability that will allow you to execute in more trades even while you go about your other daily activities.

The second problem for the online brokers is declining transaction volume. Even while their customer base is expanding, trading transactions per customer are declining. Why? Because inexperienced, uneducated, and unprepared traders are not making consistent profits. Because we can no longer count on a runaway bull market to give a profit to everyone with the nerve to "buy and hold on." Because the inexperienced trader has no idea how to profit in a flat market or, even worse, in a *(gasp!)* bear market.

If these traders don't "win," the thrill is gone, so they cut back on their trading.

Online brokers know that profitable customers will solve this problem, so they really want their customers to profit in the market—bull or bear. Brokers really want their customers to be trained and educated.

*But*—and this is a huge *but*—the online brokers cannot train their own customers. Do you remember our comments about *suitability* above? The regulators have expanded their definition of *suitability* to include "teaching or encouraging a style of trading." If your online broker provides you with any form of trading education, that broker is encouraging a style of trading, and that broker becomes responsible for the *suitability* of every trade you make using that style.

In the online, real-time world, it is not feasible for your online broker to gauge the suitability of every trade you make. The broker simply cannot take that liability. To avoid that liability, the online broker must make no recommendation to you *at all*.

Beyond the liability, the potential for conflict of interest is staggering. Do you think it is possible that an online broker that makes its money from commissions on the number of trades you make just might train you to make lots of trades? Is that activity really good for you?

The solution is for the online brokers to develop "third party" relationships with training firms. The online broker will allow a few training firms to access its customer database for the purpose of promoting training programs. The online broker will *not* recommend one training company, it will not own one share of a training company, and it will remain completely separated from all training activity.

Online brokers who own, or otherwise have an interest in, firms that train their customers, are prime targets for regulatory sanctions. They will be required to divest themselves of the training company or the brokerage company. They will not be allowed to continue both functions.

## THE ONLINE TRADER

Do you know what the online trader really wants? Of course you do—just look in the mirror every morning. You want to make money in the market. You want to enjoy the freedom to make your own trades. And you want to have fun doing them.

So what's the problem? It has been estimated that almost 95 percent of today's online traders do not really know *how* to trade. That is, you do not have the knowledge and experience to consistently profit in the market. You are not prepared.

Traders come up with many excuses for not making the effort to build their skill levels:

- I'm too old to learn.
- The skills required are too complicated or difficult for me to learn.
- It will take too much time and effort for me to learn how to trade.
- It is not possible to teach trading skills at all.
- The training available today is simply not effective.

So you rely on hunches, tips, and luck. This is not a recipe for success; quite the opposite, in fact.

Over the next few years, several training companies will emerge as leaders in building credibility with the public. They will show that almost anyone can learn trading skills. They will show that the needed skills can, in fact, be taught effectively. And, they will show that good training has a direct, positive impact on profitability.

In other words, they will prove that you can be taught to consistently profit in the market, that the skills are not difficult to learn, that it can be done quickly and easily. They will eliminate all of your excuses!

As a result of this, education will take center stage in the future. The online trader will not put his money at risk without a solid educational foundation for trading. The insistence on effective training programs will signal the beginning of the real growth in online trading.

When the general public finally demands to learn skills to help them profit in the market, we will see an explosion in new traders that will make past growth seem positively anemic.

As we will show in later chapters, effective training is readily available today. You would not think of trying to fly an airplane without the proper training. Why would you risk your hard-earned money without an effective trading education?

Answering the questions in this chapter, what do *you* need to do to prosper—right now—in the Sixth Market?

# PART II

# Getting Ready to Jump into the Sixth Market

CHAPTER | 4

# The Prepared Trader

*"It wasn't raining when Noah built the Ark"*

HOWARD RUFF

*As is always the case, it was the early adapters who came running. Rumors of exciting, new, electronic ways to trade stocks were being spread everywhere. Here was a chance to get in early and to make a killing. All it took was an account at one of these day trading brokerages, and some luck.*

*They all had stars in their eyes—and greed in their hearts, and they all got clobbered! These poor people were simply not prepared to compete against the market professionals.*

That may be a bit of an exaggeration but, sadly, it's mostly true. From 1992 through 1998, it has been estimated that eight out of every ten people who tried "day trading" lost money—sometimes big money.

Isn't that the way it always goes when hopeful humans think they have found a new foolproof way to "make a killing"? Whoever said that there are no free lunches was truly guilty of understatement.

When the new online brokers such as E*Trade, Schwab, DLJ*direct,* and the others, first arrived on the scene, a similar thing happened.

Many of their customers lost money as they tried to trade for themselves. Then, the worst possible thing happened: a bull market emerged, driven by *irrational exuberance!* Traders thought all you had to do was buy some stock and hold on. It was so easy. It was so profitable. It was so much fun. There was even talk that it would never end.

Why do we say that this was the worst thing that could happen? Because it did end in March and April of 2000. When it did, lots of money was lost in a big hurry. Shellshocked, dazed, and confused were the emotions of the day. Guts were wrenching as naïve traders quickly learned about margin calls when they were forced to sell heavily-leveraged positions.

The run-up in stock prices, particularly in the technology sector, had masked a serious weakness in the entire premise of self-directed, online trading. That weakness was that most people didn't really know how to trade.

In an unscientific survey taken in April 2000, we concluded that well under 10 percent of those with online trading accounts had actually ever executed a *short sale.* Let's be blunt: if you don't understand, and are not comfortable with, playing the shorts, you simply don't understand the markets well enough to call yourself a trader . . . or to put your money at risk.

Consider the implications. If all of these online traders really don't know how to trade, and if it was just the bull market that was carrying them along, what is going to happen to this entire industry in an extended bear market?

How many of you are old enough to remember when absolutely *everyone* had to be in an oil drilling partnership? Or, when *everyone* had to invest in an apartment limited partnership? When the music stopped, and the profits weren't there, the firms that specialized in these financial products just dried up and blew away, taking their clients with them.

Is that what's going to happen to the online trading industry? Is this just one more passing fad, a brief blip on the financial radar screen that fades to nothing? We think not, because of the success of one particular group of traders.

While most people with online accounts do not know yet how to trade, there is one group that is different. This group has been determined not only to make money in the markets, but to understand how they were making it. They have learned how to make money in both a rising and a falling market. They have learned how to read charts, interpret market maker moves, and use key indexes to anticipate price movements. They have learned the value of patience and discipline. This group is made up of active, successful day traders.

OK, we've all read in the press that day trading is a *bad* business, that day trading companies encourage *too many* trades, that *everyone* loses money, that you would have to be brain dead to try day trading, and on and on. The problem with those stories is that they just are not true.

Certainly there are some bad day trading firms, and certainly there are people who lose money. But don't condemn the whole industry. There are some excellent firms and some remarkable traders who have shown everyone what day trading could—and should—be.

One of the authors of this book was the president of the largest day trading firm in the country, Cornerstone Securities (now ProTrader Securities). Cornerstone has long been a responsible industry leader. Taken directly from the ProTrader Web site are these ProTrader statistics for 1999:

| | |
|---|---|
| Number of offices | 19 |
| Number of traders | 550 |
| *NET Profit of All Traders* | *$174 million* |

Yes, that's million, as in gobs of money. As the commercial says: *"These guys are good."*

These experienced traders have discovered how to consistently make money in the market, regardless of what the market throws at them. These groundbreaking day traders are showing the rest of us the way.

They have proven that trading isn't hard. It's not some complicated mystery decipherable only by the few geniuses among us. Successful trading can be taught to almost anyone.

They have taught us that it doesn't matter what trading style you use. It doesn't matter what your trading rules are. Discipline is the key to success.

They have really taught us that—to succeed in the markets, all that matters is that you learn three vitally important things:

1. *Where to trade:* making the right choices about your online broker, your Internet service provider, and your hardware configuration.
2. *How to trade:* learning about trading psychology, market mechanics, trading strategies, risk management, capital management, and trading with a plan.
3. *What to trade:* developing an ability to spot—and to act on—high-percentage trading opportunities.

When you are proficient in all three areas, you will be *the prepared trader* and you will be ready to take on the market!

Figure 4.1 shows how each of these three areas contribute to creating the prepared trader.

**FIGURE 4.1** Three Steps to Becoming the Prepared Trader

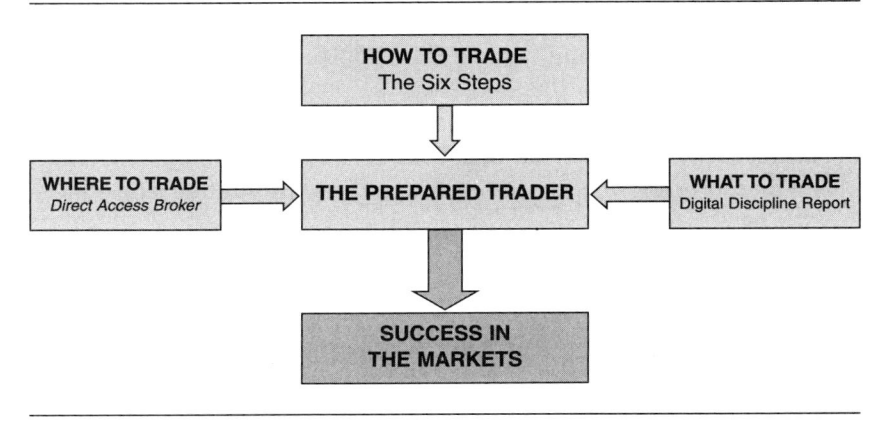

```
                    ┌─────────────────┐
                    │  HOW TO TRADE   │
                    │  The Six Steps  │
                    └────────┬────────┘
                             │
                             ▼
┌──────────────────┐  ┌─────────────────┐  ┌──────────────────────────┐
│  WHERE TO TRADE  │─▶│ THE PREPARED    │◀─│    WHAT TO TRADE         │
│ Direct Access    │  │    TRADER       │  │ Digital Discipline Report│
│    Broker        │  │                 │  │                          │
└──────────────────┘  └────────┬────────┘  └──────────────────────────┘
                               │
                               ▼
                    ┌─────────────────┐
                    │   SUCCESS IN    │
                    │   THE MARKETS   │
                    └─────────────────┘
```

Yes, it's true. You can learn to become the prepared trader. In the next chapter, we will look at the first of the three things you need to know: how you can make the right choices about where to trade.

CHAPTER | 5

# I Just Spent a Fortune, and All My Stuff Is Obsolete

*"The historical records show that humans have never, ever, opted for slower."*

STEVEN KERN, HISTORIAN

*E*xactly one week ago, I finally broke down and bought the latest, fastest, most reliable computer system on the market . . . the Whizbang 2000. *After all, I need power to be a better trader. This baby has it all—the fastest processor, the largest video cache, and the most RAM ever seen in one place. It's also in the latest designer color, and the price had been slashed by almost $90. I just couldn't pass it up.*

Then, last night we went to the neighbor's house for dinner, and his teenaged daughter couldn't wait to show me her latest prize . . . the Whizbang 3000! *It is not only faster, bigger, and more powerful, it was actually in a much prettier color. It's so fast it can guess real-time quotes before they've been posted, it can anticipate trades before they've been made, and it will meet your margin calls for you. And it's $100 cheaper than this* dog *I bought last week. I could throw up!*

D̲o you ever feel like this? Once again the technology has changed underneath your feet, and you don't even know what a *video cache* is! Do you have an unspoken suspicion that you might not actually need all of these advancements? Wouldn't you—just once—like to see some facts that would let you know what you really need? Well . . . let's try to do just that.

First, we are going to assume that you will be using a "direct access" broker, which is discussed in more detail in the next chapter. The important thing here is that, to take advantage of direct access, you will need a computer that is capable of processing a considerable amount of "real-time" data. Real-time means right now, instantly, with as little delay as possible.

What kind of real-time data are we talking about? The trader wants the fastest dynamic display possible of the "big three":

1. *Quotes.* These are the changes in posted prices. They aren't of much value if they are even a few seconds old. To get the best possible pricing in the market, you need quotes to be current within milliseconds (thousandths of a second).
2. *Executions.* If you are ready to make a trade, you want the very best price you can get, and the first order in line is the first to get filled. When you hit the button, you want the fastest possible speed to the market.
3. *Confirmations.* You want to know when a trade has been completed. There is *nothing* more frustrating than not knowing whether your trade has been executed or not.

Let's look at what you really need to handle the speed needed for direct access today.

## INTERNET SERVICE PROVIDER

First, you will need an Internet service provider (ISP), which is the link between you and everyone else on the Internet.

Your ISP is your link to the rest of the world. It does a lot of important things for you, and all ISPs are not alike. Here are some of the things that are important to consider as you choose your ISP:

### Bandwidth

Bandwidth is a measure of the size of the "pipe" through which data moves between your computer and your ISP. "Bandwidth" and "connection speed" are the same thing.

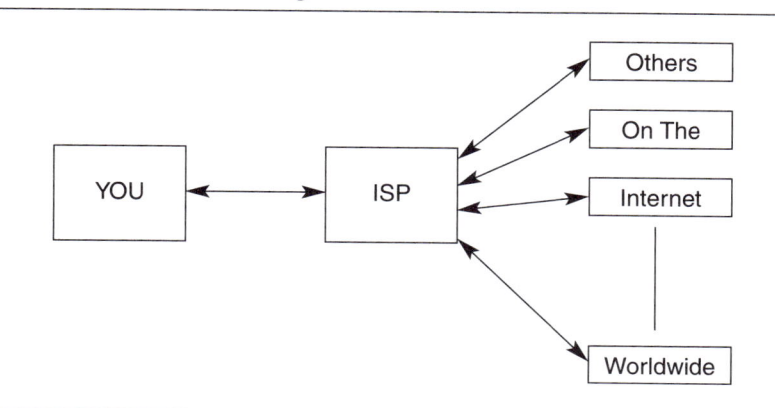

**FIGURE 5.1** Understanding the ISP

Get all the bandwidth you can. It is reasonably inexpensive now, and you cannot get too much bandwidth. Your processor easily will handle all the data you can shove into it.

## Type of Bandwidth Connection

There are three types of connection:

**"Point-to-point" connection.** A dedicated circuit between you and your ISP. These are the fastest connections, like T-3, T-1, DSL, cable, or ISDN. In our experience, these are the most stable connections as well. All of these choices will usually give you as much speed as you need for direct access trading, with two caveats:

- A *cable connection*, which is shared by others on the same cable line in your neighborhood, can suffer serious reductions in speed at those times when many of your neighbors are online with you.
- An *ISND connection*, while dedicated, runs at speeds from 64kbps to 128kbps. The 64kbps may be too slow for the most powerful trading systems.

A point-to-point connection is the type of connection you want, if it is available in your area.

**"Wireless" connection.** A satellite hook-up. The latency, which is the time it takes for the signal to travel to the satellite and bounce back to earth, renders these connections a bit slow for direct access trading. But, if point-to-point is not available in your area, a satellite hookup is preferable to a dial-up connection.

**"Dial-up" connection.** The older, and slower, technology, consisting of a regular telephone line connected to the Internet by modem, with speeds up to 56k. If you are serious about trading, even for only a few trades a month, do not settle for a dial-up connection. They are simply too slow . . . and they crash way too much!

### Actual Connection Speed

Your ISP will publish the connection speed for your connection. You will find that different ISPs will publish different speeds for the same technology. Not every T-1, DSL or Cable connection delivers the same published bandwidth. Check carefully.

On top of that, in many cases the connection speed you actually achieve will be slower (less bandwidth) than advertised. As noted above, this can be particularly true with the cable connection, but is also true with all dial-up connections. The "truest" connection speeds are with T-1 and ADSL/DSL.

### Internet Connection Speed

In the past, this was more of a concern because undercapitalized ISPs tried to save money in this area. Today, most established ISPs are connected from their servers to the Internet via T-1 or greater. Be sure your ISP can affirm that all of its servers have T-1 or greater access to the Internet.

### Communications Redundancy

Look for an ISP that has more than one communications "path" from its servers to the Internet. If your ISP only has connections through your phone company and that firm experiences a network outage, you are cooked. Multiple carriers are a must for the ISP you choose.

## Server Redundancy and Backup

Ask about server redundancy and backup; that is, the ability of your ISP to give you uninterrupted service even if one or more of its servers "goes down."

## Customer Service Staff

Is anybody home? If you have any kind of problem, will someone take care of you—*right now?* You should talk to some existing customers to find out how good your prospective ISP is at solving problems. Remember, to trade you need to be up and connected. "After hours" trading is already a reality, and it soon will become an important part of your trading business. Will your ISP be there for you 24/7?

## Price

Forget about it. Price is not an important issue; ISP charges are never that expensive. If you find an ISP with fast connections, layers of redundancy, and a customer service staff that can read your mind, sign up now! It will be more than worth it for your peace of mind and the lack of hassles during the trading day. Remember that just one good fill on one good trade can pay for your monthly ISP charges many times over.

## COMPUTER EQUIPMENT

Must you have the very latest "Flash Gordon" technology to be competitive in the markets? In a word, *no!*

In this section, we want to sort out what you really need and should be willing to pay good money for, from the bells and whistles that don't help you one bit as a trader.

## Processor Type

Every direct access trading system today runs on an IBM-compatible, Windows-based platform. We have heard rumors of the development of a direct access system for the Mac, but have not been able to confirm it. For our purposes, we will confine our discussion to the former.

### Processor Speed

How fast is fast enough? A 250 mhz Pentium-class processor should do it. Frankly, your processor is not the critical link in the "speed chain."

### RAM

The amount of RAM (memory) on board is much more important to you as a trader than processor speed. Handling streaming quotes, direct orders, and instant confirmations requires your computer to cache (temporarily store) a considerable amount of data. You want that process to be as fast as possible, and the best way to speed it up is to give it more RAM. For the serious, direct access trader, we believe that 128 Mg is a minimum (although we will concede that you can operate with less RAM). If you can push it up to 256 Mg, your speed will improve. Face it, speed can translate into money for you because you can perform more functions. Invest in RAM.

### Hard Drive

The time-sensitive processing in your electronic, direct access system does not require much of the hard drive. Quotes, executions, and confirmations display to you without delay before writing anything to the hard drive.

However, important information is written to the drive for recall on demand—price and time data for constructing charts, fundamental statistics, news headlines, trading history, open positions, etc. You don't want to limit any of these functions because of lack of space on your hard drive. Generally one gigabyte is more than enough dedicated space for your trading activities.

### Video Monitor

Come on now; if you plan to be even a mildly active trader, you are going to spend a lot of time looking at that screen. This is one place to spend some money.

## 5 / I Just Spent a Fortune, and All My Stuff Is Obsolete  45

**Screen size.** The larger the screen the better. Don't worry, every bit of that real estate will be used to display important information.

Take a look at the sample screen layout shown in Figure 5.2. The figure is not to suggest the layout you should choose to construct. Instead, we want you to see that, by the time you put up market maker windows, time and sales, boardview, tickers, charts, trade blotter, open position manager, and order entry window, your screen is packed!

A single 19" color monitor is a minimum in our opinion, but you will not easily be able to display everything you want on a single screen. A 21" monitor will do a considerably better job, but if you are an active trader, you still will have to make compromises in your layout.

Recently, we have been trading with twin 19" displays which give them the room to put up almost everything we need to trade at our best! Remember that you will likely be doing other things on your computer during the day—Internet access, banking, e-mails—which means you need even more space.

**FIGURE 5.2** Sample Screen Layout

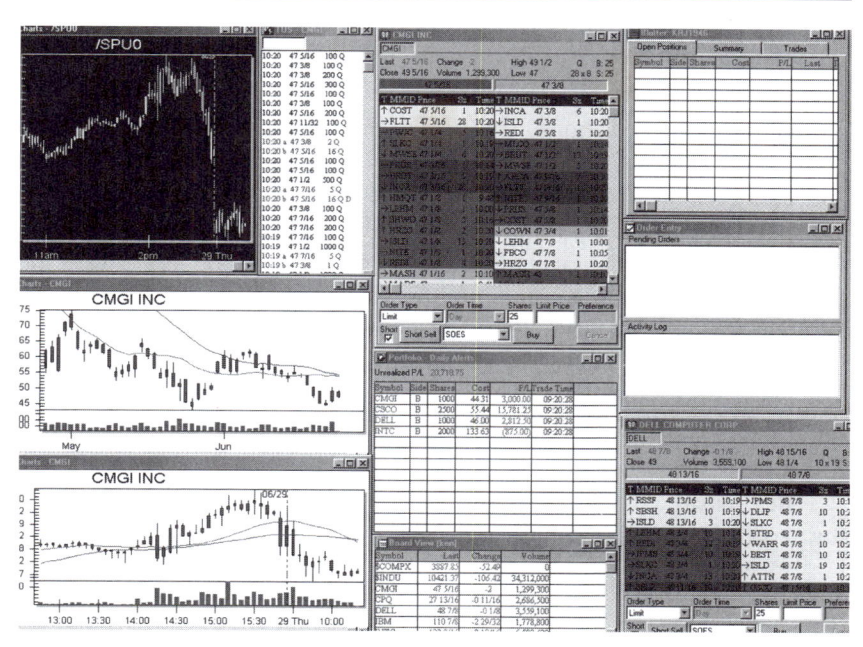

*Copyright 2000, TradeCast® Ltd.*

We can't wait for the day they come out with triple 25″ displays. We'll finally be able to see everything we ever wanted at one time, but we'll need to move to larger offices to accommodate that "wall of monitors."

**Resolution.** Interestingly, we have found that you can't really take advantage of the finest resolution available on today's monitors. In order to read everything on the screen, we trade with a setting of 1280 x 1024. If we try to move up to 1600 x 1200, we simply can't read the smaller fonts. Even bifocals don't help.

**Video card and video cache.** Guess what? This stuff really does matter. Without getting too technical, the speed of the video card controls how quickly information paints to your display, and the size of the video cache controls how much information is available to paint right now. The faster the card and the bigger the cache the better. This is another area where spending an extra $100 to $200 when you configure your computer can pay big dividends in speed.

## Other Applications

While your computer is set up to multi-task (run more than one program at a time), you should try to keep this action to a minimum while you are trading. You don't want any other computer processes going on that can slow down your critical time-sensitive information—quotes, executions, and confirmations. Try not to have any other active video graphics applications up and running on the screen. You don't want the processor busy painting something on your monitor at the wrong time.

The bottom line here is that you don't have to rush out to "keep up with the technology Joneses" each time a new gadget is introduced. Spend your money on bandwidth, RAM, and video technology where you will see the payback.

After taking care of bandwidth and your computer equipment, it's time to choose the right online broker.

CHAPTER 6

# Is One Broker Better than Another?

*"To get what you want, stop doing what isn't working."*

DENNIS WEAVER

*The first online trade was arguably made almost 20 years ago by a Michigan physicist and inventor named Bill Porter. His foresight created the company which eventually became E\*Trade.*

*As online trading developed, the promise was for lower transaction costs, more efficient pricing and faster executions. By and large that promise has not been delivered.*

*There are two reasons that the original model for online trading is not working: the "payment for order flow" broker and the "browser-based" trading systems.*

*Now, a new breed of online broker—the direct access broker—has emerged. Is this what we have all been waiting for? Will this make a difference to us as traders?*

*You bet it will. The most important decision you can make as you take advantage of the Sixth Market is to choose a direct access broker with a software-based trading system.*

*If that sounds pretty blunt, it's meant to be. If you continue to trade with an order routing broker and a browser-based system, you are throwing away your money in the market.*

*But there is more to choosing the right broker than just direct access and software-based systems. In this chapter we will lay out everything you should consider before you give a broker your money.*

## WHY YOU NEED THE RIGHT BROKER, RIGHT NOW

In this chapter we will introduce you to concepts and tools which, until recently, were of interest only to the full-time professional trader.

Now, we realize that most of you who are reading this book are not professional traders. Instead, you are most likely investors who trade occasionally. It would be logical for you to be thinking, "I am not a full-time trader. I don't need advanced tools. I don't need you to be educating me about this stuff!" But you would be wrong!

Has this happened to you? You decide to buy a stock. You see that the price is climbing so you connect to your online broker. You place your buy order. Then one of two things happens:

1. Forty-five minutes later you get notification that your order could not be executed, or
2. Forty-five minutes later you get notification that your order was executed at a price $2 above where the stock is trading right now.

We have talked to hundreds of people who have had experiences such as these. If you haven't, you have been lucky. And, unless you take the information in this chapter to heart, these things will happen to you soon enough.

If your account is with the typical online broker, you are being held hostage by ineffective tools and outdated resources. Your online broker is content to let you compete in the market at a disadvantage. The vast majority of online brokers today do not even offer the tools we are going to be discussing.

Even if you make just one trade a year, you want that trade to be at the very best possible price. There is no reason to go to the market today without the proper information and the proper execution tools.

As you will see, this information is easy to understand and the tools are easy to use. You need to know what tools are available and where to find them. Let's get to work.

## PAYMENT FOR ORDER FLOW BROKER

The dominant order handling method is called payment for order flow. It is practiced by all but a handful of the almost 200 online brokers in existence today.

This method is slow and does not get you the best execution price. The brokers who practice payment for order flow do not provide you with the trading tools used by professionals and active traders. In most cases, they don't even provide you with real-time data.

What they do, however, is decide where your order will be executed. They send your order to a trading firm that will pay them for your order instead of to the place where you will get the best price. Does that sound good to you?

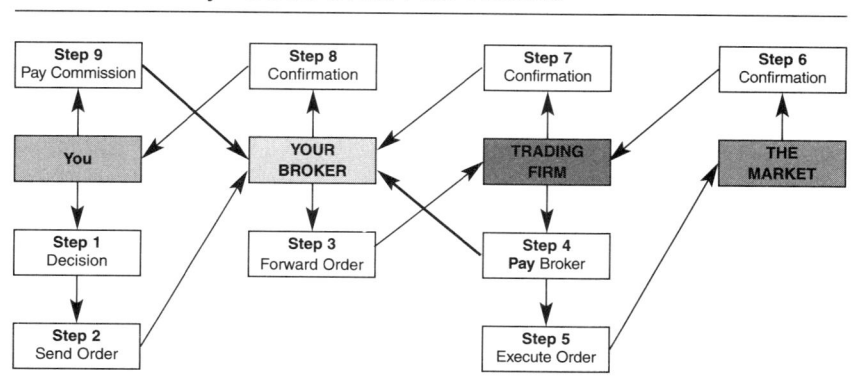

Figure 6.1 shows the payment for order flow process. It can be summarized as follows:

*Step 1.* You decide to buy 100 shares of XYZ. The quoted price that you see is 40 bid and 40¼ ask. You don't have access to information about the depth of the market, and you can't be sure that you are seeing the very best prices available.

**FIGURE 6.1** Payment for Order Flow Process

*Step 2.* You fill out the order window to buy 100 XYZ with a market order, and you send the order electronically to your broker.

*Step 3.* Your broker receives your order as an e-mail and forwards your order to a trading firm. This is a needless step that wastes time. This trading firm is usually an active market maker that has entered into an agreement with your broker to provide the "payment for order flow." What that means is that your broker has agreed to sell your order to the trading firm.

*Step 4.* The trading firm pays your broker for *your* order, usually one to three cents per share.

*Step 5.* The trading firm is now free to execute your order against the market when and where it chooses. This also takes additional time. To make up for the payment to your broker, the trading firm fills your buy order at a price slightly higher than the going market price, and your sell order at a slightly lower price. Today, this practice is legal according to the SEC.

*Step 6.* The trading firm receives confirmation of the execution.

*Step 7.* The trading firm now manually sends confirmation of the execution back to your broker.

*Step 8.* Finally, your broker manually sends confirmation of the execution back to you.

*Step 9.* You pay your broker a commission. The broker is being paid by both you and the trading firm. Is there a potential conflict of interest here? Which of these two is the broker's biggest customer? Certainly not you!

This process can take from 15 seconds to several minutes. The result is that, if you pay ¼ of a point more than the best price at the time of order on 100 shares, you just paid an extra $25. On 1,000 shares, you would pay an extra $250!

As Bill Burnham, a venture capitalist at Softbank Capital Partners, recently wrote in the *Financial Commentator:* "Everybody's happy with $9.95 trades, but they're not looking at what their broker *really* costs them." How good does that low commission rate look now?

## DIRECT ACCESS BROKER

The direct access broker, on the other hand, provides professional-level tools to investors. It allows its clients to direct where their orders will be filled.

Figure 6.2 shows a direct access trade, which can be summarized as follows:

*Step 1.* You decide you want to buy 100 shares of XYZ. The quoted price that you see is 40 bid and 40¼ ask. These are the actual, live prices at this instant.

*Step 2.* You fill out the order window to buy 100 XYZ at 40¼ because you have real-time quotes and therefore you know where the best price is. You send the order electronically to the execution servers at your broker.

*Step 3.* In milliseconds, the execution servers check your order for a series of compliance and margin issues and instantly routes it to the correct exchange or ECN for the fastest possible execution. There is no time wasted with human intervention.

*Step 4.* Confirmation of the execution is sent electronically to your broker; and

*Step 5.* Confirmation is electronically sent to you.

*Step 6.* You pay your broker a commission. The broker has no conflict from being paid by a trading firm, too.

This process can take from under one second to just a few seconds. However, no system is immune to an overcrowded market. At such times (like the "open" each morning), it can take several minutes.

The direct access process is efficient, fast, and results in consistently better price execution. That equals more money in your pocket.

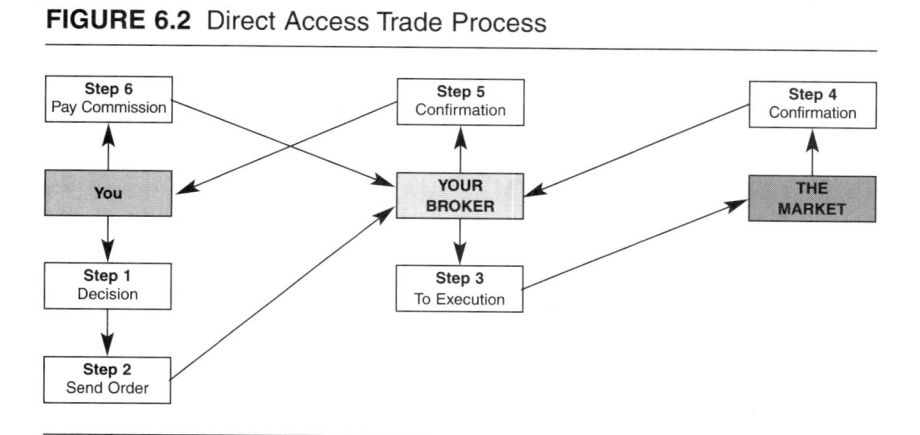

**FIGURE 6.2** Direct Access Trade Process

Let us say it again: If you are not using a direct access broker, stop reading this book and go open an account with a direct access broker—*now!*

Who are the direct access brokers? As of August 2000, there are at least five direct access brokers:

1. TradeCAST.com
2. CyBerCorp.com
3. Datek.com
4. RealTick.com
5. TradeScape.com

The rest of this chapter will give you some insight into how to choose the right direct access broker for you.

## SOFTWARE TRADING SYSTEM

All of the direct access brokers provide you with a software-based trading system (as opposed to a browser-based system). A software-based system loads the trading software on your hard drive. The only thing you are moving over the Internet connection is a compressed stream of numbers (price quotes, order information, and confirmations). Your machine does all calculations and screen painting.

A browser-based system keeps all software in a central server and must send much more information over the Internet. Just sending information for video display takes time and bandwidth. The result is a much slower process. As we have said time and again: time is money. You can't afford the slow speeds of a browser-based system.

Virtually all of the "payment for order flow brokers" use a browser-based system. This is one more reason to choose a direct access broker.

## THE RIGHT TRADING TOOLS

The electronic trading platforms that are offered by the direct access brokers all come with very effective trading tools—tools that can help you make more money. Throughout this book, we have chosen to use sample screen shots from TradeCAST *Elite*™ v3.2.5, which we rank as the most advanced and most stable electronic trading platform in the industry.

Let's review some of the most important tools in an electronic trading platform.

## Stock Window

This window is used to read detailed pricing information for one stock at a time. It will be your source to find the very best price in the market, which is your key to saving or making money on every transaction.

The top section of each stock window is the basic quote, which is called *level I* information and includes: the last trade, up or down tick, yesterday's close, today's open, today's high, today's low, and today's volume. A sample window is shown in Figure 6.3.

**FIGURE 6.3** Sample Stock Window

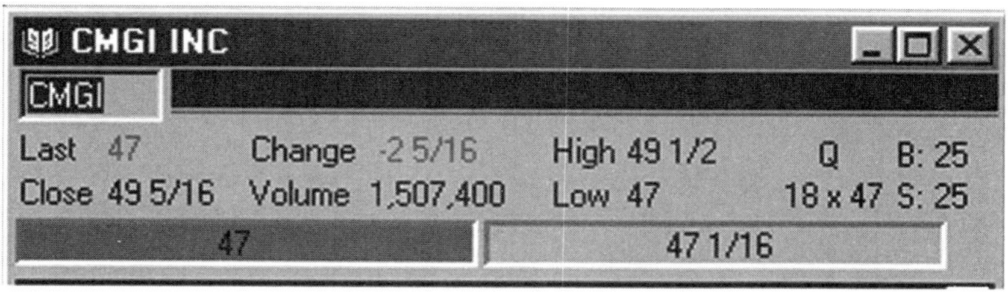

```
CMGI INC                                              _ □ x
CMGI
Last  47        Change -2 5/16     High 49 1/2      Q    B: 25
Close 49 5/16   Volume 1,507,400   Low  47          18 x 47  S: 25
                47                             47 1/16
```

*Copyright 2000, TradeCast® Ltd.*

The bottom section of this window will display one of two configurations, based on the market you have chosen:

**Nasdaq Level II Window.** When you choose to display information about a Nasdaq stock, this screen, shown in Figure 6.4, gives you more than just real-time quotes, it provides you with a look at the limit order book for the entire Nasdaq market, showing all posted bids and offers, along with order sizes. This depth of market display gives you valuable information about the direction of the market. The prices quoted by market makers and ECNs show you where to execute your trade for the best possible price.

**FIGURE 6.4** Sample Nasdaq Level II Window

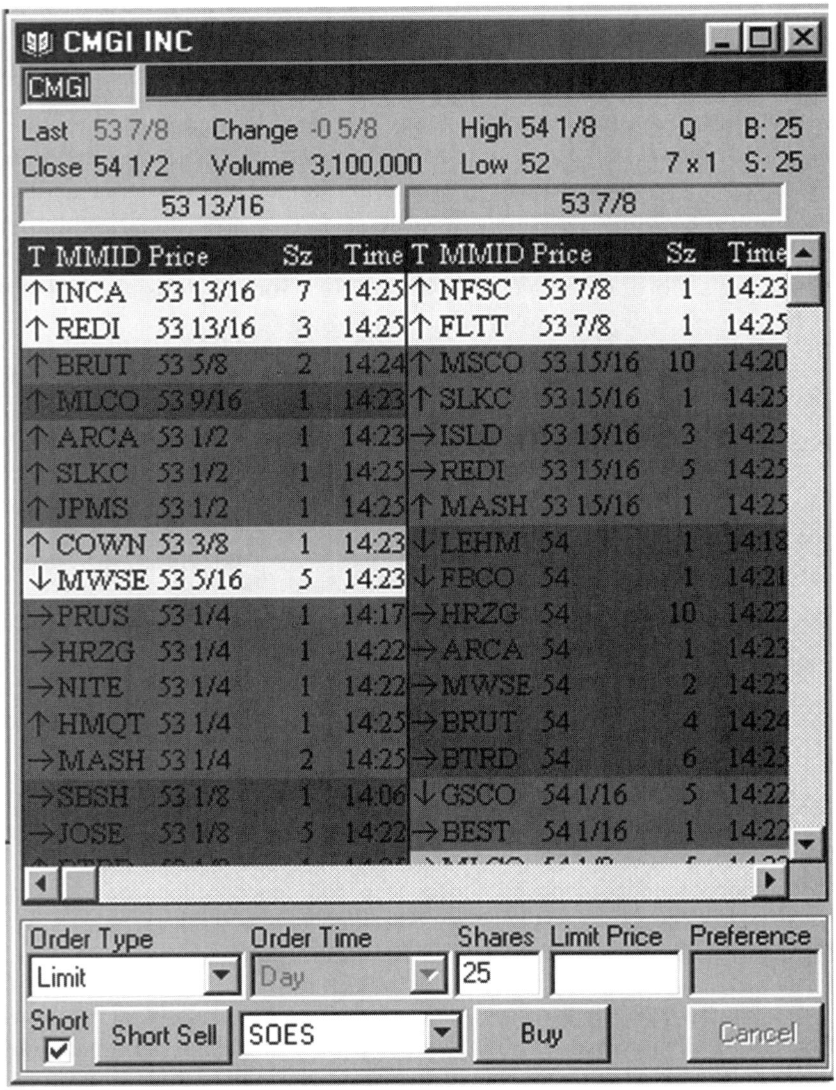
CMGI INC
CMGI
Last 53 7/8 Change -0 5/8 High 54 1/8 Q B: 25
Close 54 1/2 Volume 3,100,000 Low 52 7 x 1 S: 25
53 13/16
53 7/8
T MMID Price Sz Time T MMID Price Sz Time
↑ INCA 53 13/16 7 14:25 ↑ NFSC 53 7/8 1 14:23
↑ REDI 53 13/16 3 14:25 ↑ FLTT 53 7/8 1 14:25
↑ BRUT 53 5/8 2 14:24 ↑ MSCO 53 15/16 10 14:20
↑ MLCO 53 9/16 1 14:23 ↑ SLKC 53 15/16 1 14:25
↑ ARCA 53 1/2 1 14:23 → ISLD 53 15/16 3 14:25
↑ SLKC 53 1/2 1 14:25 → REDI 53 15/16 5 14:25
↑ JPMS 53 1/2 1 14:25 ↑ MASH 53 15/16 1 14:25
↑ COWN 53 3/8 1 14:23 ↓ LEHM 54 1 14:18
↓ MWSE 53 5/16 5 14:23 ↓ FBCO 54 1 14:21
→ PRUS 53 1/4 1 14:17 → HRZG 54 10 14:22
→ HRZG 53 1/4 1 14:22 → ARCA 54 1 14:23
→ NITE 53 1/4 1 14:22 → MWSE 54 2 14:23
↑ HMQT 53 1/4 1 14:25 → BRUT 54 4 14:24
→ MASH 53 1/4 2 14:25 → BTRD 54 6 14:25
→ SBSH 53 1/8 1 14:06 ↓ GSCO 54 1/16 5 14:22
→ JOSE 53 1/8 5 14:22 → BEST 54 1/16 1 14:22
Order Type Order Time Shares Limit Price Preference
Limit Day 25
Short Short Sell SOES Buy Cancel

Copyright 2000, TradeCast® Ltd.

**Exchange Window.** This same section of the stock window becomes an exchange window when you call up a listed security, and provides relevant bid and offer information for listed stocks across all of the exchanges. Figure 6.5 shows an exchange window.

**FIGURE 6.5** Sample Exchange Window

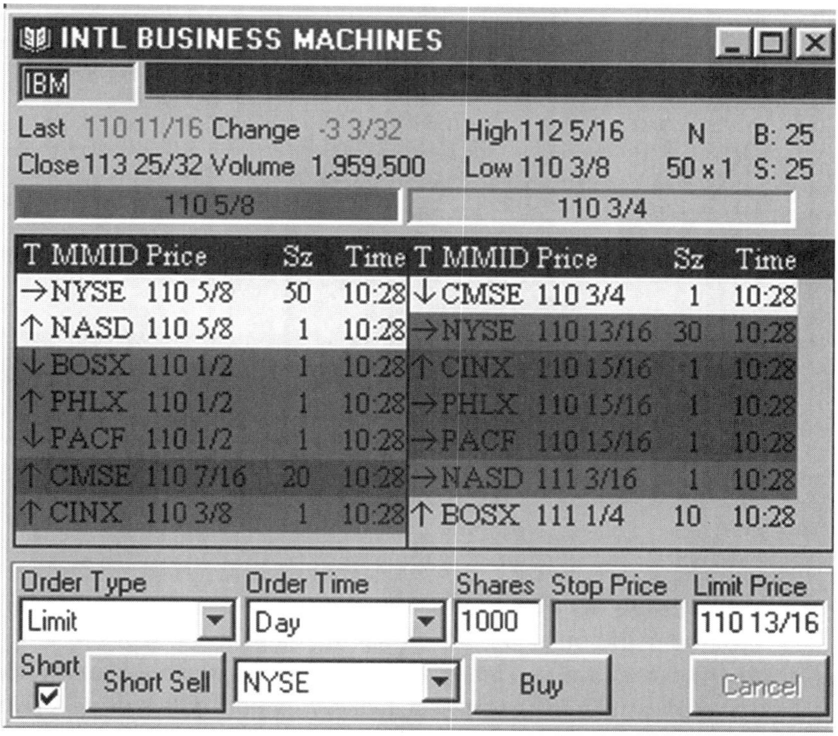

*Copyright 2000, TradeCast® Ltd.*

## Time and Sales Window

Usually you will "link" a time and sales window to your stock window, as shown in Figure 6.6. This window displays every buy and sell transaction in a particular stock, by price, share size, and time. Time and sales is extremely valuable because it shows the relative buying pressure or selling pressure in the market. For example,

**FIGURE 6.6** Sample Time and Sales Window

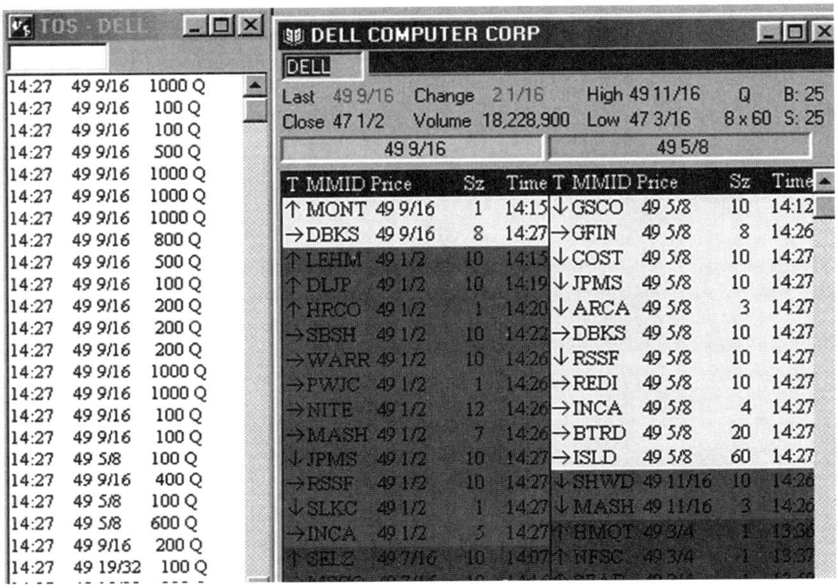

*Copyright 2000, TradeCast® Ltd.*

- *If most prices are executing at the offer price,* outsiders are buying from the market makers, which will tend to drive prices up.
- *If most prices are executing at the bid price,* holders of this stock are selling back to the market makers, which will tend to drive prices down.

In Figure 6.6, there is considerable action at the bid price of 49 9/16. Which way do you expect the price of DELL to move in the next few minutes? (Down, because holders of the stock are selling it to the market makers at their bid price.) This kind of information is invaluable in helping you time your orders.

### Ticker Window

This is where you spot quote changes in stocks you choose to watch. These are highly-customizable windows that allow you to create your own list of stocks to watch, and that allow you to color-code the quote changes (rising quotes in one color, falling quotes in another) so that you can easily see when quoted prices are rising or falling. Again, this information, as shown in Figure 6.7, helps you time your orders.

**FIGURE 6.7** Sample Ticker Window

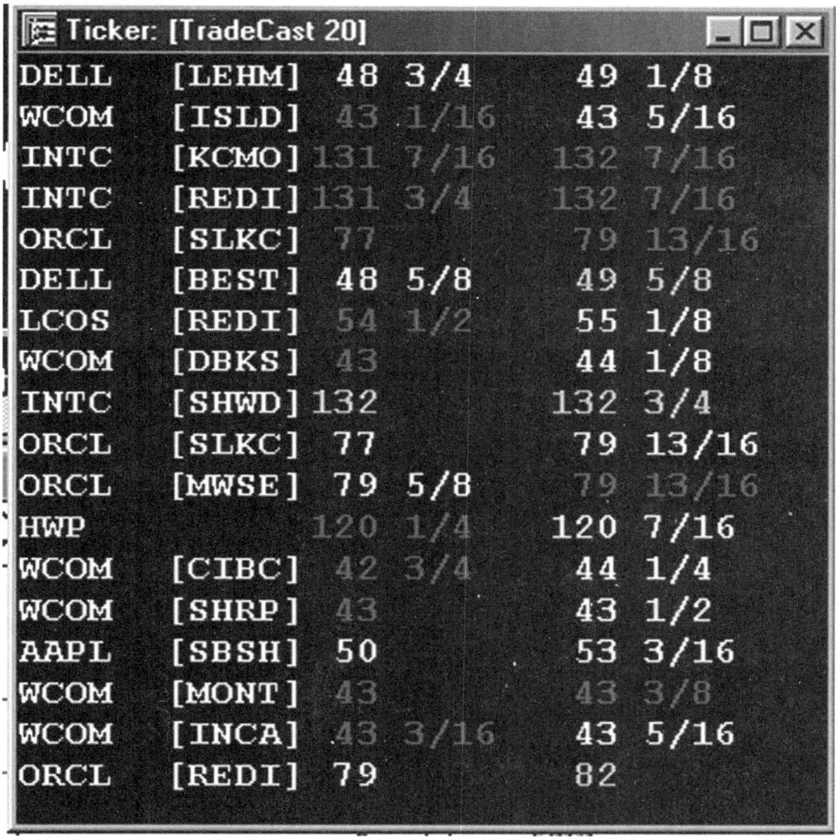

```
Ticker: [TradeCast 20]
DELL    [LEHM]   48 3/4        49 1/8
WCOM    [ISLD]   43 1/16       43 5/16
INTC    [KCMO]   131 7/16      132 7/16
INTC    [REDI]   131 3/4       132 7/16
ORCL    [SLKC]   77            79 13/16
DELL    [BEST]   48 5/8        49 5/8
LCOS    [REDI]   54 1/2        55 1/8
WCOM    [DBKS]   43            44 1/8
INTC    [SHWD]   132           132 3/4
ORCL    [SLKC]   77            79 13/16
ORCL    [MWSE]   79 5/8        79 13/16
HWP              120 1/4       120 7/16
WCOM    [CIBC]   42 3/4        44 1/4
WCOM    [SHRP]   43            43 1/2
AAPL    [SBSH]   50            53 3/16
WCOM    [MONT]   43            43 3/8
WCOM    [INCA]   43 3/16       43 5/16
ORCL    [REDI]   79            82
```

*Copyright 2000, TradeCast® Ltd.*

## Real-Time Charts

Charts are used for identifying trends and, as we will see in Chapter 11, finding high-probability chart patterns. These are fully-customizable charting packages that allow you to display charts, as shown in Figure 6.8, in various formats, in selected time periods, and with a range of chart studies.

**FIGURE 6.8** Sample Real-Time Chart

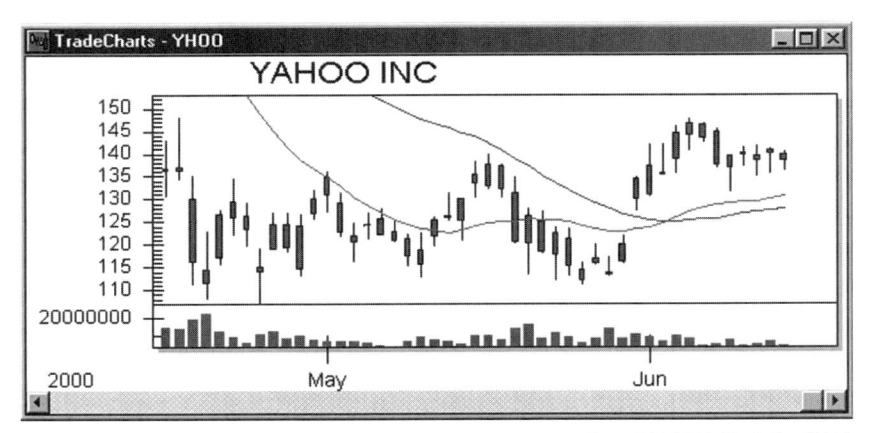

*Copyright 2000, TradeCast® Ltd.*

### Board View

As shown in Figure 6.9, this comprehensive display tool shows you selected data on a group of chosen stocks and indexes you like to watch. For example, you might create a real-time display of last price, yesterday's close, change from close, today's open, change from open, and volume. All of these can be valuable indicators to the prepared trader.

### Top Ten Window

Another aid for choosing stocks to trade is a window that will display, in real-time, a list of the top ten in such categories as: volume, gainers, losers, percentage gainers, percentage losers, etc., as shown in Figure 6.10.

## FIGURE 6.9  Sample Board View

| Symbol | Change | Last | Close | Volume |
|---|---|---|---|---|
| $COMPX | 89.37 | 3949.93 | 3860.56 | 0 |
| $INDU | 99.35 | 10548.65 | 10449.30 | 109,665,000 |
| CMGI | 0 1/8 | 54 5/8 | 54 1/2 | 3,270,500 |
| CPQ | 0 3/16 | 27 11/16 | 27 1/2 | 8,412,400 |
| DELL | 2 1/16 | 49 9/16 | 47 1/2 | 19,355,100 |
| IBM | 3 13/16 | 117 1/16 | 113 1/4 | 3,427,800 |
| INTC | 8 11/16 | 134 3/4 | 126 1/16 | 19,054,900 |
| MSFT | 0 3/8 | 72 15/16 | 72 9/16 | 14,564,800 |
| YHOO | -2 5/8 | 138 5/16 | 140 15/16 | 4,981,000 |

*Copyright 2000, TradeCast® Ltd.*

## FIGURE 6.10  Sample Top Ten Window

**NASDAQ NMS Gainers**

| Symbol | Change | Last | Bid | Ask | Volume |
|---|---|---|---|---|---|
| FAUX | 1 | 6 1/4 | 6 1/4 | 6 5/16 | 19,500 |
| INSO | 0 29/32 | 5 15/32 | 5 15/32 | 5 17/32 | 812,300 |
| INTF | 2 13/16 | 12 5/16 | 12 1/4 | 12 3/8 | 249,000 |
| JMIC | 0 5/8 | 2 7/8 | 2 3/8 | 2 7/8 | 2,900 |
| PRTK | 0 3/4 | 4 | 3 1/2 | 4 | 1,300 |
| SAMC | 0 3/4 | 5 1/8 | 4 7/8 | 5 1/8 | 17,800 |
| SGNT | 2 5/8 | 11 3/8 | 11 3/8 | 11 7/16 | 2,583,600 |
| SOLP | 1 | 4 7/16 | 4 7/16 | 4 15/32 | 151,400 |
| UTLX | 1 7/16 | 5 13/16 | 5 13/16 | 5 27/32 | 660,200 |
| XGNT | 0 7/16 | 3 | 2 13/16 | 3 | 19,100 |

*Copyright 2000, TradeCast® Ltd.*

### News Window

Use a news window, as shown in Figure 6.11, to catch late-breaking developments, or to research why a particular stock is moving. Generally this window will have two sections: the top section is to display breaking headlines about selected stocks or topics; the bottom section will be displayed only when the text of the article is desired.

**FIGURE 6.11** Sample News Window

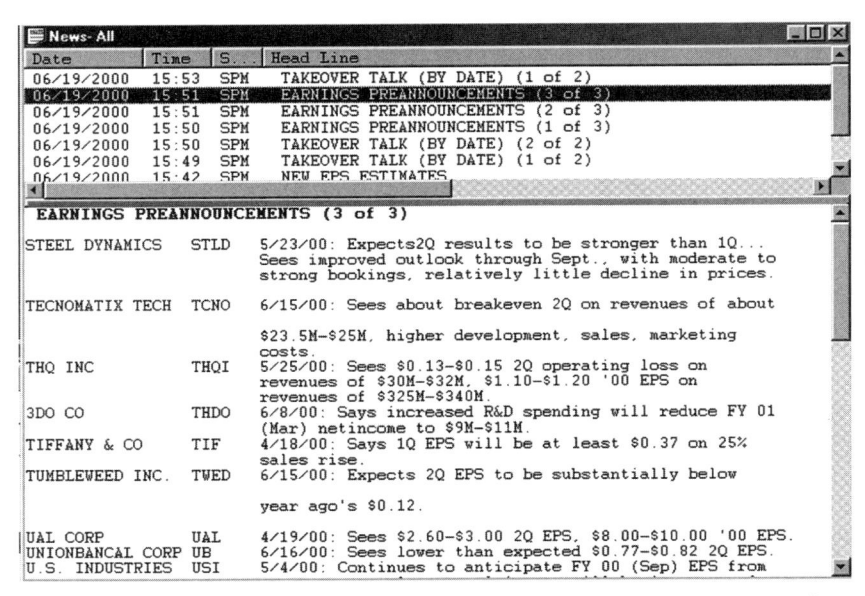

*Copyright 2000, TradeCast® Ltd.*

### Order Entry Window

When you are ready to place an order, this window allows you to direct your order to the point of execution you choose—the market maker, ECN, or exchange with the best price in the market.

As shown in Figure 6.12, this window also shows all execution and confirmation information, including buys, sells, pending, and cancellations. This is essential for managing the order process.

**FIGURE 6.12** Sample Order Entry Window

*Copyright 2000, TradeCast® Ltd.*

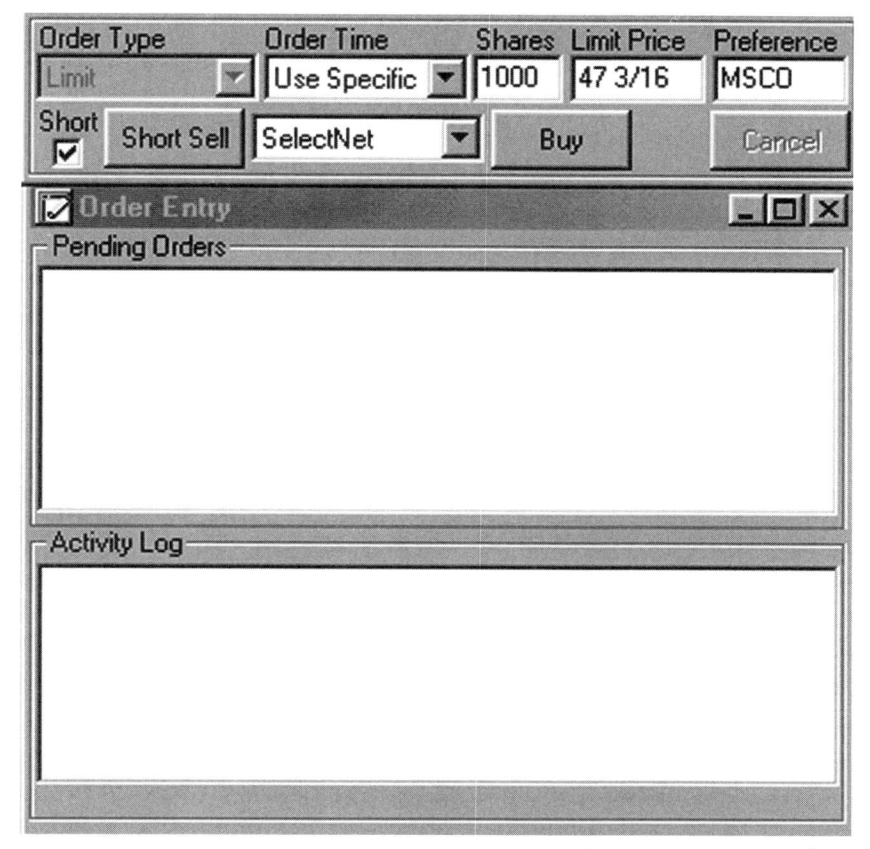

## Smart Logic

The leading software packages also include "intelligent routing logic" that uses the computer to go through the Internet to find the best price for you. TradeScout™, by TradeCAST®, is an example of an intelligent routing logic capability. Figure 6.13 shows that you can select the order in which the computer searches for the best possible price for you. Using TradeScout greatly simplifies the execution task while it gives you the best chance to find the best price in the market.

**FIGURE 6.13** Sample Intelligent Routing Logic Screen

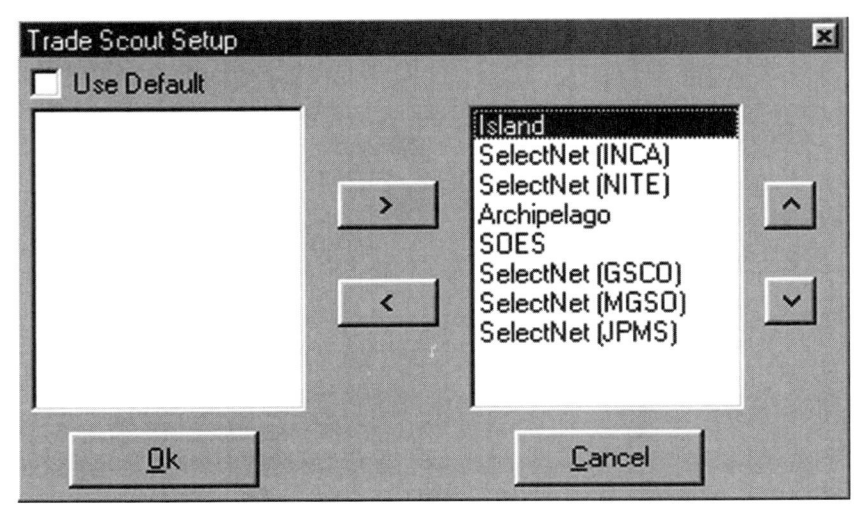

*Copyright 2000, TradeCast® Ltd.*

### Alert Window

This window allows the trader to create alerts for selected stocks. The trader will be notified by message, sound, or remote access when a desired price point has been reached. Figure 6.14 shows an alert window.

This is a benefit for the busy person who still wants to make a few trades. You can set up the alerts you want, then go about your other business. The computer will call you back to the screen when the event you are looking for has occurred.

Some examples of possible alerts would be

- if you want to be notified when DELL executes at a price of 48½.
- if you want to be notified when more than 10,000 shares of MSFT trade in a single block.
- if you want to know when CMGI declines by more than 5 percent today.

### Conditional Order Logic

This capability is being developed on the most-advanced systems to take the trader one giant step beyond alerts. Simply, you give the com-

**FIGURE 6.14** Sample Alert Window

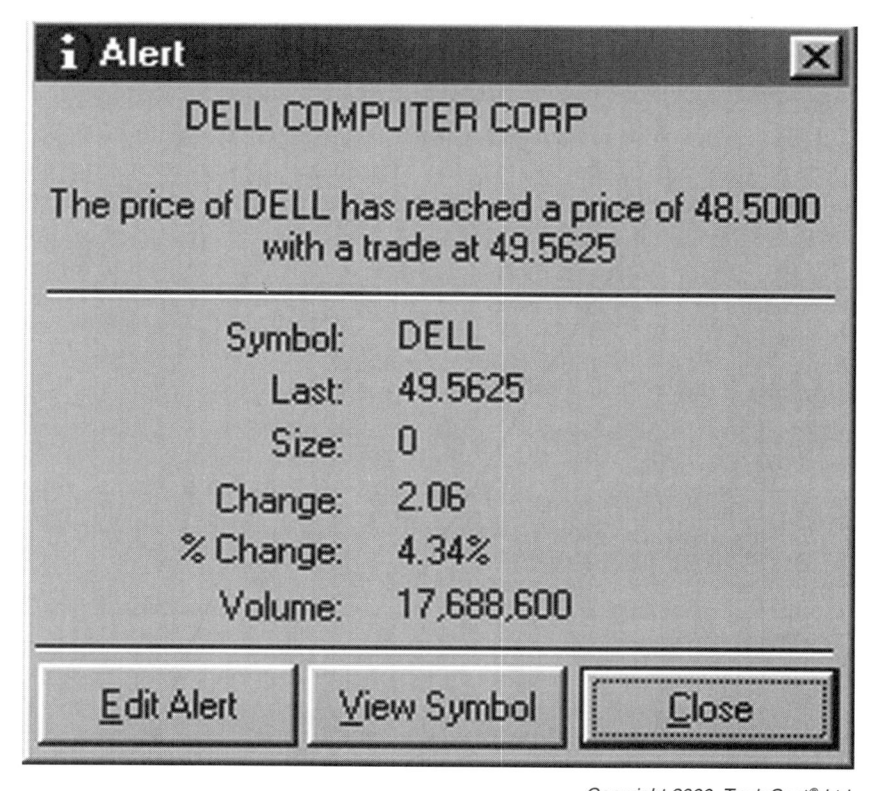

```
┌─ Alert ──────────────────────────────── × ─┐
│                                             │
│            DELL COMPUTER CORP               │
│                                             │
│   The price of DELL has reached a price of  │
│              48.5000                        │
│         with a trade at 49.5625             │
│                                             │
│           Symbol:   DELL                    │
│             Last:   49.5625                 │
│             Size:   0                       │
│           Change:   2.06                    │
│         % Change:   4.34%                   │
│           Volume:   17,688,600              │
│                                             │
│   [ Edit Alert ] [ View Symbol ] [ Close ] │
└─────────────────────────────────────────────┘
```

*Copyright 2000, TradeCast® Ltd.*

puter a target price. When your target price has been reached, the computer will execute the trade for you, without any intervention on your part. For example, you could set up a trading plan with the following conditions:

1. If Dell executes a trade at 50, send out an order to buy 1,000 shares of Dell at 50 for me.
2. Once I have bought DELL, if it declines to 49, sell it and I will take a $1 loss on the trade. (This is how I control my risk.)
3. Once I have bought DELL, if it rises to 52 sell 500 shares at 52. (This is how I will take some profit off of the table.)
4. Once I have sold 500 shares, put in a trailing stop to sell the remaining 500 shares anytime DELL drops ¾ of a point below its

high for the day. (This is how I let the stock "run" for more profit, but still protect myself in case it starts falling back.)
5. If I still own any shares of DELL ten minutes before the close of the market three days from now, sell all my shares. (This is how I put a time limit on this trade.)

This is a very powerful tool for the trader who is busy with other responsibilities during the trading day. With the computer managing all the required executions for you, you will be able to become much more active and much more productive in the market. For an untrained or uneducated trader, however, these automatic executions can lead to a fast downfall.

## Open Position Window

Once you have executed a trade, this window—as shown in Figure 6.15—is used to show your open positions—the number of shares, your cost, the current value, and your net profit or loss at this moment. This is invaluable for managing your trades.

**FIGURE 6.15** Sample Open Window

Portfolio - Blotter Ken

Unrealized P/L  13,625.00

| Symbol | Side | Shares | Last | Cost | P/L |
|---|---|---|---|---|---|
| CMGI | B | 2000 | 54 5/16 | 52.63 | 3,375.00 |
| CSCO | B | 2500 | 68 5/16 | 67.19 | 2,812.50 |
| DELL | B | 1000 | 49 1/2 | 48.75 | 687.50 |
| INTC | B | 1000 | 135 | 132.50 | 2,437.50 |
| ORCL | B | 1500 | 84 13/16 | 84.00 | 1,125.00 |
| SUNW | B | 1000 | 93 15/16 | 91.06 | 2,812.50 |
| YHOO | B | 1000 | 137 15/16 | 137.50 | 375.00 |

*Copyright 2000, TradeCast® Ltd.*

## Fundamental Data Window

For a longer term view of your stock, this window displays comprehensive fundamental data, such as Cusip number, published financial data, stock price history, fundamental ratios, etc. See Figure 6.16.

---

**FIGURE 6.16** Sample Fundamental Data Window

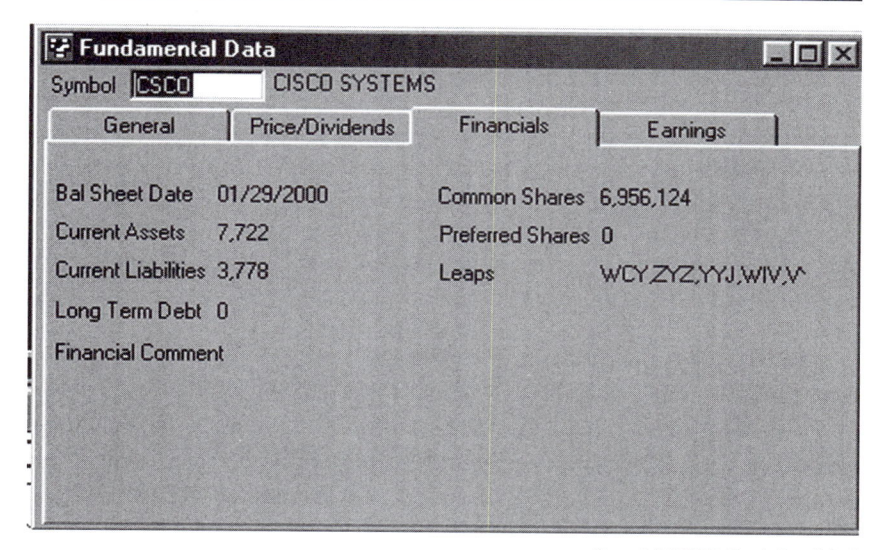

```
Fundamental Data                                    _ □ ×
Symbol [CSCO]      CISCO SYSTEMS
┌─────────┬────────────────┬──────────┬──────────┐
  General   Price/Dividends  Financials  Earnings

Bal Sheet Date   01/29/2000      Common Shares  6,956,124
Current Assets   7,722           Preferred Shares  0
Current Liabilities  3,778       Leaps          WCY,ZYZ,YYJ,WIV,V^
Long Term Debt   0
Financial Comment
```

*Copyright 2000, TradeCast® Ltd.*

---

## HOW TO CHOOSE AN ONLINE BROKER

No matter what your level of experience, you must insist on certain capabilities so you can trade effectively.

### Access to the ECNs

In order to take advantage of the ECNs—with their liquidity and attractive pricing, you must be able to execute directly to their computers. That means that your online broker must have direct connections to the ECNs. As of August 2000, the most active ECNs are Instinet (INCA), Island (ISLD), and Archipelago (ARCA).

### Avoiding Downtime

Even if you only make one trade every year, you cannot afford for your broker's network to be "down" when you want to make that trade. Network redundancy, communications redundancy, backup procedures, and manual error recovery systems are key criteria when choosing a broker. Ask to see their downtime reports and speak with some of their customers about their reliability record.

### Customer Service

Systems will fail. Will there be anyone there to help you when they do? When choosing a broker, ask if it has automated systems to take care of the most common problems quickly. Does it have specialists to take care of unusual or difficult problems in a timely fashion?

Most important, does it have an experienced team, with advanced support systems, to help you solve a trading problem? The worst thing that can happen is for a trade to be "lost"—it is your money at risk while your broker is trying to find the problem. Is it good at finding trades quickly?

**Pay attention to this next point!** You must realize that a network failure, a systems failure, or a customer service failure can result in a loss, sometimes a very big loss! That risk is yours; it is a risk of trading. Don't proceed under the mistaken impression that your brokerage will absorb this loss—it won't!

It is imperative that you find the broker with the very best network and customer service possible. It could be worth a lot of money to you.

### Other Types of Securities Services

Are you interested in electronic trading of options or futures? What about a preferential ability to purchase shares of IPOs? What about an ability to buy and sell mutual funds online? What about extended hours trading? What about trading on exchanges around the world?

The need for these other types of services is a choice of the individual trader. If one or more of these capabilities are important to you, then seek out the broker who can serve your particular needs.

If you think these might be things you want to trade in the future, don't worry about whether your chosen broker can support them now. In the near future, before mid-2001, all of the good direct access brokers will be able to handle all of these types of securities.

## Other Financial Services

In the beginning of this book, we might have come down a bit hard on the online brokers who are trying to provide a broad range of financial services to their customers. After all, who are we to say that the online auction of brownie recipes is not valuable to some of you?

But, we repeat, what do all of these services have to do with trading? Are they really just a way to divert your attention from trading services? Are these firms admitting that they don't have leading-edge trading capabilities?

If you intend to trade, then find the best direct access, software-based broker you can find.

## Training and Suitability

Of course you want help learning how to trade. But the regulators have ruled that there is a conflict of interest if a broker also teaches you how to trade. Brokers earn their money from commissions on trades, so there is simply too much temptation for them to teach clients to do lots of trades.

As Arthur Levitt, chairman of the SEC, said in a speech to the National Press Club on May 4, 2000:

> These firms should be on notice that they are still broker-dealers and must operate within the existing rules. Any firm, whether day trading or online, that recommends a type of investment strategy or customizes research should ensure that it is suitable for its customers.

That simply means that if your broker trains you, it must ensure that every trade you make is suitable for you, your knowledge level, your experience level, and your financial situation. As an astute trader, you will not subject yourself to that conflict of interest. Never choose to take training from the same broker that will charge you commissions for trading. Seek out competent, independent training resources.

## Commission Rates and Other Charges

We emphatically put this criteria last on the list. The stated prices you are charged for commissions, real-time quotes, or other fees are not that important. That's right . . . they are not that important.

If you choose the broker with direct access to more ECNs, a software-based system with top quality trading tools, fast quotes, stable network and communications facilities, and experienced technical support and customer service staff, your improved trading will more than offset an extra few dollars in fees.

Choose your broker by looking for value, not cost.

That's it for Part Two. Now you know how to choose *where* to trade, the first step in becoming the prepared trader. Let's move on to learning *how* to trade.

# PART III

# Winning in the Sixth Market through Education

CHAPTER 7

# Aw, Mom. Do I Really Have to Go to School Today?

*"If you think education is expensive, try ignorance."*

DEREK BOK

**L**et's see where we are. The Sixth Market is in full swing—fueled by fast processors, abundant bandwidth, a stable Internet, great trading platforms, unlimited information, a new kind of trader, and a bright future full of wonderful progress.

We already know where to trade, we can configure our equipment, choose an ISP, and choose the right direct access broker for our needs. It's not surprising that millions of us have opened online trading accounts to take advantage of these newly found powers in the Sixth Market. Eagerly, we new traders have embarked on this exciting new online trading adventure. It can't get any better than this, can it?

Well, frankly it had better get a lot better! Don't forget the dirty little secret of the Sixth Market. Most of these self-directed traders are not making consistent profits in the market. That kind of takes all the fun out of it, doesn't it?

So, why isn't everyone making money? What's gone wrong?

**P**eople aren't making consistent profits because of a lack of effective education. Traders have to learn *how* to trade. The professionals have been studying market behavior for hundreds of years.

Go back as far as 1720, when Exchange Alley was the London stock exchange. In that year, stock of the South Sea Company opened at 128½ in January, and rose to 1,000 in July, when the directors of the company sold out, the bubble exploded, and the stock closed worthless. There is nothing new under the sun!

Incidentally, Exchange Alley is where investors were first divided into "bears" and "bulls." Another class was christened here, too. Those who were not able to meet their obligations became known as "lame ducks" because, when defeated, they looked like they "waddled out of the Alley"!

The watershed experiences of the Dutch Tulip episode, the crash of 1929, and the bull market of the 1990s, all have added to the knowledge base of the professional.

Anything that can be reduced to mathematical expression has been. The hypothesis, the modeling, the testing, the analysis, the interpretation are all part of our ongoing education.

Value theory, efficient market theory, chaos theory, and random walk theory have been expostulated to explain market behavior. We've even seen a theory tied to the alignment of the planets. Trading theories are endless.

Trading systems, magical algorithms, black boxes, and programmed trading have all been offered as ways to assure successful trading.

For years, the financial community has helped to spread the myth that trading was hard. It was complicated. It was beyond the abilities of mere mortals.

So how can you hope to compete against all of this knowledge? Isn't it obvious that the professionals have an insurmountable edge over you? Can't you see that it would be impossible to learn all of this stuff?

Baloney! What's really obvious is that no one knows everything. Each professional just knows about a special area of knowledge. Fundamental is fundamental, technical is technical, and never the twain shall meet!

Anyone can learn to trade. Look no further than the "Turtles" to demonstrate that truth.

*Richard Dennis, the legendary Chicago commodity trader, who turned $400 into $200 million in just 18 years, wanted to settle a friendly argu-*

*ment with his partner, William Eckhardt. This was the issue at hand: Can the skills of a successful trader be learned? Or are they innate, some sort of "sixth sense" a lucky few are born with?*

*In 1984 and 1985, Dennis placed ads seeking trader trainees. Twenty-three young people were hired and trained in proprietary trading methods during a two-week seminar. Dennis called his protégés the "Turtles." (He had visited a turtle "farm" in Singapore and had decided that he could "grow" traders the way this farm grew turtles!)*

*The results of his experiment have been impressive to say the very least. Today these "Turtles" collectively manage more than $2 billion for customers. Annual returns of more than 50 percent—and even more than 100 percent—have resulted. Some Turtles have had returns exceed 100 percent in a single month!*

*Dennis said, "Trading was even more teachable than I had imagined."*

The professionals have actually made our case for us. After all, it is the professionals who prove that trading is a skill that can be learned, and that the concepts for successful trading can be mastered.

If you truly want to trade, there are ways to improve your chances of market survival. You do not have to learn *everything*. You must learn a proven, solid trading method, and then consistently apply that method without emotion.

That is a manageable task, so let's get on with it.

The next chapter will explore the six steps that you need to cover to learn how to trade.

CHAPTER | 8

# OK, I'm Ready to Learn. Now What?

*"Knowledge is the antidote to fear."*

RALPH WALDO EMERSON

*James kept thinking about the money. He saw some of the traders around him making big profits every day and he was beside himself with envy. "Why can't I make that kind of money?" he would ask himself. "Is today the day I finally get it all together and start getting rich?"*

*He had taken several good training courses and read a dozen books on trading. Certainly he knew how to trade after all that effort. By now, he was beyond just thinking about the money; he was obsessed with it. Yet, it seemed that the more he focused on making money, the more money he lost. Almost out of trading capital, James was in a real bind.*

*At just the darkest moment, one of his most successful pals on the trading floor took him aside and gave him this advice: "Thinking about the money is getting in your way. Quit it. Instead, focus on learning about the markets and mastering your trading style. Get passionate about the process of trading. If you will leave it alone, the money will take care of itself."*

*James remembers: "Somehow, that advice clicked in me. The next day, I actually felt a sense of physical relief. The doubts and fears were gone; instead of worrying about my P&L, I was really focused on the trading process." He had one of his best days ever. Over the course of the next three weeks, his profits exceeded $15,000, and he was on his way.*

**W**hat is the secret to making money consistently in the markets? Isn't that what you really want to know? Isn't that what you really bought this book to find out? Aren't you thinking that if you only had that secret, everything would be great? Don't you see . . . there is no secret!

## THE THREE STEPS TO SUCCESSFUL TRADING

To make money consistently in the markets, you only need three things:

1. A statistically valid trading plan
2. Effective money management techniques
3. The discipline to put your plan and techniques to work.

In reality, the questions you should be asking yourself are:

- How do I get those three things?
- How do I learn a statistically valid trading plan?
- How do I learn effective money management techniques?
- How do I develop the discipline to put them both to work?

Until now, there has not been a readily-available answer to that question.

Training for the securities trader has been greatly fragmented. The truth is that you have had to learn about trading psychology from one authority, technical analysis from another expert, trading strategies from three or four different specialists, money management from still another source, and on and on.

There has been no single source for a curriculum that gives a complete education in trading. There has not even been agreement on what should be taught. None of the pieces of this puzzle worked together. Without a coordinated roadmap to tell you everything you need, key concepts, and proven techniques are sure to be missed entirely. Consider Janie's story to illustrate this point:

*Janie was determined to become a good golfer. She wanted her handicap to be in single digits. She reasoned that the best way to achieve this goal was through instruction.*

*So, she sought out the very best instructor at her local golf course. After weeks of individualized sessions working with her driver and fairway woods, he had her making a very nice "full shoulder turn" and she began to see real improvement in those areas. But her irons and her putting were terrible—something would have to be done about that!*

*So, Janie found a golf clinic in a nearby city that specialized in iron play. Full of hope, she made four trips to the clinic over the next month. Sure enough, after learning how to "stay behind the ball," her iron shots were improving.*

*In the back of her mind, Janie realized that this new instructor had very different thoughts about the golf swing from her original instructor. Somewhat confused by conflicting messages, she noticed that her driver seemed much more erratic than it had been. But, she had no time to worry about that; she still needed help on her putting.*

*Luckily, a respected "putting guru" was about to start a week-long putting camp at a beautiful resort in another state. If she acted now, she could get the last spot. She was almost trembling with excitement as she boarded the jet.*

*And what an instructor this guru was. Eloquent, patient, and experienced, he made several immediate changes in her grip and alignment. She saw the results almost immediately.*

*But he also told her that the natural pendulum motion in the putting stroke was the key to every good golf shot. So, Janie started experimenting with a pendulum move with her other shots.*

*When she returned home, Janie couldn't wait to get with her regular foursome for their weekly game. She just knew that all of this instruction and all of this dedicated effort would pay off with much lower scores.*

*As she stepped up to the first tee, she tried to remember all she had been taught.*

*Let's see . . . "full shoulder turn" . . . "stay behind the ball" . . . "pendulum motion." Each instructor's words flooded back to her. With supreme willpower, she did her best to apply everything they had taught her all at once.*

What's wrong with this picture? How do you think Janie played that day? Of course she had a miserable day. She was trying to integrate the teachings of three very different instructors, each with a very different perspective on the swing, and each with no knowledge of what the others had taught her. The result was that the conflicting messages caused confusion, frustration, and eventually paralysis. She could barely even begin her swing!

This is how too many people have had to learn to trade. They took different courses from different instructors, each with a very different perspective on trading, and each with absolutely no knowledge of what others might have already taught them. Is it any wonder that many people conclude that trading is difficult, confusing, and impossible to learn?

It doesn't have to be that way. There is a better way—one that works. We call this approach the Six Steps—*Trading Fitness for Life.*

With this program, you study trading as a process, learning to integrate a set of specific skills to produce the results you want from the market. Each step is designed to be a building block for the steps to come. You learn the skills you need in a sequential and logical order.

Figure 8.1 shows the logical flow through the Six Steps. It describes each step in detail, and suggests the basic classes which make up each step.

The real value of the process is that for the first time you have a basic, organized curriculum that you can follow to learn all of the things you will need to know to trade effectively and with confidence.

This is not to suggest that your learning stops when you complete the Six Steps . . . go back and read Step Six! Your learning has only begun. Once you have begun to trade with that *core* knowledge, you will begin to develop and perfect your own trading style. Your motivations and goals, your trading temperament, your risk propensity, and your money management skills will help you quickly see the areas where you need to concentrate further education.

For more information on the Six Steps, visit <www.sixthmarket.com>. Each of the classes is delivered over the Internet with streaming video presentations and comprehensive graphics. They are organized into 10- to 15-minute segments to match the optimum human attention span.

In this online format, you can use time to your advantage. Rather than trying to "cram" all of this education into a weekend seminar—or even a two-week camp, take your time to learn, to digest, to reflect, and to revisit classes for deeper understanding. Best of all, all of these classes are *free*.

# 8 / OK, I'm Ready to Learn. Now What? 79

**FIGURE 8.1** The Six Steps

| THE SIX STEPS™ | Description | The Basic Classes |
|---|---|---|
| **STEP ONE** Building Self-Awareness | Trading "fitness" begins with self-awareness: an honest appraisal of your motivation for trading and your particular investment goals. Determine the trading style that best fits your needs. Probing deeply here maximizes your effectiveness and gets you on the road to becoming a disciplined trader. | • Your Personal Motivation<br>• Your Investment Goals<br>• Your Trading Style<br>• Characteristics of Successful Traders<br>• Beliefs, Anxiety, and Confidence<br>• Personal Discipline |
| **STEP TWO** Learning Trading Fundamentals | Develop a thorough grounding in market mechanics, basic and advanced trading tools, and the rules of trading. Every skill you acquire as a trader depends on the foundation you build at this stage. | • Basic Market Mechanics<br>• Nasdaq Level II<br>• Basic Trading Tools<br>• Advanced Trading Tools<br>• Short Selling<br>• Proven Trading Rules<br>• Choosing the Right Broker |
| **STEP THREE** Understanding Charts | Charts reveal market psychology. Learn how to construct, read, and interpret price charts. There are many types of charting studies for you to consider before you find the ones that best suit your trading style. | • Market Psychology and Price Movements<br>• Japanese Candlesticks<br>• Basic Chart Formations<br>• Trends<br>• Support and Resistance<br>• Moving Averages<br>• Oscillators |
| **STEP FOUR** Trading from Reliable Chart Setups | Profitable trading strategies derive from understanding proven, high-probability chart patterns that are predictable and repeatable. | • High-Probability Chart Patterns<br>• The "Opportunity Spotting" Report<br>• The Trading Plan<br>• Gaps<br>• Other Trading Tips<br>• Exit Strategies |
| **STEP FIVE** Mastering Your Trading Plan | As you progress through the first four steps, you will have learned the skills needed to make a trade. In this vital fifth step, you will learn to master the principals of risk/reward and money management, which are essential for consistent profits. You will revisit your own psychology to better understand your trading discipline and emotional control. | • Risk and Reward<br>• Money Management<br>• Personal Discipline— Revisted |
| **STEP SIX** Committing to Your Education | Trading success has no limits. To continue to grow and prosper as a trader, you must commit to continue to learn about yourself and the market. Knowledge and research are your ultimate edge. | • Self-directed study |

This is not, however, a commercial for any particular educational firm. You can choose to use the Six Steps as a checklist to put together a series of courses from teachers you select. The main thing is to be sure that you cover all of the topics contained in the Six Steps.

In Part Four we will look more closely at the educational course material that will be covered in each of the Six Steps.

# PART IV

# The Six Steps™

CHAPTER 9

# Step One: Building Self-Awareness

*"The beginning is the most important part of the work."*

PLATO

*The proper place to begin to learn to trade is with yourself. Successful trading begins and ends with self-awareness. Who you are—your strengths, your weaknesses, your likes, your dislikes, your needs, your desires. All of these have an important bearing on the trader that you can become.*

*Many traders resist this notion. They believe they can succeed by reading another book, subscribing to another newsletter, purchasing another black box system, listening to another chat room, or taking another seminar.*

*Certainly, some of those things are useful, but they are of little value until you know who you are as a trader. This is where the series of "self awareness" classes comes in.*

*The ground we will cover in this area applies to all traders—the part-time or the full-time trader. Whether trading is an avocation or a vocation, the nature of the challenge is the same: you are competing against the pros! If you want a chance to make consistent profits in the market, you need to get serious about learning to trade.*

*Think of the local club champion in tennis. She may be a full time lawyer or teacher, but you can bet that her commitment to winning and to improvement is very strong!!! She practices, reads the latest tennis magazines, and talks tennis with her buddies.*

*Your commitment should be no less !!!*

## YOUR PERSONAL MOTIVATION

Let's look at why the best traders succeed. They all share a burning, unquenchable desire to become successful. But there is more to it that mere desire. Desire alone will not sustain a dream.

We all want things, but we are not necessarily willing to work for them. Do you want to be a great piano player, but are not willing to commit untold hours to practice? You may have a desire to succeed at trading, but without a sustaining motivation, you cannot—you will not—commit to the effort nor rebound from the disappointments.

The simple fact is that the markets have a stark way of revealing exactly who you really are. They exaggerate all of your weaknesses . . . fear . . . greed . . . emotional meltdowns.

So, the first thing to know about yourself is *why* you desire to succeed as a trader.

- *Is it to get rich quick?* You would be better off buying a lottery ticket or starting a "dot-com" business.
- *Is it for excitement?* Take up hang gliding.
- *Is it to impress others with your skill and daring?* Try rock climbing.

These reasons are simply not enough to sustain you. As you learn to trade, you will suffer losses. If you are only in this to make money, you will conclude that "trading is not for me" and you will quit a loser. You will get frustrated with your confusion and your emotions and, if you are only in this for excitement, you will quit a loser. You will get discouraged when you have a series of losing days and, if you are only in this to impress others, you will quit a loser.

Some trading days are tough and the "why" reasons above will not sustain you. You need more compelling reasons. For example, what if you were determined to find and master a satisfying intellectual challenge? Or do you want to solve one of life's most intriguing puzzles, how to take advantage of stock movements? Do you want to build a base of knowledge and skill to help you compete on a level playing field against committed, determined, experienced, disciplined people who are all trying to take advantage of endless opportunities for profit? Without an overarching, compelling, almost noble reason to trade, you cannot summon the intensity and the commitment to master the learning process.

Let us illustrate with the story of Wilma Rudolph. Do you remember her?

She was born in 1940 with polio. She had pneumonia and scarlet fever before she was four years old. She was so crippled she could not attend public school. She was told she would never walk normally. It was a giant challenge just to stay alive.

But in 1960, at age 20, in Rome, Italy, Wilma Rudolph became the first American woman to win three Olympic gold medals. She was the fastest woman alive!

How did she do it? Wilma had an overriding motivation. She had a dream. It was no ordinary dream, for no ordinary dream would have sustained her to bear years of painful heat treatments, to endure years of wearing numbing leg braces, or to suffer insults as a crippled black girl in the 1950s south. Her dream was the ultimate in motivation—she dreamed of winning an Olympic gold medal. That dream was larger than all of the hurt in her life. That dream kept her going when any reasonable person would have quit.

Few of us will ever find a motivation to match Wilma's, but your own powerful motivating purpose is still essential to success in trading, and in the rest of your life. So, be honest with yourself. Take a few minutes and ask yourself: What is my motivation to trade? What will keep me going when the going gets rough? What will keep me determined in the face of adversity?

If your dream can meet the challenges in those questions, you have made an important discovery about yourself. You now know why you want to trade. You can articulate your reasons for trading. That is the first step toward true trading success. Write your reasons for trading on a piece of paper as a constant reminder to yourself, and refer to it often to keep your motivation alive.

## YOUR INVESTMENT GOALS

Once you know your motivations for trading, the second thing you must know about yourself is: What you want from trading.

What are your investment goals? You have heard it before: Setting written goals is important—even vital—in reaching your dreams. This is especially true for trading. To significantly change your life, you first must know the outcome you desire. If you don't know where you are going, you will end up nowhere!

We love the story of the two lumberjacks in the north woods, working side by side. After several hours, one noticed that his partner was not even $\frac{1}{16}$ of an inch into the tree!

"Hey Bob," he said. "You're not making any progress."
"I know, I know. Don't bother me," said the other.
"But," said the first, "you've got to stop and sharpen your blades."
"Stop? I can't stop! I've got to cut down this tree!"

Here is a man consumed by *activity* instead of being focused on achieving his goal. That's the problem with too many traders. They're too busy trading to sharpen their skills. They don't define their goals. You should create two kinds of goals:

1. Goals for skills and performance.
2. Goals for results.

### Goals for Skills and Performance

These are targets to improve your skills and performance. They need to be specific, realistic, and measurable. For example:

- To take a specific class, by a certain date
- To devote a certain amount of time to chart review each day
- To trade every trading signal
- To set a stop loss before entering any trade, and to hold to that stop loss without exception

### Goals for Results

These are targets for desired results. Again, they need to be specific, realistic, and measurable. For example:

- Liquidity, working capital, acid test
- Operations, products, market position
- Management
- Strategy

This style requires much attention to detail, concentrated research, and a long learning curve. Patience is rewarded. Many of you are already long-term investors in mutual funds, managed accounts, and retirement funds.

## The Long-Term Trader

This is a variation on the long-term investor. The time horizon is shorter: usually one week to about one year. The entry decisions are often similar to those of the long-term investor, but the exits are most often based on more immediate market conditions such as changes in market indexes or targeted price levels being reached. This style requires the attention to fundamentals of the long-term investor coupled with the ability to conduct sophisticated technical analysis.

## The Swing Trader

This trader seeks "pivot points" in the market—gaps, breakouts, and reversals—with a one-day to five-day time horizon. Trades chosen have proven, high-probability chart patterns.

The educated swing trader enjoys a high percentage of winning trades because one's chart patterns have been back-tested and their winning percentages are known. One's risk parameters are highly defined. The swing trader is an aggressive user of trading stops.

This style is especially well-suited for online trading because

- it is the easiest of all styles to learn, due to the fact that the underlying market psychology of chart patterns is easy to understand.
- it is fun, and it can be very profitable since the educated swing trader enjoys a high percentage of winning trades.
- it is the easiest to manage in terms of time commitment. The disciplined swing trader can trade as actively, or as sporadically, as one chooses without detriment to one's results.
- education and practice can really pay off.

## The Day Trader

The day trader looks to exploit very short-term price movements. This style is characterized by speed, fast executions, small gains, and many trades. While day trading can be quite thrilling, it also produces high tension because this style produces many losses. It requires extreme focus and discipline, and generally requires full-time participation in the market.

For most people there is one strategy that will be right for them. Consider Warren Buffet. He is renowned as a long-term investor, characterized by his endless research, intimate knowledge of management and strategy, and his remarkable patience. He would be a terrible day trader! Choosing the right strategy for him was what made him successful.

This decision will be just as important for you. How do you decide the right strategy for you? You decide on a style that fits your personality, fits your motivation, helps you reach your trading goals, gives you a realistic chance at a profit, and feels right to you.

## Your Style Must Fit Your Personality

Take the time to answer these questions:

- What do I enjoy most about trading?
- What do I enjoy least?
- What do I find most interesting?
- What do I find least interesting?
- What are my greatest strengths as a trader?
- What are my greatest weaknesses as a trader?
- How much time and effort am I willing to commit to trading?
- How much money am I willing to commit to the learning curve?
- Do I want to trade by feel?
- Do I want to trade with a mechanical system?
- What does my ideal trading system look like to me?

Only you can answer these truthfully in order to decide what fits your personality. If you cannot stand fast action, don't be a day trader. If you need fast feedback, don't be a long-term trader.

## Your Style Must Fit Your Motivation for Trading

Remember that you must be seeking more than just profit. Does your chosen style meet your need for intellectual stimulation? Does it meet your need for conquering a challenging opportunity? There's no need to get started if you will only be bored to death with your choice.

## Your Style Must Help You Reach Your Goals for Trading

The fit must be precise here or you will be miserable. Does your chosen style meet your profit expectations, your time commitment expectations, your expectations for the education required, and your lifestyle expectations.

If one of your goals is to buy and hold, don't get into swing trading. If your goal is to make $2,000 in cash each day, don't go into long-term trading. If your goal is to trade part-time, don't go into day trading.

## Your Style Must Give You a Realistic Chance at Profits

Trading is about performance, not theory. Are you willing to learn the success tactics in your chosen style? Do you really want to apply them with discipline? Do you truly believe you can make money with this style?

## Your Style Must Feel Right to You

The tactics you will use in your strategy must be comfortable to you, must be understandable to you, and must make you believe that you can master those tactics. It must help you spot opportunities easily, encourage you to trade with confidence, and encourage you to accept full responsibility for your results.

You must decide which strategy is right for you. Don't take another step until you work this out to your satisfaction.

Once this is done, you have three steps completed: you know why you trade, you know what you want from your trading and, you know what style of trading is for you.

These first three sections have helped you to build a solid foundation for trading. You may not even realize just how important this preparatory work has been. But our experience shows that the time and effort you have spent here is certain to pay dividends.

## CHARACTERISTICS OF SUCCESSFUL TRADERS

Can we learn from the great traders? What characteristics do they possess? What are their capabilities? Can we model them?

Over the years, when we ask traders to describe the very best traders they know, we always hear the same descriptions. The best traders are:

- *Motivated*. They clearly understand why trading is important to them and they are in it for more than just the money.
- *Goal-oriented*. They clearly understand what they want to achieve and their goals are realistic and measurable.
- *Self-aware*. They know their strengths and weaknesses and have learned to take advantage of both.
- *Self-reliant*. They take full responsibility for all of their actions.
- *Knowledgeable*. They understand the markets and use strategies and tactics that work for them.
- *Confident*. They are optimistic. The knowledge they possess allows them to expect positive results.
- *Focused*. They are intense and are not distracted by the "noise" in the market.
- *Disciplined*. They stay on their plan and within their trading rules.
- *Positive*. They have a positive state of mind and can "roll with the flow" without emotion or confusion.
- *Independent*. They are not trading to please others.
- *Flexible*. They can adapt and adjust unemotionally.
- *Realistic*. They can separate a loss from being a loser.
- *Winners*. They play to win instead of "not to lose."
- *Automatic*. They react automatically. They internalize their trading concepts, then save time by acting unconsciously according to their chosen strategy.

- *Good Managers*. They manage risk and are great at money management. They protect their capital to ensure they will be able to trade tomorrow.
- *Committed*. They are determined to succeed, and are willing to do what is needed for success.
- *Having Fun*. They enjoy trading and they make it look easy.

Isn't this a very impressive list? Do you think that all of these characteristics are fully-developed in one person? Probably not, but there is a little bit of each in everyone—even you!

We call each of these characteristics an "ability" and we all have the ability to develop each of these characteristics. When we have developed one of these abilities, it becomes a capability.

You must accept that developing capabilities such as these takes time. Even the best traders go through periods of loss and frustration at first. Then, they all tell a similar story: one day they found a plan that consistently worked, that gave them confidence, and that allowed them to stay disciplined to their plan. And then came trading success.

Do you believe that you can develop these characteristics in yourself? Anthony Robbins says, *"Our beliefs about what we are and what we can be precisely determine what we will be."* If you can't see these success characteristics in you, you will not put in the effort or make the commitment to succeed.

Ask yourself these eight questions:

1. Do I really want to be a successful online trader? Why?
2. Do I possess the internal skills necessary to succeed?
3. Am I willing to pay the price in terms of effort and commitment?
4. Am I willing to suffer financial losses while I learn to trade?
5. Am I willing to take full responsibility for my trading actions?
6. Am I capable of thinking for myself?
7. Am I willing to start right now, right where I am?
8. Am I willing and able to live up to my full potential?

Were you able to answer "yes" to all of those questions? If so, you have arrived at another important stage in this process. Let us summarize: you now clearly understand your motivation to trade, you have written the goals you want to achieve from trading, you have selected the right trading strategy for yourself, and you have made the commitment to develop many of the personal characteristics of great traders.

If you have not done all of these things, we promise you that you are only hurting your chances to succeed. But, if you have come this far with us, you truly are on the path to success as a trader!

## WINNING IN THE MARKET

Now it's important to start talking about winning in the market. After all, it's profits we are after.

As Winston Churchill said: *"It is a socialist idea that making profits is a vice. I consider the real vice is making losses."*

To talk about winning, we want to start with some of our beliefs about trading:

- *Security prices are not random.* There is underlying order to price movements that can be discerned. You CAN learn
- *Effective trading and investing can be taught.* We have proven this time and time again over the years.
- *The psychological side of trading* is more important than any trading system. Understand and adjust your state of mind, belief system, focus, and discipline.
- *Knowledge breeds confidence, confidence breeds discipline.* You've learned that building one's ability leads to another capability.

To win as a trader, we think that you must first understand why so many people lose. Here are the most common barriers to successful trading:

- *Not defining the loss.* The trader has no idea where to get out of the trade. Before entering any trade, define the downside and set the stop loss.
- *Not taking the loss.* The trader wants to avoid the pain of a loss, which leads to bigger losses. Losing trades are a major part of trading. Take the loss when you hit the stop.
- *Not defining the profit.* This is just the other side of number one above, the trader still doesn't know where to get out of the trade. Before entering the trade, define the target exit point.
- *Not taking the profit.* This is a result of getting confused or greedy. When the target is reached, take the profit. The market may not give you a second chance.
- *Getting locked into a belief about the market.* Here is where the trader starts destructive self-talk, like: "I just know it'll go up."

This leads straight to disaster. What you think is irrelevant. The market is your boss. Trade your plan.
- *Thinking you are "bulletproof."* In this case, the trader has made a few great trades, and he can do no wrong. Watch out.
- *Hesitation.* The trader has a plan, the market comes to the selected price, but the trader can't pull the trigger. This trader is simply leaving money on the table.
- *Not staying focused.* The trader lets the *noise* of the market distract him or her. To succeed, stay attentive to your plan.
- *Being right instead of making money.* Trading is about making money . . . *period!* Yet trading is overpopulated with people who go to great lengths to justify how they were right and the market was wrong. Who cares? Take the money!
- *Not consistently applying tactics.* How can the trader guess which signal is best? When you have chosen a good plan, you must take every signal possible.
- *Not preserving capital.* Rule number one is to protect your trading "stake." Yet we have seen so many fledgling traders risk—and lose—it all on just one trade. The saddest words on the trading floor are: "The trade looked so good," or "I just knew it would come back."
- *Not being in the right state of mind.* The trader who is distracted or upset is just giving money away. Stay away from trading unless you can concentrate.

How do you overcome these problems? The very best traders always talk about "having the edge." What do they mean by "having the Edge"? The *Edge* is the overriding capability to deal with what the market presents you with no emotional impact.

*Say it again!* The *Edge* is the overriding capability to deal with what the market presents you with no emotional impact.

That's great, but how do these great traders get the Edge? Consider the chart in Figure 9.1. Compare those with the Edge to those without the Edge.

Now that you've had a chance in Figure 9.1 to compare trading with the Edge and without the Edge, use the following questions to review the advantages of proper preparation and mental attitude:

- Do you see the progression in this chart: from motives → to goals → to trading style → to educated tactics → to risk control and money management → to discipline → to state of mind?

**FIGURE 9.1** Winning with the Edge

| Trading Characteristic | Having the Edge | Not Having the Edge |
|---|---|---|
| Motives | Compelling motive, e.g., intellectual challenge | To make money, instant gratification |
| Goals | Clearly defined | Ill-defined |
| Trading Style | Fits personality and goals | Does not fit personality or goals (if any) |
| Trading Tactics | Highly planned, consistent application of tactics | Little planning, no consistent methodology |
| Expertise | Well prepared, has done homework | Little market knowledge, unprepared |
| Patience | Waits for proven opportunities to materialize | Reacts according to whim |
| Risk Control | Highly controlled risk/reward ratio | Little or no understanding of risk/reward |
| Money Management | Highly controlled capital deployment and preservation plan | Little or no understanding of capital deployment or preservation |
| Discipline | Dispassionate | Emotional, anxious, often confused |
| State of Mind | Positive, resourceful, relaxed, confident, enjoys trading | Nervous, unfocused, expects the worst, afraid of trading |

- Do you see that gaining a capability in one area is the foundation to gaining a capability in the next area?
- Do you recognize this as the building process of a great trader?
- Do you recognize that this is exactly how the Six Steps are organized? Following that process will help you gain skills in each of these areas, and will help you build the Edge—if you commit to your education.

Let's move on to some of the psychological underpinnings to your success as a trader.

## BELIEF SYSTEM

We have all heard that our belief system is important to our success in anything we do. Here is a simple test to help you understand your beliefs about yourself as a trader. Look in the mirror and say: "I am a trader." Now, do you believe it? If you do, then you are! If you don't, then we have work to do.

Here are some other common beliefs of good traders:

- I believe I will be a successful trader.
- I believe trading is a process.
- I believe I am personally responsible for all of my trading results.
- I believe I can be successful without being perfect.
- I believe my performance as a trader does not reflect my self worth.
- I believe if I make one bad trade that is all I have done.
- I believe I can identify and execute winning trades.
- I believe I can trade with confidence.

Which of these do you share? Can you see that with education and practice, you can come to believe similar things about yourself?

## ANXIETY

Another psychological element is anxiety. Anxiety is driven from four sources:

1. *Fear of failure.* There are at least four fears here, all of which can be debilitating.
   i. You tie your self-worth to trading.
   ii. You are concerned about what others think about you.
   iii. You are striving for perfection.
   iv. You feel pressure to perform.
2. *Fear of success.* You don't feel you are worthy of good things. You sabotage yourself.
3. *Fear of inadequacy.* You doubt yourself and your abilities. You have a loss of self-esteem and diminished self-confidence.
4. *Fear of loss of control.* You feel you are not the master of your fate. You lose your sense of personal responsibility. You feel the market is out to get you.

The key to controlling anxiety is to focus on your methodology. The more you can concentrate on a sound strategy and proven tactics, the less anxious you will feel. As we develop your methodology in later classes, these anxious feelings should dissipate.

## CONFIDENCE

Let's talk about confidence. You have certainly heard that confidence is important to success as a trader. But what is confidence?

- Confidence is the expectation of a positive outcome. (Fear is just the opposite—it is the expectation of a negative outcome.)
- Confidence is *knowing* that you will have a positive outcome instead of *thinking, wishing* or *hoping*.
- Confidence is conviction, not arrogance.

Obviously, confidence—this expectation of a positive outcome—has its roots in a picture of success. This picture could have been experienced before through successful trades with your methodology. Or, this picture could be clearly visualized because your preparation has been so thorough.

## POSITIVE STATE OF MIND

Finally, we want you to think about, and to begin to work toward, developing a positive state of mind. Top trading is the result of competence and the ability to control one's state of mind.

Your state of mind is simply how you are feeling at the time.

- The positive state of mind is optimistic, resourceful, calm, and focused. The result is a high level of performance.
- The negative state of mind is anxious, fearful, angry, uptight, unfocused, and confused. The result is a low level of performance.

How valuable is a positive state of mind? Answer four questions:

1. How much money have you lost because you traded with a negative state of mind?
2. How much more would you make if you always trade in a positive state of mind?

3. How much more fun would you have if you managed your state of mind?
4. How would the quality of your life be enhanced if you were in a positive state of mind every day?

## PERSONAL DISCIPLINE

The concept of discipline is central to any discussion about profitable trading. When we talk about discipline we are not talking about raw willpower—the ability to make your mind do something it does not want to do. Instead, we are talking about a disciplined state of mind that is unemotional, focused, and effective.

In an earlier section in this book we stated that success in trading only requires:

- A statistically valid trading plan.
- Good money management skills.
- The discipline to trade your plan.

We can and will teach you how to achieve the first two in other parts of this book.

In this section, we will discuss how to build up your discipline. The end result, however, is totally up to you. We have proven that the real battle is within yourself. It is not you against the market; it is just you against you!

Think about some of the tried and true rules of trading:

- Buy low, sell high.
- The trend is your friend.
- Take big profits.
- Take small losses.
- The first loss is your best loss.
- Preserve your capital.

This list goes on and on. We will explore more of these rules in more detail in Chapter 10. Rules like these are correct and they are easy to understand.

So, why doesn't everyone simply apply them and achieve immediate and enduring success? The answer is because for most people emotions get in the way.

Success in trading takes more than just a few rules. It needs an attitude that fosters decision making based on logic, research, and method—not emotions.

Emotions almost never help a trade. They destroy your discipline, your ability to make clear-headed decisions, your ability to follow your plan, and your ability to do the right thing.

Emotions almost always hurt your results. In an emotional state, traders get on an endless circle, like that shown in Figure 9.2.

- Your lack of knowledge intensifies your emotions because you are confused and unsure of your capabilities.
- Your emotions cause you to lose focus.
- Lost focus causes you to lose discipline.
- Lost discipline leads to poor trading decisions and poor results.
- Poor results increase emotion.
- And on and on.

**FIGURE 9.2** Emotional Cycle

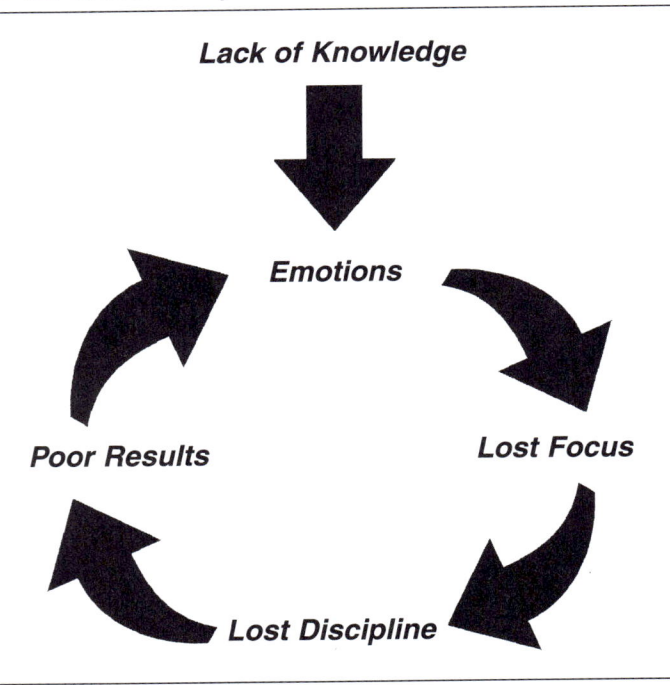

**Lack of Knowledge** → **Emotions** → **Lost Focus** → **Lost Discipline** → **Poor Results** → (back to Emotions)

So, how do you break this cycle? First, you must overcome your own psychological and emotional biases. These biases induce emotional reactions and prevent us from peak performance. What are the biases that cause us to be emotional?

## Bias toward Certainty

Our human nature demands certainty. We abhor making decisions under uncertainty. The market, however, will never give you certainty.

How can you cope with your bias toward certainty? The answer is to think in probabilities. Learn and use proven (winning) trading tactics. Select high probability trades. Those probabilities themselves become your certainty. For example, through back testing, you can be "certain" that a particular chart pattern will result in winning trades 63.6 percent of the time. That's all the certainty you need. You can control your emotions if you think in probabilities.

## Bias toward Control

Our human nature demands control. We are very uncomfortable when we are out of control. But the markets will never give you control.

How can you cope with your bias towards control? The answer is to control those things you can—your knowledge; preparation; planning and, most importantly, the execution of your plan. Don't worry about price movements. You cannot control them.

The best way to control those things that are under your control is to act in certainty. That is, don't hesitate, don't second guess. You know what to do because you think in probabilities. You can take control if you act in certainty.

## Aversion to Loss

This bias is unbelievably strong. From birth we are taught to avoid loss and that mistakes are bad. Now you start trading and you see losses all the time.

How can you cope with your aversion to loss? We have identified four *bad* ways to handle losses:

1. *Denial.* The refusal to face a loss and to let the trade continue against you is a real recipe for disaster. The attitude that "it's not a loss until I sell" has ruined more traders than we care to think about.
2. *Inaction.* Rather than risk a loss, you just don't trade. This is the fallacy of "if I sleep on the floor, I won't fall out of bed." You miss out on the whole game.
3. *Confusion.* Confusion is caused by trading without a clear plan at the time you enter the trade. Not knowing what to do creates hesitation, which increases your emotions, which gets you back on that cycle to poor decisions and more emotion.
4. *Anger.* Some traders take losses personally and claim "the market is out to get me." Wrong! The market doesn't care about you. Your little trades are but a drop in the ocean. But anger certainly increases emotion, and you are on the cycle again.

We have identified only one *good* way to handle losses. This four-step process brings success:

1. *Plan your trade* based on a high-probability chart pattern.
2. *Identify your signal*—your entry signal, your stop loss, and your exit target.
3. *React automatically* by following your strategy to take decisive action with no second-guessing.
4. *Feel good about the trade.* Your decision and your execution were based on methodology, not emotion. You must feel good because you did the right thing according to your plan. Regardless of the outcome of this one trade, you know that your high-probability trades will succeed over time.

Take a healthy view of losses. They happen. If you don't make mistakes, you won't learn. Your motto should be: "Win or lose, it's another step forward."

Those of you who admire Winston Churchill know that his life was an unending series of failures until fate thrust him into the role of Prime Minister of England during World War II, where he rose to the challenge perhaps better than any before him.

Sir Winston understood losses. He understood losing and his perspective on handling failure is timeless: *"Success is the ability to go from one failure to another with no loss of enthusiasm."*

So, to get and to keep the disciplined state of mind, we form another endless circle, as shown in Figure 9.3:

- Knowledge of our proven plan breeds confidence.
- Confidence in our plan gives us focus.
- Focus eliminates the distractions and makes it easy to remain disciplined to our plan.
- Discipline to our plan leads to great results.
- Great results give us more confidence.
- And on and on.

This is an endless chain, self-reinforcing and ultimately self-fulfilling. Discipline is not some supreme test of willpower. Knowledge is the key to starting this positive chain of events. If you know your plan will work, why would you do anything but stay disciplined to that plan? If you *know* your plan will work, discipline to it becomes easy!

**FIGURE 9.3** Discipline Cycle

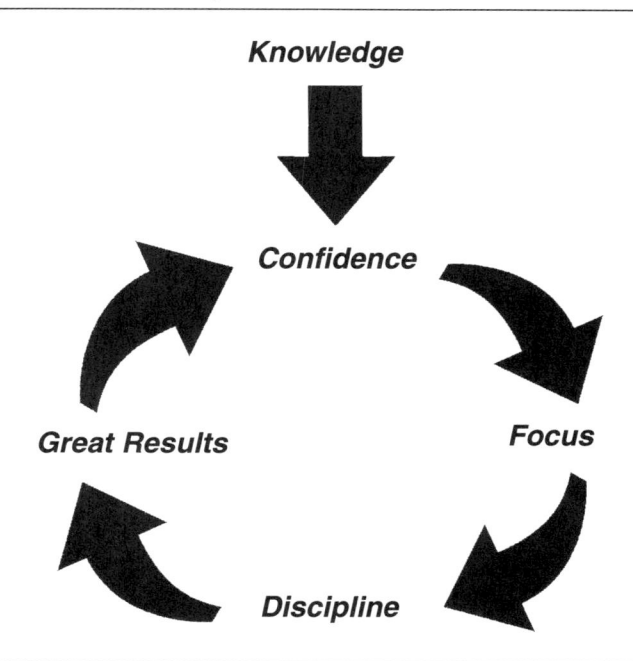

Knowledge → Confidence → Focus → Discipline → Great Results → Confidence

We know what you are thinking: All of this is great. It really makes a lot of sense. Now if these guys will just tell me how I can know that my plan will work!

Have patience, we'll get to that detail in Chapter 12.

For now, you have a good grounding in *Step One: Building Self-Awareness.*

Let's now move on to *Step Two: Learning Trading Fundamentals.*

CHAPTER | 10

# Step Two: Learning Market Fundamentals

> *"Learning is not compulsory . . . but, then neither is survival."*
>
> W. EDWARDS DEMING

**O**K, by this time you have put together all of your resources: a good processor with plenty of RAM and a great video display, a terrific ISP with a rock-solid Internet connection; and a direct access broker who provides you with a software-based trading platform. On top of that, you are motivated. You have written goals. You are comfortable with your trading style. You accept that knowledge is the key to building confidence, increasing focus, and staying disciplined. You are ready to go! What power you have at your command!

But wait just a minute before you jump in with both feet. What in the world are you actually going to do with all of this stuff? Do you really know how to trade, or have you just put together an engine to help you lose money faster?

Let's think again about this business of learning.

The second of the Six Steps is all about learning the fundamentals that will help you to interact with the market in the most effective way possible.

Too often, we see the experts make all of this stuff too complicated or too confusing or too boring. Our purpose is to tell you what you need to know to consistently make money in the market. No more, no less!

Remember, we trade using a particular group of proven chart patterns. Our goal is to show you how to consistently profit using those same methods. With that goal in mind, we are going to cover only those areas that are needed to understand and profit from that type of trading.

If there is an area or discipline or technique that we don't cover in this book, it is simply because you don't need it to prosper with the methods we use.

## THE MARKETS

Let's look at where stocks are traded in the United States.

### The New York Stock Exchange (NYSE)

When most people think of stock trading, they have a vision of the New York Stock Exchange. They see the huge trading floor, the scurrying people, the endless scraps of paper, the shouts and hand signals among the traders, the energy, and the palpable chaos. What excitement!

It's not as chaotic as it seems. In fact, the NYSE is quite well organized. Companies that meet stringent financial and operating requirements may be granted approval for their equity securities to be listed and traded on the NYSE. More than 3,000 companies are traded on NYSE.

The NYSE is an "auction market" where trading takes place between exchange members who act as agents for institutions or individual investors. Prices are determined by supply and demand, in an auction process, on the trading floor. This auction process is sometimes called "open outcry," where the traders shout and gesture to one another to indicate their buys and sells.

Each stock that is listed on the NYSE is assigned to a "post" where a specialist oversees the auction process. All orders for that particular stock are brought to that one post to be "exposed" to the market so that all trading in that stock is centralized in one spot.

Let's look at the two ways orders get to the floor of the NYSE: manually or electronically.

**Manual orders.** The first way orders come to the floor is through the *floor brokers* who work from one of the 1,500+ trading booths that surround the trading floor. You give your order to your brokerage firm, which sends it to its booth on the floor. Once the floor broker has received that order, that floor broker physically goes to the post and represents your order as agent to the market. In that way, buyers and sellers, represented by these individual floor brokers, literally "meet" at the specialist's post on the trading floor to seek the best possible prices.

**Electronic orders.** The second way to get an order to the floor is through an electronic system, called NYSE Super Dot, which sends your order directly from your brokerage house to the specialist's electronic "book."

The specialist is charged with maintaining an orderly market in the stocks traded at his post. Floor brokers meet at his post to expose their buy and sell orders through open outcry. In this way, a competitive determination of prices is possible.

When a bid gets high enough—or an offer gets low enough—for the prices to match, a trade is made.

If there are temporarily more buy orders than sell orders, the specialist will sell shares from his or her inventory to bring the market back into balance. If there are more sell orders than buy orders, the specialist will use her or his capital to buy shares, again to bring the market back into balance.

In most cases, orders are filled without the intervention of a specialist; in fact, it has been estimated that specialists are involved only in about 10 percent of the shares traded through their posts.

The chart in Figure 10.1 shows how two floor brokers, one representing a buyer and one representing a seller, come together to effect a trade at the specialist's post.

An interesting question is: do the buyer and seller get the "best price" possible in an auction market? Think about it. Certainly the price at the instant the trade is consummated has been exposed to a group of willing buyers and sellers around the specialist's post who have declined the opportunity to improve upon that particular price. Isn't that a pretty good definition of best price?

**FIGURE 10.1** Making Trades Happen

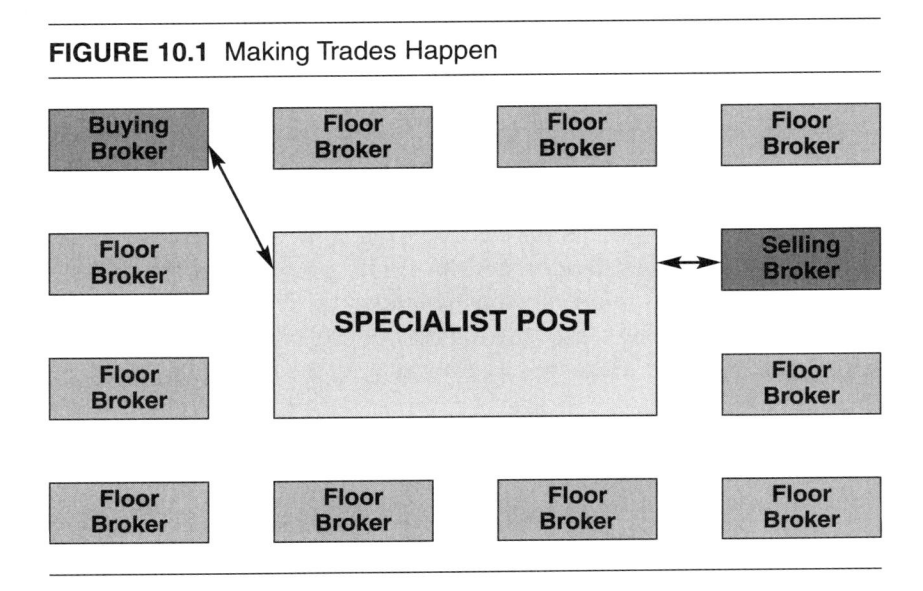

[Diagram: Buying Broker and Selling Broker connected to a central SPECIALIST POST, surrounded by multiple Floor Brokers]

## Nasdaq

The National Association of Securities Dealers Automated Quotation System is better known as Nasdaq. It arose from quite humble beginnings.

In 1963, the over-the-counter market (the "OTC") was a collection of little-known and little-traded companies that the SEC characterized in a report to the U.S. Congress as "fragmented and obscure." Determined to bring relevance to this market, the SEC charged the NASD with creating an automated market.

On February 8, 1971, the Nasdaq came online, displaying median quotes for more than 2,500 securities. Executions were not done electronically at that time, they were still made over the telephone.

What a difference today! The Nasdaq National Market is made up of more than 4,400 companies, and the Nasdaq Small Cap Market is an additional 1,800 companies. Trading information is simultaneously transmitted to more than 500,000 computer terminals across the globe. About one billion shares are traded each day, creating the largest electronic marketplace in the world.

Nasdaq trading is done entirely on computers, with no exchange floor or trading specialists. Instead of floor brokers, orders are transmitted directly through a computerized network to the Nasdaq computers for execution.

A note: you will hear the term "listed stock" that refers to stocks traded on the Exchanges, primarily the NYSE. This term is not used with Nasdaq stocks. The Nasdaq is not a physical exchange and it's stocks are not called "listed."

Instead of specialists who are involved in a small percentage of the total trades on the NYSE, every execution on the Nasdaq computers is made by a market maker. *(Don't let us confuse you here . . . later in this chapter you will see that with ECNs you can execute Nasdaq orders without using the Nasdaq computers or the market makers.)*

## BID AND ASK

For every stock traded, there are two prices quoted: a *bid* and an *ask*.

- A *bid* is an indication of a willingness to buy a security.
- An ask (or an *offer*) is an indication of a willingness to sell a security.

Sounds simple enough, doesn't it? But new traders often get confused when they go to the market. This is because stocks are sold to you at one price and they are bought back from you at a slightly lower price. The difference between these two prices is called the *spread,* which will be discussed shortly.

Specialists and market makers make money by filling customer orders as follows:

- When someone wants to *buy,* they sell the trader the stock at the higher price, the *ask*.
- When someone wants to *sell,* they buy the stock at the lower price, the *bid*.

They do this all day long, essentially making the spread in exchange for providing liquidity to the market.

Figure 10.2 shows a stock window showing the ask and bid prices for Microsoft shares. To buy MSFT at this moment, you would pay 120½ because you have to buy at the price the market maker (in this case ABSB) is asking to sell its shares to you.

To sell MSFT, you would receive 120⅜ because that is the price the market maker (either GSCO or MSCO) is bidding for your shares. That is all they are willing to pay for your stock at this moment.

**FIGURE 10.2** Sample Ask and Bid Price Window

| MarketMakers: MICROSOFT CORP | | | | | | | |
|---|---|---|---|---|---|---|---|
| MSFT | | 120 1/2 | | + 1/2 | down | | |
| Hi | 121 3/4 | | Lo | 119 3/4 | Vl | 2356000 | |
| ID | Bid | | Size | ID | Ask | | Size |
| GSCO | 120 3/8 | | 1 | ABSB | 120 1/2 | | 1 |
| MSCO | 120 3/8 | | 1 | LEHM | 120 9/16 | | 1 |
| FBCO | 120 5/16 | | 1 | SALB | 120 9/16 | | 1 |
| DMGL | 120 5/16 | | 1 | DLJP | 120 5/8 | | 1 |
| CANT | 120 1/4 | | 1 | MONT | 120 11/16 | | 1 |
| RPSC | 120 3/16 | | 1 | NITE | 120 11/16 | | 1 |
| RSSF | 120 3/16 | | 1 | PWJC | 120 11/16 | | 1 |
| PRUS | 120 1/8 | | 1 | TSCO | 120 3/4 | | 1 |
| OLDE | 120 1/8 | | 1 | DEAN | 120 3/4 | | 1 |
| WEED | 120 1/8 | | 1 | HRZG | 120 13/16 | | 1 |
| MASH | 120 | | 1 | SBSH | 120 13/16 | | 1 |

The spread is the difference between those two prices, in this case 1/8 of a point. If you buy this stock and the price never moves before you sell it, your loss will equal the spread.

Figure 10.3 displays how the spread affects your P&L.

**FIGURE 10.3** How the Spread Affects P&L

YOU BUY at the price the market maker is asking
YOU SELL at the price the market maker is offering, or bidding

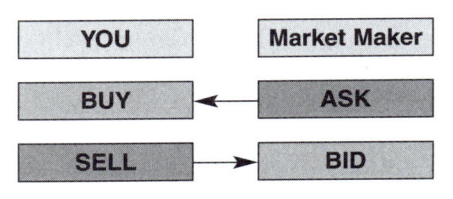

| YOU | Market Maker |
|---|---|
| BUY | ← ASK |
| SELL | → BID |

It's important to understand clearly the spread, and its effect on your potential profit.

The good news is that there are ways to get around this rule of always buying on the ask and selling on the bid, and thus "giving up" the spread.

## TYPES OF ORDERS

If you want to buy or sell a security, you need to know about the different kinds of orders you can give to your broker.

### Market Order

A market order is an instruction to your broker that you want to buy or sell at the best price that can be obtained at the current time. Market orders are given execution priority over other types of orders.

This sounds just fine, doesn't it?

The problem is that, the minute you issue a market order, you have lost control. You don't know what price you are going to get; it could be very far from the price you wanted.

Imagine what would happen to your market order in a very busy market when delays may be 5, 10, or even 20 minutes. There is no way of telling what that price might be.

Or imagine you placed a market order just before the market opens and the price for your stock opens six points higher than yesterday's close (called a "gap up"). You would be executed at a price very far from the one you had in mind.

On second thought, *don't* imagine—you will get depressed! As a rule, experienced traders don't use market orders very often; they set limits on their prices.

### Limit Order

A limit order does just what it says, it sets an upper limit on the price you are willing to pay to buy a stock, or it sets a lower limit on the price you are willing to accept to sell a stock. If your order is executed, you will receive either the limit price or a better price. You cannot receive a worse price.

The problem with limit orders is that your order may not get filled at all, particularly in a fast-moving market. The price may simply move beyond your limit before you get executed.

### Stop Order

A stop order is an order to buy or sell a security once the security has traded at, or better than, the price you state. Stop orders tell your broker to initiate a trade at some time in the future. Nothing happens until your stop price is reached.

For example, suppose IBM is trading at 74 and you want to buy it when it reaches 75. You can place a stop order to buy IBM at 75. Once IBM trades at 75 (the stop price), your stop order becomes a market order.

Most of the time we don't like to use "plain" stop orders because they become market orders. (You *DO* remember how we feel about the risks associated with market orders, don't you?)

### Stop Limit Order

A stop limit order solves that market order problem. You give your broker the stop price—IBM at 75. Then you state a limit price—75⅜. The effect of this order is that once IBM trades at 75, your stop limit order becomes a limit order at 75⅜. The result will be either an execution between 75 and 75⅜ or no execution at all. Stop limit orders give you maximum control over your price execution.

Oops . . . there's a problem. You can't issue stop orders to Nasdaq or to the ECNs! That's where an advanced electronic trading platform (see Chapter 6) from your direct access broker will prove to be a lifesaver. Virtually every direct access electronic system we have tested has some form of "alert" that will allow you to set and manage your own stop orders. As soon as the desired price level has been reached, the system will alert you and you can place your execution order immediately.

Here is a simple suggestion that will be worth a lot of money to you: *Do not trade without the ability to use stop limit orders!*

In addition to the above types of orders, you also can specify how long they are in effect:

- *Day orders.* This order is cancelled if not executed on the day it is issued.

- *Good-till-canceled orders.* This order remains in effect until cancelled by the trader.
- *Fill-or-kill order.* This instructs the broker to fill the entire order immediately, or cancel the entire order. It does not allow a partial execution.

## SPECIALISTS

Trading listed stocks is a much simpler proposition than trading Nasdaq stocks. Your direct access broker (of course you are using one by now!) will have arrangements for directly connecting to, and executing through, NYSE SuperDot as well as the various other exchanges. You simply look on the exchange screen (described later in this chapter) and select the exchange with the best price. Price movements are generally not as rapid or volatile as they are on the Nasdaq, so you submit your order and wait to see if you are executed. You usually don't know the name of the specialist firm but it just doesn't matter.

## MARKET MAKERS

Trading on the Nasdaq is much different. The market maker does matter, primarily in terms of liquidity. NITE or GSCO generally have a much bigger "appetite" for shares than SWST and MONT. Knowing that kind of information can make a big difference in your profitability. Because your goal is to get the number of shares you want at the very best possible price, it pays to understand which market makers will serve you best.

The primary purpose of the market maker is to provide liquidity to the Nasdaq market, much as the specialist does on the NYSE. To maintain their market maker designation, they must be active in the market almost all of the time. That means that the market makers will "be there" to buy from you when you want to sell and to sell to you when you want to buy, providing that the price is marketable. Oh . . . did I mention? The market makers set the prices. They decide what a marketable price is. Cozy little arrangement, isn't it?

Market makers earn their profit from the spread. They buy from you at one price, and they sell to you at a slightly higher price. Take a look at the published financial statements of many of these market maker firms; they are paid quite handsomely for "being there." If you trade Nasdaq stocks, you will do business quite often with market makers, and you will pay them the spread for the privilege.

Much has been written about the "tricks" market makers use to affect prices in the short term. Knowledge of these tricks can be quite important if you are an active day trader because you make your living off of minute-to-minute price movements. However, because this book is aimed at traders with a longer time horizon these market maker tricks will have virtually no effect on your profitability.

The problems most of you will have in dealing with market makers will be related to "size" and "liquidity." As of August 2000, a market maker is not required to post the *real* size of its interest. For example, it may post a bid on MSFT at 68½ and it may show "size" of 100 shares. You have no way of knowing if it is only interested in 100 shares or if it wants many more shares at that price. How does this affect you? Profoundly.

This "blind spot" means you cannot discern the strength or depth of the market. Let's say you want to sell 1,000 shares at 68½. You want to know: What is the real liquidity at 68½? How deep is the market at that price?

You may get an execution of all 1,000 shares at 68½, or you may just get 100 shares at 68½, and the rest at 68¼. You cannot get the information you really need! That can cost you money—sometimes a lot of money.

## ECNS

It was precisely this problem with market maker size and liquidity that fueled the growth of the ECNs. As we discussed in Chapter 1, the Electronic Communication Networks are the Fifth Market. They are viable alternatives to the Nasdaq. Many times they are preferable alternatives to the Nasdaq.

If you trade through an ECN, you are not actually trading "on" the Nasdaq, and you are not trading with a market maker. Instead you are posting your bid or offer directly to the computers of the ECN for electronic matching against someone else who has posted a bid or offer.

The advantage of the electronic matching of orders on an ECN is that many times you can get improved pricing between the spread. How does that work, and what does that mean for you?

Say the market makers are quoting 45 bid and 45⅛ ask on a particular stock. This is very straightforward: you can buy at 45⅛ or you can sell at 45.

However, on an ECN at that same instant you may be able to electronically match a trade at 45 1/16—between the spread. The buyer pays only 45 1/16, the seller gets 45 1/16. Whether you are buying or selling, your price is 1/16 better! You win on either side of that transaction. Both sides of the transaction on an ECN have an incentive for price improvement. Is this a great world or what?

Advantages to using ECNs are

- the participants in the ECN have an incentive to give one another mutual price improvement.
- the participants in the ECN provide liquidity to one another.
- the participants in the ECN post their actual "size" interest so you have a better indication of market liquidity and price support.

Sounds perfect, doesn't it? But nothing ever is.

Here's the problem with ECNs: no one is being "paid" to maintain liquidity, so there may not be a suitable bid or offer on your favorite ECN every time you want to trade.

That was a pretty big drawback three years ago, but today there are ten ECNs, so even if your favorite ECN is not posting the price you want right now, chances are another of the ECNs might be.

Here is the list of the ten ECNs which are active as of August 2000:

| | | |
|---|---|---|
| Archipelago, LLC | ARCA | <www.tradearca.com> |
| Attain | ATTN | <www.attain.com> |
| B-Trade Services, LLC | BTRD | <www.bloomberg.com> |
| The BRASS Utility | BRUT | <www.sungard.com> |
| Instinet Corporation | INCA | <www.instinet.com> |
| The Island ECN | ISLD | <www.isld.com> |
| MarketXT | MKXT | <www.marketxt.com> |
| NexTrade | NTRD | <www.nextrade1.com> |
| Spear, Leeds & Kellogg | REDI | <www.redi.com> |
| Strike Technologies | STRK | <www.strk.com> |

As you learn to trade, you will find the ECNs to be an important part of your business. Because ECNs lack liquidity, *never* submit a market order on one. Use limit orders with ECNs!

To learn more about trading with, and against, market makers and ECNs, you can access a wealth of information about their trading patterns through the Nasdaq, at: <www.nasdaqtrader.com/static/tdhome.stm>.

For example, you can research a particular stock to learn which market makers and ECNs are the largest traders in that stock. There are two reasons you want to know who the larger players are in a particular stock:

1. They will be your best source of liquidity.
2. They will be the most aggressive on price.

You also may research a particular market maker or ECN to learn which stocks they are most active in. This is just another way to discover where the best liquidity and price will be.

Figure 10.4 shows the Nasdaq Web site, showing the ten biggest traders in CSCO. Can you see how important that information can be for you? Doesn't this information encourage you to look to ISLD, MASH, SBSH, and GSCO when you want liquidity in CSCO?

## SHORT SELLING

There are two ways to describe your position in a stock:

1. You can be *long*—which means you own the shares. To close out a long position, you sell your shares.
2. You can be *short*—which means you have agreed to sell shares you did not own so you have a negative position in the stock. To close out a short position you buy shares.

Are you a short seller? Have you ever made a short sale? If your answer is *no,*

- we would tell you that you are not yet even "in the game."
- we would tell you that you are leaving about 50 percent of your profit opportunities "on the table."
- we would tell you that you are fighting a battle against a very strong adversary, but you have "one arm tied behind your back."
- we would tell you some more things, but we have run out of cliches.

Let's start with the basic concept of short selling—it is selling something that you do not own. Sure, we know that sounds like something

## FIGURE 10.4 Sample Nasdaq Web Site

**TOTAL VOLUME - MARKET HOURS**
**CSCO   Cisco Systems, Inc.**

| Total # of MPs: 392 | MP Type | May-00 Volume | Rank | % | Apr-00 Volume | Rank | % | Year to Date Volume | Rank | % |
|---|---|---|---|---|---|---|---|---|---|---|
| **Totals** | | 1,288,171,542 | | | 1,282,030,385 | | | 3,880,538,201 | | |
| **ISLD** THE ISLAND ECN | C | 109,403,730 | 1 | 8 | 92,636,767 | 2 | 7 | 320,130,975 | 2 | 8 |
| **MASH** SCHWAB CAPITAL MARKETS L.P. | M | 100,390,656 | 2 | 7 | 101,690,640 | 1 | 7 | 328,365,483 | 1 | 8 |
| **SBSH** SALOMON SMITH BARNEY INC. | M | 85,618,637 | 3 | 6 | 78,820,402 | 3 | 6 | 283,632,127 | 3 | 7 |
| **GSCO** GOLDMAN, SACHS & CO. | M | 74,301,137 | 4 | 5 | 65,821,438 | 5 | 5 | 112,907,259 | 10 | 2 |
| **MSCO** MORGAN STANLEY & CO., INCORPORATED | M | 64,362,769 | 5 | 4 | 78,254,056 | 4 | 6 | 217,243,976 | 4 | 5 |
| **NITE** KNIGHT SECURITIES, INC. | M | 63,212,097 | 6 | 4 | 46,618,547 | 8 | 3 | 163,126,164 | 6 | 4 |
| **MLCO** MERRILL LYNCH, PIERCE, FENNER & SMITH INCORPORATED | M | 56,400,232 | 7 | 4 | 59,723,322 | 6 | 4 | 181,705,816 | 5 | 4 |
| **INCA** INSTINET CORPORATION | C | 41,592,893 | 8 | 3 | 51,537,531 | 7 | 4 | 149,920,573 | 7 | 3 |
| **MADF** BERNARD L. MADOFF | M | 34,871,798 | 9 | 2 | 37,063,450 | 9 | 2 | 117,707,431 | 8 | 3 |
| **NFSC** NATIONAL FINANCIAL SERVICES CORPORATION | M | 33,692,871 | 10 | 2 | 36,323,012 | 10 | 2 | 117,669,317 | 9 | 3 |

that is illegal, but when you are dealing with stocks, it's not only legal, it is an accepted and honorable practice. Best of all, selling short can make you a lot of money!

**118** THE SIXTH MARKET

Here is a more formal definition:

*Short Sale:* The sale of shares of a security that the seller does not own. Such sales are made in anticipation of a decline in the price of the security. They enable the seller to cover the sale with a purchase at a later date, at a lower price, and thus at a profit because delivery of the current sale is in the future.

For those of you who are not yet short sellers: What is the difference between these two approaches to the market?

- *Buy low, sell high.*
- *Sell high, buy low.*

Does the "order" of the transaction matter? Of course not. The answer is obvious. The math doesn't change so the order of the transaction is immaterial.

Short selling is just the reverse of "going long," buying first and selling later. Many new traders get confused by this whole concept, but it is really so simple. You are trying to accomplish the same thing, buy

**FIGURE 10.5** Sample Short Sale

|  | Trade A | | Trade B | |
|---|---|---|---|---|
| **Symbol** | CSCO | | CSCO | |
| Shares | 1,000 | | 1,000 | |
| **Entering Trade** | BUY | | SELL | |
| Price per Share | (65.00) | | 68.00 | |
| Total | | (65,000.00) | | 68,000.00 |
| **Exiting Trade** | SELL | | BUY | |
| Price per Share | 68.00 | | (65.00) | |
| Total | | 68,000.00 | | (65,000.00) |
| **GAIN** | | $3,000.00 | | $3,000.00 |

low and sell high; you have just reversed the order of the transaction. Don't make it any more difficult than that!

Another potential profitable phenomenon associated with short sales is that stock prices tend to move in a smoother fashion when prices are falling than when they are rising. As prices rise, there are always sellers looking to take their profit along the way instead of waiting for the highest peak. This selling activity tends to interrupt the upward movement in stock prices. As you study a price chart, such as shown in Figure 10.6, you will see an upsurge—followed by the selling-induced pullback—even in the strongest rally. As a trader, you never know when one of these pullbacks will be the start of a true price reversal to the downside. Often traders exit those trades too soon.

As prices fall, many times there are simply no buyers in sight and the price falls in a fairly uninterrupted fashion. Again, on the price charts you can watch the price decline in a smooth, linear fashion. You can sell short and just hang on for a nice long profitable ride. Look at the chart

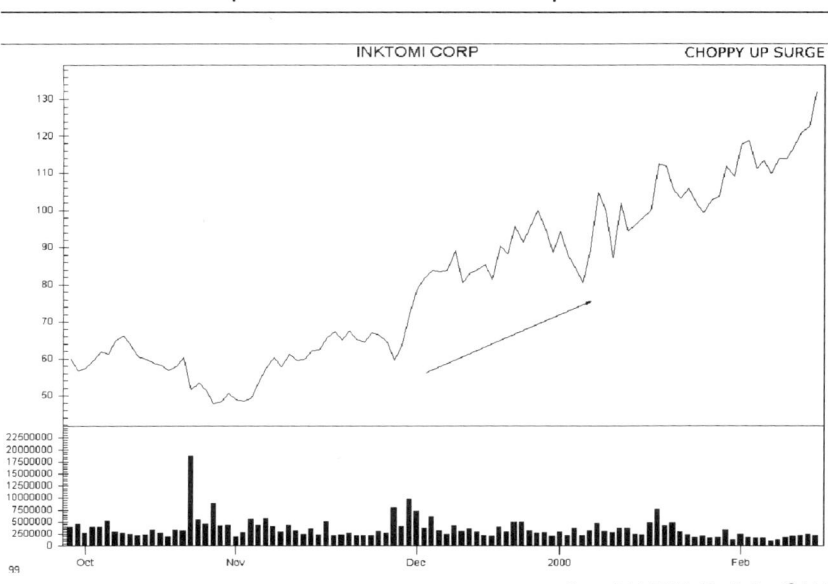

**FIGURE 10.6** Sample Price Chart with Interrupted Rises

*Copyright 2000, TradeCast® Ltd.*

in Figure 10.7. It shows the same stock but on a much less stressful ride down!

Now that you can read a price chart, there are still three mysteries about executing short sales:

1. *Where do you actually get these shares* you are selling if you don't own them? You know you have to deliver the shares you are selling in just a few days. Where will you get them?

   The answer is that you are borrowing them from other customers of your broker or its clearing firm. Little did you know that when you opened your account and signed several agreements, one contained a little-noticed, unexciting provision that creates the mechanism to let all of this happen. You can borrow shares from other customers of the broker/clearing firm and they can borrow your shares. Everyone wins!

   One note: some stocks are not "borrowable" (there are no shares available for you to use for a short sale). Generally these are low priced (under $5) or very thinly traded stocks. All direct

**FIGURE 10.7** Sample Price Chart with Smooth Decline

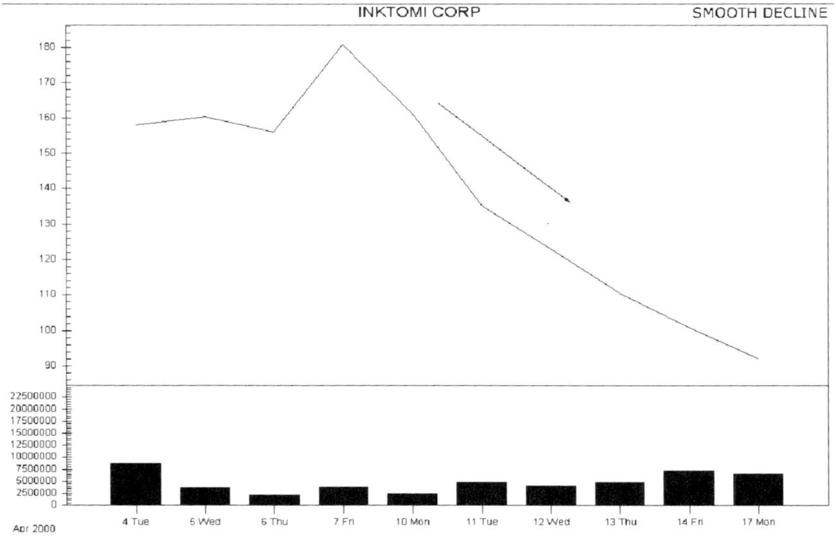

*Copyright 2000, TradeCast® Ltd.*

access brokers have a list programmed into the electronic trading platform so that you can quickly short most stocks but you cannot inadvertently short stocks that are not borrowable.

2. *What happens if the price goes up* instead of going down like you had planned? You lose! But this is similar to buying a stock and seeing the price go down instead of up.

   There is a pretty important difference, however. If you buy a stock and the price goes down, it can only go to zero. That's all you can lose. It may be a lot of money, but it is a finite amount of money.

   On the other hand, if you sell a stock short and the price rises, there is no limit to how far it can rise. Your loss, theoretically, can be infinite. There is a big difference between finite and infinite!

3. *How do you actually execute a short sale?* Well, first you have a good reason to believe that the price will decline. Then you wait for an uptick. Securities and Exchange Commission rules allow investors to sell short only when a stock price is moving upward to prevent investors from destabilizing the price of a stock when the market price is falling.

   On your level II screen, you will see the green indicator or an up arrow, depending on the direct access system you are using. That is when you can enter a short order.

   What this all means is that although you think the stock is going to decline in price, you can only short it when the price is actually rising!

   Don't worry—this is not as frightening as it sounds. When trading against proven chart patterns, you simply wait for an uptick within your target entry price range and execute the sell. As you gain more experience you will learn to short offer the stock during a downtick at a price at least $\frac{1}{16}$ above the inside bid to actually create the uptick yourself.

Certain index instruments—such as Spiders (SPY—which mirrors the S&P 500) and Diamonds (DIA—which mirrors the Dow Jones Index)—can be sold short without adherence to the uptick rules. If you find yourself in a rapidly falling market these instruments may be your best way to quickly take advantage of the short selling opportunities.

One last thing about short selling: Have you heard the term "short squeeze"? This occurs when a particular stock has experienced considerable short selling. All of those short sellers are going to have to buy back those shares in the future. If the price of that security starts to rise, short sellers will begin to rush into the market to buy their covering positions. This buying activity forces the price even higher, which brings in more of the short sellers to cover, and on and on. The price keeps climbing. The short squeeze can happen very suddenly and have a devastating affect on the short seller who is slow to react.

## MARGIN

A quick word about your margin account. Current regulations issued by the Federal Reserve allow investors to have up to one-half of their portfolio on margin. For example, a trader with $100,000 in a trading account could buy up to $200,000 worth of stock. The risk of investing or trading on margin is that it is possible to lose more than your investment, as discussed in selling short.

When should you or should you not use your margin privileges?

- If you are not consistently profitable, why would you accelerate the amount of your losses with leverage?
- If you are consistently profitable—if you can earn more than the interest charge on the margin loan—why would you not accelerate the amount of your gains with leverage?

## TO FIND OUT MORE

### Glossary

If the terminology in this chapter seems a bit overwhelming, have a look at the glossary at the end of this book. It may not sound exciting to read a bunch of definitions, but it's a little too exciting to lose a lot of money because you don't understand the instructions here.

### Recommended Reading

Following the glossary is a recommended reading list. You can dig deeper into those subjects of interest to you, or those subjects on which you feel you need additional understanding.

As promised, we have covered quite a bit of ground in this chapter, giving you practical trading knowledge that you can put to use immediately.

The next chapter digs more deeply into Nasdaq Level II and helps you learn how to really go out and get the best price available.

CHAPTER | 11

# More Step Two: Nasdaq Level II

*"What's money? A man is a success if he gets up in the morning and goes to bed at night and in between does what he wants to do."*

BOB DYLAN

**W**hat we want to do is help you learn to take money out of the market consistently. Learning how to read, interpret, and act on price information is vital to that mission.

## STOCK WINDOW

Figure 11.1 shows a window that you will use to see key pricing information for any stock. In this case, it is IBM, which is a stock listed on the NYSE.

In the top section of this box, we see level I information, which is a summary of key facts about the chosen stock:

| | |
|---|---|
| 119 7/16 | Price of the Last Trade |
| +1/8 | Change from the Close Yesterday |
| 120 | High for Today |
| 118 3/4 | Low for Today |
| | (The difference between the high and the low is the trading range for today, in this case 1 1/4.) |

**FIGURE 11.1** Sample Stock Window

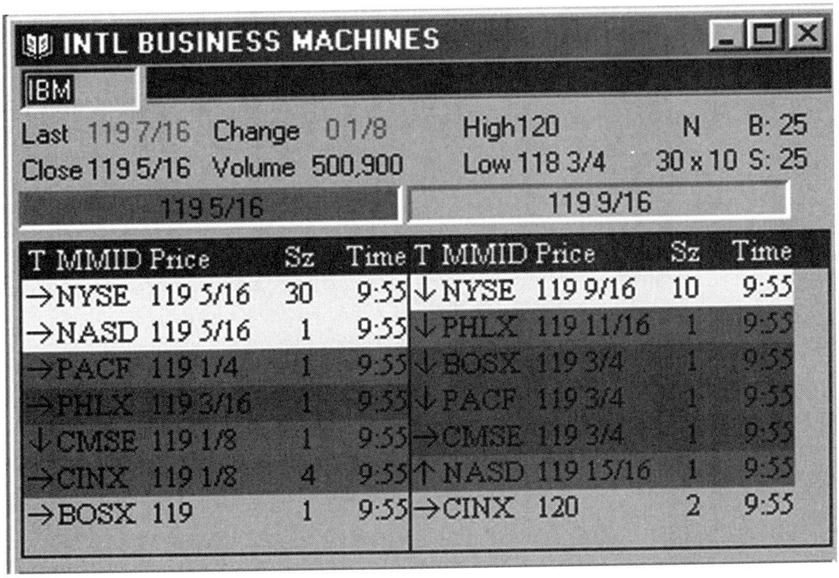

```
INTL BUSINESS MACHINES                    _ □ X
IBM
Last 119 7/16  Change  0 1/8    High 120         N    B: 25
Close 119 5/16 Volume 500,900   Low 118 3/4   30 x 10  S: 25
          119 5/16                     119 9/16
 T MMID Price      Sz   Time  T MMID Price     Sz   Time
→NYSE  119 5/16    30   9:55  ↓NYSE  119 9/16   10   9:55
→NASD  119 5/16     1   9:55  ↓PHLX  119 11/16   1   9:55
→PACF  119 1/4      1   9:55  ↓BOSX  119 3/4     1   9:55
→PHLX  119 3/16     1   9:55  ↓PACF  119 3/4     1   9:55
↓CMSE  119 1/8      1   9:55  →CMSE  119 3/4     1   9:55
→CINX  119 1/8      4   9:55  ↑NASD  119 15/16   1   9:55
→BOSX  119          1   9:55  →CINX  120         2   9:55
```

119 5/16    Close Yesterday
500,900     Share Volume Today

Take the time to learn to read level I. You'll quickly get a clear picture of how this stock is trading right now!

In the lower section, we see specific price quotes:

- The left side of this section contains the bids, arranged by price with the highest bid on top.
- The right section contains the offers, arranged by price with the lower offer on top.

This is exactly how you, the trader, want to see the prices arranged. You want to know who will sell you the stock at the lowest price. And you want to know who will buy your stock at the highest price.

At a glance you can see the best (highest) bid and the best (lowest) offer. These figures together are often referred to as the "inside market."

The quotes are grouped by color to indicate price levels. Importantly, we see the size of the bids and offers expressed in hundreds of shares (e.g., 30 means 3,000 shares).

In this example, these are exchange quotes—the bids and the asks from the various exchanges that quote IBM: the New York Stock Exchange (NYSE), Nasdaq (NASD), Pacific (PACF), Philadelphia (PHLX), Chicago Mercantile (CMSE), Cincinnati (CINX), and Boston (BOSX).

This window gives us useful information about the current price for IBM, but it omits one very important piece of information: the level of support below the prices listed on each exchange. This is particularly important for NYSE quotes because so much of the liquidity in these listed stocks in on the NYSE.

For example, we see that NYSE is bidding 3,000 shares of IBM at 119$\frac{5}{16}$, and offering 1,000 shares of IBM at 119$\frac{7}{16}$.

- Would you want to buy IBM right now at 119$\frac{7}{16}$ if you knew that the IBM specialist on the NYSE had offers to sell another 75,000 shares at 119$\frac{5}{8}$? Don't you see how this selling pressure would act to keep the price from rising very far?
- Would you like to buy IBM right now at 119$\frac{7}{16}$ if you knew that the specialist had no other offers to sell IBM, but did have offers to buy another 75,000 shares at 119$\frac{1}{2}$? Don't you see how this buying interest could help to drive the price up?

Without seeing the depth of the market, you are missing valuable clues to the future direction of a stock's price that can affect the timing of our orders.

For exchange listed stocks, that information is simply not available. The specialist keeps that information to himself.

## NASDAQ LEVEL II

On the Nasdaq, it is a different story. You can see the depth of the market through a service called Nasdaq Level II, which shows price quotes from every market maker and ECN trading a stock. Level II takes you to the very pricing soul of your selected stock!

Figure 11.2 shows what Nasdaq Level II looks like:

**128** THE SIXTH MARKET

**FIGURE 11.2** Sample Nasdaq Level II Window

| INTEL CORP | | | | | | | |
|---|---|---|---|---|---|---|---|
| INTC | | | | | | | |
| Last 129 5/16  Change -2 3/16 | | | High 131 5/16   Q    B: 25 | | | | |
| Close 131 1/2   Volume 3,935,400 | | | Low 128 1/2   26 x 26  S: 25 | | | | |
| 129 1/4 | | | | 129 5/16 | | | |
| T | MMID | Price | Sz | Time | T MMID Price | Sz | Time |
| ↑ | ARCA | 129 1/4 | 2 | 10:08 | ↓ MLCO 129 5/16 | 10 | 10:08 |
| ↑ | MASH | 129 1/4 | 7 | 10:08 | → MSCO 129 5/16 | 8 | 10:08 |
| → | INCA | 129 1/4 | 3 | 10:08 | → ISLD  129 5/16 | 26 | 10:08 |
| → | REDI | 129 1/4 | 26 | 10:08 | → WARR 129 3/8 | 1 | 10:08 |
| ↑ | BRUT | 129 1/4 | 5 | 10:08 | → INCA 129 3/8 | 25 | 10:08 |
| ↑ | DKNY | 129 1/4 | 1 | 10:08 | → DKNY 129 3/8 | 1 | 10:08 |
| ↑ | CHIP | 129 3/16 | 1 | 10:07 | ↓ DEAN 129 1/2 | 1 | 9:38 |
| ↓ | ISLD | 129 3/16 | 4 | 10:08 | ↓ SLKC 129 1/2 | 1 | 10:06 |
| ↑ | LEHM | 129 1/8 | 10 | 10:07 | → CHIP  129 1/2 | 1 | 10:07 |
| ↑ | NFSC | 129 1/16 | 1 | 10:07 | → REDI 129 1/2 | 2 | 10:08 |
| ↑ | FLTT | 129 1/16 | 1 | 10:07 | ↑ PRUS 129 9/16 | 1 | 10:03 |
| ↑ | DLJP | 129 | 10 | 10:07 | ↑ SBSH 129 9/16 | 10 | 10:07 |
| ↑ | PWJC | 129 | 1 | 10:07 | → SHWD 129 9/16 | 1 | 10:07 |
| ↑ | GSCO | 129 | 10 | 10:07 | → BTRD 129 9/16 | 1 | 10:08 |
| → | ALLN | 128 15/16 | 1 | 10:06 | ↑ MONT 129 5/8 | 10 | 10:06 |
| → | BEST | 128 7/8 | 1 | 10:06 | ↑ LEHM 129 5/8 | 10 | 10:07 |
| ↑ | MONT | 128 7/8 | 10 | 10:06 | ↑ JPMS  129 5/8 | 1 | 10:07 |
| ↑ | NITE | 128 7/8 | 1 | 10:07 | → FLTT  129 5/8 | 1 | 10:07 |
| ↓ | NTRD | 128 7/8 | 12 | 10:07 | ↑ RSSF  129 3/4 | 10 | 10:07 |
| ↑ | JPMS | 128 7/8 | 1 | 10:07 | ↑ GSCO  129 3/4 | 10 | 10:07 |
| ↑ | RSSF | 128 3/4 | 10 | 10:07 | ↑ MADF 129 13/16 | 1 | 10:07 |
| → | MWSE | 128 3/4 | 5 | 10:08 | ↑ NFSC  129 13/16 | 1 | 10:07 |
| ↓ | SWST | 128 11/16 | 1 | 9:52 | → BEST  129 7/8 | 1 | 10:06 |
| ↑ | MADF | 128 11/16 | 1 | 10:07 | ↓ CANT  130 | 1 | 9:58 |
| → | MSCO | 128 11/16 | 10 | 10:08 | ↓ PERT  130 | 1 | 10:05 |
| → | COST | 128 5/8 | 1 | 10:05 | ↑ HRZG  130 | 1 | 10:07 |
| → | SELZ | 128 5/8 | 1 | 10:05 | ↑ DLJP  130 | 10 | 10:07 |
| ↓ | SLKC | 128 5/8 | 1 | 10:06 | ↑ WPCO 130 | 1 | 10:07 |
| → | BTRD | 128 5/8 | 1 | 10:08 | → MASH 130 | 1 | 10:08 |
| ↑ | PRUS | 128 9/16 | 1 | 10:03 | → BRUT  130 | 5 | 10:08 |

This window shows a great deal of information about INTC (Intel). The MMID column shows the four-letter identifier for each of the various market makers or ECNs. Again, we see the inside market. The price levels will be identified by different colors, and we can see the size (in hundreds of shares) of the various bids and offers.

You can instantly see the strength of interest at a particular price by the number of market makers and ECNs, and by the posted share size. Remember that earlier we talked about size and the fact that while the market makers disguise the real size of their interest, the ECNs tend to disclose the true size of their interest.

Level II is so COOL. What you are really seeing as you watch the level II screen is prices responding to supply and demand, in real-time action.

Figure 11.3 shows a snapshot of a stock.

What does this snapshot tell you about the market? Not much, because you have no frame of reference. You learn what a stock is doing by watching the movement on this level II screen.

**FIGURE 11.3** Snapshot of MSFT at 11:00 AM

MarketMakers: MICROSOFT CORP

| MSFT | 120 1/2 | | + 1/2 | down | |
|------|---------|---|-------|------|---|
| Hi | 121 3/4 | Lo | 119 3/4 | Vl | 2356000 |

| ID | Bid | Size | ID | Ask | Size |
|------|---------|----|------|-----------|-----|
| ISLD | 120 3/8 | 8  | BTRD | 120 1/2   | 110 |
| INCA | 120 3/8 | 25 | REDI | 120 9/16  | 40  |
| GSCO | 120 5/16| 3  | ISLD | 120 9/16  | 25  |
| NITE | 120 5/16| 5  | INCA | 120 5/8   | 13  |
| ARCA | 120 1/4 | 10 | MONT | 120 11/16 | 2   |
| ATTN | 120 3/16| 15 | COWN | 120 11/16 | 1   |
| LEHM | 120 3/16| 1  | PWJC | 120 11/16 | 4   |
| PRUS | 120 1/8 | 1  | TSCO | 120 3/4   | 1   |
| DEAN | 120 1/8 | 1  | DEAN | 120 3/4   | 1   |
| WEED | 120 1/8 | 1  | HRZG | 120 13/16 | 1   |
| MASH | 120     | 1  | SBSH | 120 13/16 | 1   |

What if just one minute later the screen looks like this Figure 11.4?

**FIGURE 11.4** Snapshot of MSFT at 11:01 AM

MarketMakers: MICROSOFT CORP

MSFT  120 1/2  + 1/2  down
Hi 121 3/4  Lo 119 3/4  VI 2356000

| ID | Bid | Size | ID | Ask | Size |
|---|---|---|---|---|---|
| ISLD | 120 3/8 | 26 | BTRD | 120 1/2 | 4 |
| INCA | 120 3/8 | 25 | REDI | 120 9/16 | 5 |
| GSCO | 120 3/8 | 3 | ISLD | 120 5/8 | 6 |
| NITE | 120 3/8 | 16 | INCA | 120 11/16 | 7 |
| ARCA | 120 3/8 | 22 | MONT | 120 11/16 | 2 |
| ATTN | 120 3/8 | 36 | COWN | 120 3/4 | 1 |
| LEHM | 120 3/8 | 1 | PWJC | 120 3/4 | 4 |
| PRUS | 120 5/16 | 1 | TSCO | 120 3/4 | 1 |
| DEAN | 120 5/16 | 1 | DEAN | 120 3/4 | 1 |
| WEED | 120 5/16 | 1 | HRZG | 120 3/4 | 1 |
| MASH | 120 3/16 | 1 | SBSH | 120 3/4 | 1 |

Notice what has happened:

- The bid has strengthened because there is increasing buy pressure. Five market makers have joined the best bid. Displayed size has increased by 8,600 shares. It seems that *everyone* suddenly wants to buy at 120⅜!
- The offer is moving up. Several market makers have increased their offer price and the shares offered at the best offer price have declined by 10,600. *No one* seems to want to sell at these prices!

If you are watching level II and you see pressure increasing on the bid side and shares disappearing on the offer side, don't you expect the price of that stock to rise? You are seeing demand in action, and prices should rise accordingly.

Or you may see just the opposite movement. If the bids are disappearing—no one wants to buy, and you see more and more shares available on the offer (for sale) at lower and lower prices. Isn't it clear that the price of that stock is declining? More shares available equals more supply, and prices should drop accordingly.

### Rotation

The visual clues on the level II screen are even simpler to read once you learn how to read the "rotation" on the screen:

**Start.** You have just pulled up a level II screen for MSFT. One is shown in Figure 11.5.

Whenever you pull up a new screen—a start—it is in a neutral position. You are watching to see how the stock moves from this point.

**FIGURE 11.5** Start of Rotation in Level II Screen

MarketMakers: MICROSOFT CORP

| MSFT | 120 1/2 | | + 1/2 | down | |
|------|---------|---|-------|------|---|
| Hi | 121 3/4 | Lo | 119 3/4 | VI | 2356000 |

| ID | Bid | Size | ID | Ask | Size |
|------|----------|------|------|----------|------|
| ISLD | 120 3/8 | 26 | BTRD | 120 1/2 | 15 |
| INCA | 120 3/8 | 25 | REDI | 120 1/2 | 15 |
| GSCO | 120 3/8 | 3 | ISLD | 120 1/2 | 25 |
| NITE | 120 3/8 | 16 | INCA | 120 1/2 | 13 |
| ARCA | 120 1/2 | 22 | MONT | 120 9/16 | 2 |
| ATTN | 120 1/2 | 36 | COWN | 120 9/16 | 1 |
| LEHM | 120 1/2 | 1 | PWJC | 120 9/16 | 4 |
| PRUS | 120 7/16 | 1 | TSCO | 120 5/8 | 1 |
| DEAN | 120 7/16 | 1 | DEAN | 120 5/8 | 1 |
| WEED | 120 7/16 | 1 | HRZG | 120 11/16 | 1 |
| MASH | 120 7/16 | 1 | SBSH | 120 11/16 | 1 |

**Clockwise movement = prices falling.** As you watch the level II screen, it may look like it is moving in a clockwise motion, as shown in Figure 11.6.

**FIGURE 11.6** Clockwise Movement of Level II Screen

| MarketMakers: MICROSOFT CORP | | | | | |
|---|---|---|---|---|---|
| MSFT | 120 1/2 | | + 1/2 | down | |
| Hi | 121 3/4 | Lo | 119 3/4 | Vl | 2356000 |

| ID | Bid | Size | ID | Ask | Size |
|---|---|---|---|---|---|
| ISLD | 120 3/8 | 4 | BTRD | 120 1/2 | 26 |
| INCA | 120 1/2 | 2 | REDI | 120 1/2 | 15 |
| GSCO | 120 1/2 | 1 | ISLD | 120 1/2 | 33 |
| NITE | 120 9/16 | 6 | INCA | 120 1/2 | 13 |
| ARCA | 120 11/16 | 11 | MONT | 120 1/2 | 9 |
| ATTN | 120 11/16 | 8 | COWN | 120 1/2 | 4 |
| LEHM | 120 11/16 | 1 | PWJC | 120 1/2 | 8 |
| PRUS | 120 5/8 | 1 | TSCO | 120 1/2 | 1 |
| DEAN | 120 5/8 | 1 | DEAN | 120 1/2 | 1 |
| WEED | 120 5/8 | 1 | HRZG | 120 9/16 | 1 |
| MASH | 120 5/8 | 1 | SBSH | 120 9/16 | 1 |

What is really happening is that bids are disappearing on the left side and being replaced by lower bids on the right side because there are fewer buyers. More offers are being added on the right side as more traders want to sell. More sellers and fewer buyers result in lower prices.

The top price section is shrinking on the left and growing on the right. This gives a neat visual illusion of moving in a clockwise motion.

**Counter-clockwise movement = prices rising.** As you watch the level II screen, it may look like it is moving in a counter-clockwise motion, as shown in Figure 11.7.

What is really happening is that more bids are being added on the left side as more buyers come into the market. Offers are disappearing on the right side and being replaced by higher offers as fewer want to sell at these prices. More buyers and fewer sellers create rising prices.

The top price section is shrinking on the right and growing on the left, it gives the illusion of a counter-clockwise motion.

**FIGURE 11.7** Counter-Clockwise Movement of Level II Screen

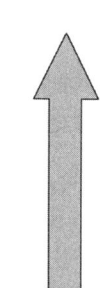

| MarketMakers: MICROSOFT CORP | | | | | |
|---|---|---|---|---|---|
| MSFT | 120 1/2 | | + 1/2 | down | |
| Hi | 121 3/4 | Lo | 119 3/4 | Vl | 2356000 |

| ID | Bid | Size | ID | Ask | Size |
|---|---|---|---|---|---|
| ISLD | 120 3/8 | 26 | BTRD | 120 1/2 | 1 |
| INCA | 120 3/8 | 25 | REDI | 120 5/8 | 3 |
| GSCO | 120 3/8 | 12 | ISLD | 120 5/8 | 2 |
| NITE | 120 3/8 | 16 | INCA | 120 5/8 | 5 |
| ARCA | 120 3/8 | 22 | MONT | 120 11/16 | 2 |
| ATTN | 120 3/8 | 36 | COWN | 120 13/16 | 1 |
| LEHM | 120 3/8 | 4 | PWJC | 120 13/16 | 4 |
| PRUS | 120 3/8 | 8 | TSCO | 120 7/8 | 1 |
| DEAN | 120 3/8 | 2 | DEAN | 120 7/8 | 1 |
| WEED | 120 1/2 | 1 | HRZG | 120 15/16 | 1 |
| MASH | 120 1/2 | 1 | SBSH | 120 15/16 | 1 |

Once you get used to seeing this rotation in the level II screen, you will be able to instantly assess price direction very easily. Wonderful! Level II can help you spot price momentum and it can clearly give you an instant look at supply and demand.

So, how do you use this information to trade?

## Help "Time" Your Entry and Exit from the Market

For the day trader, level II and related trading tools, such as time of sales and ticker, are used quite religiously to take advantage of very small, very short-term price movements. A day trader's timing must be exquisite! But we are not recommending day trading in this book, and we do not intend to dig any deeper into those techniques.

For every other trading style, you will be much less concerned about these small, short-term price movements. You will be watching for specific, preidentified price targets. You will use level II to help time your entry and exit actions.

To make the best use of these tools, ask yourself these questions:

- Can you see how you can use level II to time your entry or exit moves? As the price nears your target, can you see how to use the supply and demand information and the rotation clues on level II to anticipate when your target price will be hit?
- Can you see that if you can successfully anticipate that price move you have a better chance of moving quickly and getting the execution at the price you want?

## Find Where the Best Price and the Most Liquidity Are

Here are the steps you will go through with level II:

**Find the best price.** That's not hard—just look at the window. The best bid and the best offer are at the top of the window!

**Find the liquidity.** This one gets hard in a hurry! Remember that the market makers hide their real liquidity.

We know this is the third or fourth time we've mentioned this and you're probably getting tired of hearing about it. But, when you want to unload 2,500 shares of QCOM while its price is dropping about 5 points every 10 seconds, liquidity will suddenly become very important to you—and to your children's educational plans!

So, how do you find the liquidity?

- Remember the Nasdaq Web site; it holds good clues. Before you get into a good-sized position, take just a few minutes to go to that site and figure out who the three or four biggest market makers in your stock are.
- Look at the ECNs on the level II display: Who is showing the most size?
- Always—and we really *do* mean always—look at INCA (Instinet), ISLD (Island), NITE, and GSCO. These four are generally big players in most stocks.

**Execute the right type of order.** Once you have your price, and have determined where the liquidity is, you have four ways to execute orders on Nasdaq stocks:

1. *SOES* (Small Order Execution System). This is a Nasdaq execution method that automates execution at the inside market price:

- You send your order to the Nasdaq mainframe, which puts your order in a queue.
- Orders are processed in the order received, with market orders receiving precedence over limit orders. Limit orders must be priced at, or better than, the inside market.
- Market orders remain in the queue until cancelled or executed. Limit orders remain in the queue until the limit price is breached or until the order is canceled or executed. If shares are available when your order reaches the top of the queue, it will be executed.

2. *SelectNet Broadcast.* This is another Nasdaq execution method that automates the negotiation and execution of trades. In a SelectNet Broadcast order:
   - You send your bid or offer to the Nasdaq system.
   - It is displayed to every market maker and ECN in that particular stock.
   - You may not cancel your bid or offer for ten seconds.
   - Any of those market makers or ECNs may choose to execute your bid or offer.
   - If your bid or offer is not executed within a specified time (3 to 99 minutes) it is terminated by Nasdaq.

3. *SelectNet Preference.* This is the third Nasdaq execution method. It has the same characteristics as the SelectNet Broadcast method except that you direct your bid or offer to one or more "preferred" market makers or ECNs. You would use the Preference method when your experience tells you that the particular market maker or ECN you choose is highly likely to have the liquidity to execute against you. We always seem to come back to liquidity!

4. *ECN Direct.* This execution method does not go through Nasdaq, but it requires that your broker have direct access to the ECNs with whom you would like to trade. If your broker has that capability, you simply send your bid or offer directly to the ECN computer of your choice. Your order either will be matched against a corresponding order or held in the limit order book until executed or cancelled.

Is this starting to sound complicated? Well, we wanted you to feel like this is quite difficult because it can be.

To tell the real truth, we could have written fifty more pages about the nuances of placing orders on Nasdaq stocks. A considerable amount of experience is required to successfully juggle all of the permutations of price, liquidity, and order technique.

Without months—or even years—of daily practice, you are at a big disadvantage against the skilled professional trader. This one area has been one of—if not *the*—most difficult things to master to be a consistently profitable trader.

*Do you remember the scene in that Indiana Jones movie where a fearsome, sword-wielding assassin faces Dr. Jones in a crowded, dusty street? The tension builds as you realize that the bad guy can easily cut Dr. Jones into bite-sized morsels. Dr. Jones is just no match for this guy. So, Dr. Jones pulls out his pistol and shoots the assassin!*

We don't bring this up to encourage violence or mayhem. We bring this up to show you that there is always more than one way to skin the proverbial cat! You no longer have to be better, faster, or more experienced than all of these professional traders to compete with them on Nasdaq. You've got the computer on your side!

You see, another reason to use one of the leading direct access brokers is that they already have a better and faster way for you to execute trades on Nasdaq without worrying about this delicate and intricate balancing of price, liquidity, and order type.

Remember in Chapter 6 we talked about "smart order" logic on the direct access broker's trading platforms. You make a few choices about the order in which you want the computer to search the various ECNs or market makers and the computer can execute all of those much faster than you—or that professional trader—can. All you have to do is push one button!

So, your trading choices are to

- become an expert at the mental calculations of price, liquidity, and order type, then practice for hours every day to develop the dexterity to hit the keys just right.
- choose a good direct access broker and let the computer get the best possible executions for you!

Moving on, Chapter 12 will help you understand price movements and charting.

CHAPTER 12

# Step Three: Understanding Price Movements and Charting

*"The first and most important step toward success is the feeling that we can succeed."*

NELSON BOSWELL

*Over the years, the authors collectively have trained hundreds of professional traders. In most cases, a pattern emerges:*

- Stage One *is the "cocky" stage, generally used to hide a deeply felt feeling of inadequacy. It is accompanied by a strong reliance on native intelligence and quick reactions to get into trades and to escape when it was time to get out of trades.*

- Stage Two *is the "humble" stage, when reality sets in and the new trader realizes that natural gifts are not enough. The trader accepts that skills must be learned to succeed.*

- Stage Three *is the "eureka" stage, when the pieces come together. The trader realizes that success in trading really is both simple and achievable. This is when the trader finally "gets it."*

*More times than not, the eureka stage occurs when this new trader begins to really understand how to read and use charts.*

## TECHNICAL ANALYSIS VERSUS FUNDAMENTAL ANALYSIS

There are two main branches for the study of investments: (1) fundamental analysis studies a company or industry's earnings, and (2) technical analysis studies price and volume.

The investor who uses *fundamental analysis* operates in the longer time horizon. She or he is counting on the fundamental strengths of a particular company relative to its industry or to the whole economy to increase the value of its stock over time. Because even the very best companies will see their prices decline over periods of hours, days, weeks, or even months, and experience price swings that can be quite dramatic in the short term, fundamental analysis is not germane to the shorter term trader.

*Technical analysis* seeks to take advantage of these price movements. The technical analyst believes that there are recurring price patterns that can be identified and traded with a high degree of success. It is possible to trade technically with no knowledge of the company beyond what the chart tells you.

Remember that charts are plotting price—not value. When you trade using technical analysis you are trading price movements, not the underlying value.

CSCO is a company that you might want to own in your retirement account because you think the value will increase nicely over time. But there is nothing wrong with trading it in the short term: buy at 58—sell at 66—short at 68—buy back at 62, and on and on. You make money on CSCO going up and coming down. Your money is working harder and more productively for you.

As Arnold Bernhard, the founder of The Value Line Investment Survey, said in his book, *The Evaluation of Common Stocks,* "Stocks are not always worth what they sell for. Sometimes they are carried too high, sometimes too low, by mass excitement. Sooner or later, they move in line with value." In the interim, you can trade those price movements profitably, using technical analysis!

## THE MIRACLE OF THE MARKETS

The price of any security is set in the marketplace based on the bids and offers of many buyers and sellers. Each day, billions of shares of stock are traded in millions of separate transactions in the United States alone.

Here's the miracle: Every single one of those trades had a buyer who believed that the price was going to increase, and a seller who believed that the price was going to decrease. Imagine that! At exactly the same time these two people held exactly opposite beliefs—and one of them was totally wrong.

How can so many millions of people, with exactly opposite beliefs, come together in the market every day? Our markets really are a miracle!

## MOVEMENT OF STOCK PRICES

Let's start by stating the obvious: stock prices can only do three things—go up, go down, or stay flat. See Figure 12.1 to see how these movements are charted.

Now we need to understand what *causes* stock prices to move.

**FIGURE 12.1**  Stock Price Movement

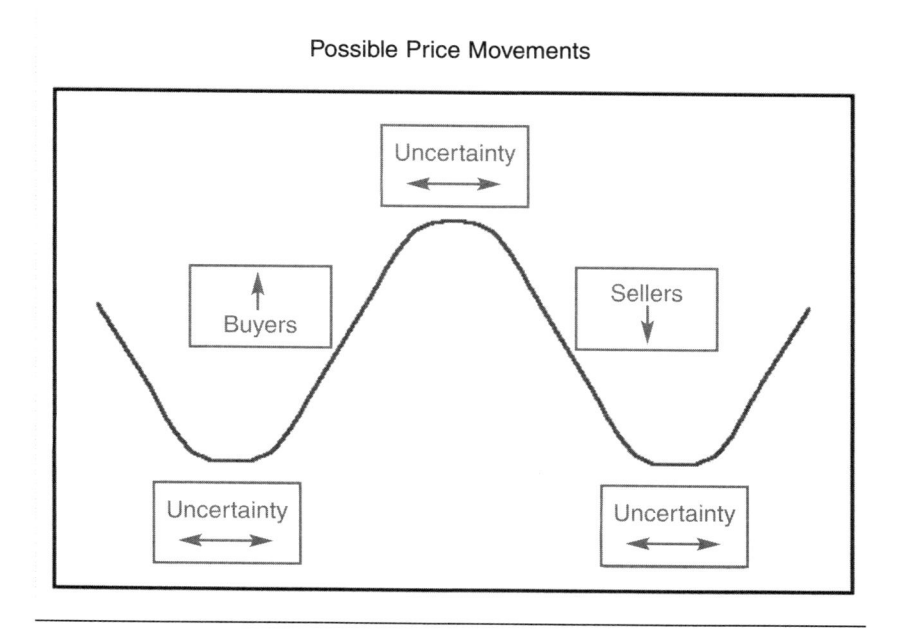

Possible Price Movements

## Stock Prices Move Because of Buying and Selling Activity

If there are more buyers than sellers, the price will rise. If there are more sellers than buyers, the price will fall. This exhibits the economic rule of supply and demand at its most basic.

- *Stock prices go up* when there are more buyers than sellers, when there is an increase in demand, and when the buyers are dominating trading.
- *Stock prices go down* when there are more sellers than buyers, when there is an increase in supply, and when the sellers are dominating trading.
- *Stock prices stay flat* when there is uncertainty—or call it ambivalence or call it confusion. When there is equilibrium in supply and demand or when neither buyers nor sellers are dominating trading, prices stay flat.

While stock prices are just an endless repetition of these three movements, there are endless *reasons* that motivate someone to become a buyer or to become a seller: earnings announcements, dividends, stock splits, interest rate changes, inflation news, research reports, product introductions, merger mania, legal actions, war and peace, solar flares, desire to get the best price, fear of getting the worst price, and on and on.

Any of these reasons may stimulate someone to take action. It is this very fact of so many reasons floating around that leads to so many people every day with exactly opposite opinions. This creates the miracle of our markets!

By themselves, however, these reasons will not move the stock price. Only the actual buying and selling activity of real traders with real money will move the stock price.

As Gary Anderson, the publisher of *EquityPM* says: "Focus on what traders do, not why they do it." The point is this: You don't care what the reasons are, you will make your money by trading against what all of those people *do!* That's where charts come in. Charts tell you very clearly what all those people out there are doing.

Here's another question for you: What do you think trading is *really* all about? Isn't it about matching your wits, education, and experience against the wits, education, and experience of someone else? To be more blunt, aren't you "placing a bet" that there is someone out there who is not as good as you are?

*Remember the story of the two guys walking in the woods when they came upon an obviously agitated and aggressive grizzly bear? Immediately one guy bends down to tighten the laces on his tennis shoes.*

*Puzzled, his buddy turns to look at him and screams in panic, "What do you think you're doing? Start running, you've got to outrun that bear!"*

*At which point his friend stands up, looks him squarely in the eye, and says, "No, I don't have to outrun the bear—I just have to outrun you!"*

Isn't that what trading is really all about? You don't have to outrun the entire market, you just have to outrun the slower traders.

And deep in your heart you know what it takes to outrun them. You need to learn the skills of making high-probability trades and to follow a trading plan.

Again, that's where charts come in. If you can learn to use charts to recognize what the market is doing, won't you have a huge advantage over the person who does not have that knowledge?

So, we are going to learn a bit about charts in this chapter. Some of this may seem a bit "dry" or "basic" or "technical," but hang in there with us. We won't get too bogged down in details. We just want to be sure you understand some basic charting concepts, and appreciate the power of Japanese candlestick charts.

Remember that the concepts we introduce here are part of a foundation for the specific trading techniques we will introduce in later chapters.

## THE BASIC PRICE CHART

For trading purposes, we use price charts that simply plot price against time. The vertical axis $(y)$ shows price, while the horizontal axis $(x)$ shows time.

Let's consider "time" first. You can construct a chart for any time period you choose. In practicality, the range will be from one minute to one year. In *The Sixth Market,* we generally will be talking about "daily charts" (that refer to a one-day time period).

Then you choose the price you want to plot. In any given time period, there are four different prices you could choose:

1. Opening price for the period
2. Closing price for the period

3. Highest price for the period
4. Lowest price for the period

Then you choose the style of chart you would like. The two choices we will look at are: (1) a line chart, or (2) a Japanese candlestick chart.

## Line Chart

Figure 12.2 shows a simple line chart for Dell. It is able to show you one piece of information. In this case it is the closing price over a period of 20 days.

**FIGURE 12.2** Line Chart

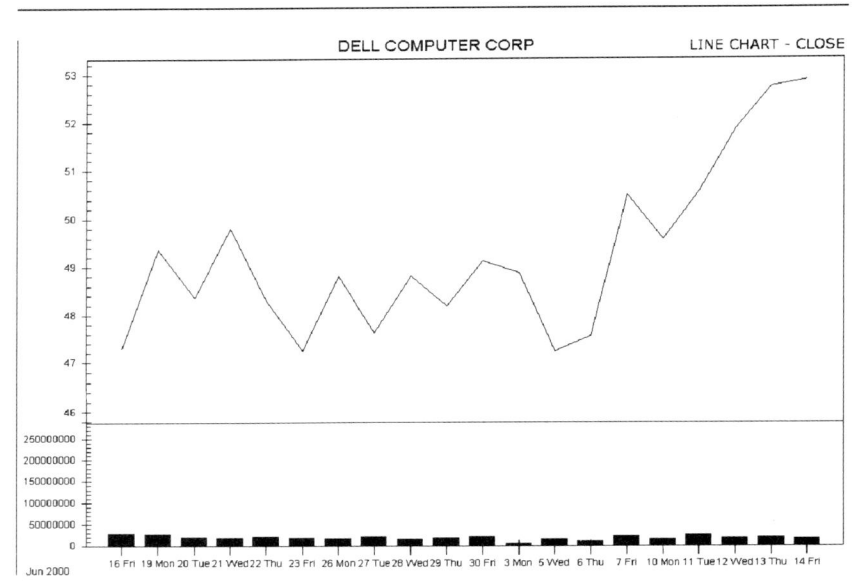

*Copyright 2000, TradeCast® Ltd.*

## Japanese Candlestick Charts

We prefer to use Japanese candlestick charts for our trading because you can get more information in the same space as a line chart. Also, you can learn to read the psychology of the market from the various candlestick formations. Figure 12.3 shows a Japanese candlestick chart for Dell for the same period as the line chart in Figure 12.2.

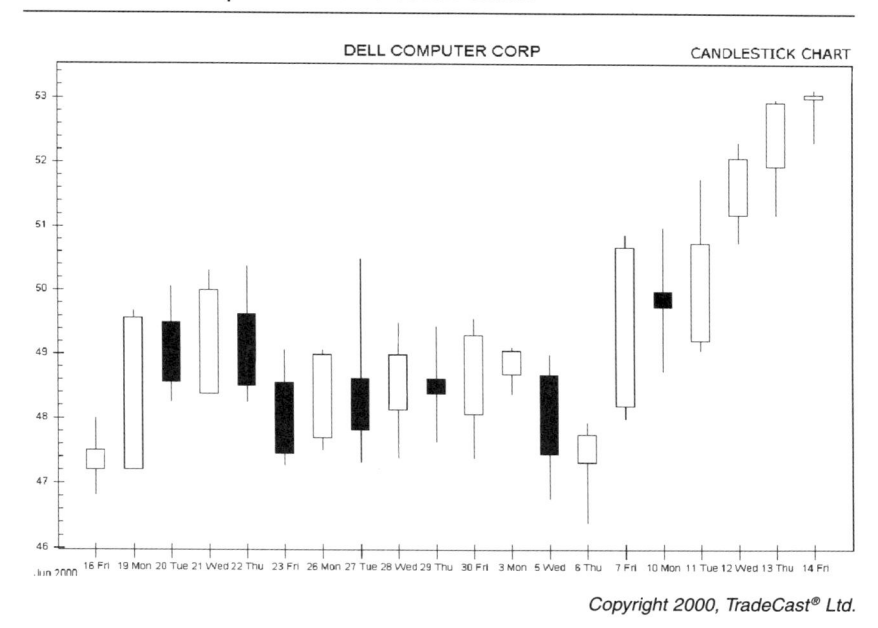

**FIGURE 12.3** Japanese Candlestick Chart

*Copyright 2000, TradeCast® Ltd.*

You can see that these two charts have a similar shape to them but there is quite a bit more information on the candlestick chart. What is it telling us?

As you look at Figure 12.4, you can see eight important pieces of information about your selected stock for the chosen time period:

1. High for the period
2. Closing price
3. Opening price
4. Low for the period
5. Trading range for the period
6. Relationship of the close to the high
7. Relationship of the open to the low
8. Net change from open to close

**144** THE SIXTH MARKET

**FIGURE 12.4** What a Japanese Candlestick Chart Shows

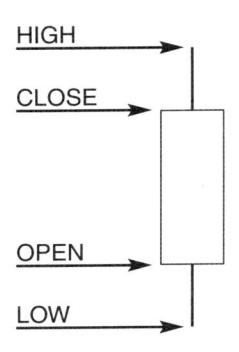

```
              HIGH  ───▶┐
                        │
              CLOSE ───▶├──┐
                        │  │
                        │  │
                        │  │
              OPEN  ───▶├──┘
                        │
              LOW   ───▶┘
```

Figure 12.4 is for a stock that closed higher than the open. You can see that because the body of the candlestick is open (white). If the stock had closed lower than the open, the body will be closed (black). All of this information will be important in learning to trade high-probability chart patterns.

Figures 12.5 through 12.21 show examples of various configurations of the Japanese candlestick. You'll be amazed at how complete a picture of the market or a stock that these charts can give you.

Figure 12.5 shows at a glance that the close was above the open because the main body of the candlestick is open (white). Because the close was above the open, this shows an up day. You can easily spot the high, the low, and the trading range for the day.

**FIGURE 12.5** Up Day Candlestick Chart

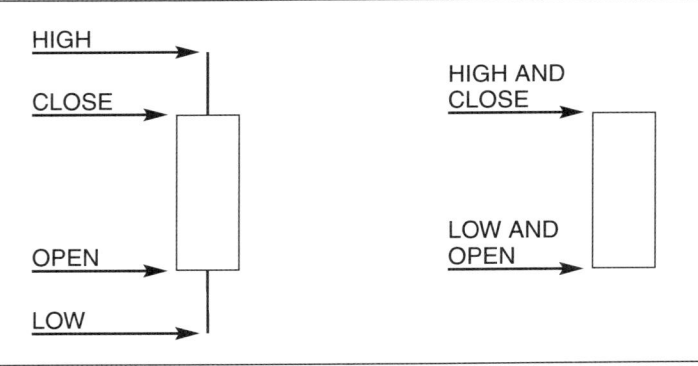

```
      HIGH   ───▶┐                HIGH AND
                 │                CLOSE   ───▶┐
      CLOSE  ───▶├──┐                         │
                 │  │                         │
                 │  │                         │
                 │  │                         │
      OPEN   ───▶├──┘             LOW AND     │
                 │                OPEN    ───▶┘
      LOW    ───▶┘
```

**FIGURE 12.6** Down Day Candlestick Chart

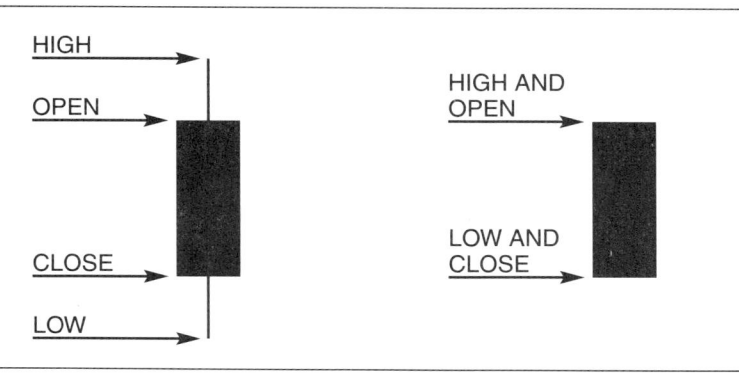

The closed (black) body in Figure 12.6 tells us that the close was below the open. That is why this is called a down day.

A flat day is one in which the open and the close are at the same price, hence it is called a flat day. Figure 12.7 shows what this chart looks like. Yet, the candlestick still gives us valuable information about trading range and the relationships among the four price points.

**FIGURE 12.7** Flat Day Candlestick Chart

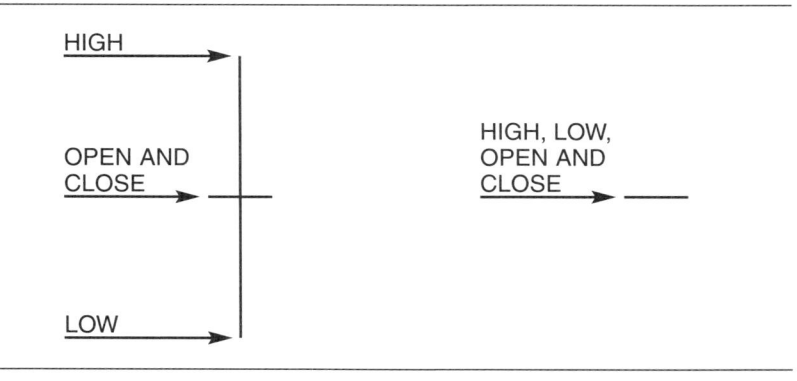

As you study these examples, be sure you can see all eight points of information in each. If you cannot, reread this section until you can easily spot all eight points.

## ARE BUYERS OR SELLERS WINNING?

Let's look at how Japanese candlesticks can help us clearly and easily see if the buyers are winning or if the sellers have the upper hand. As you study these examples, try to see how the shape of just one candlestick can give you a concise understanding of market psychology.

### Buyers in Control

On this day, the close is very near the high, showing no real selling pressure at the end of the day. The price dropped after the open and was driven up quite sharply by aggressive buyers to close near the high for the day. *Can you see that the buyers are dominating here?*

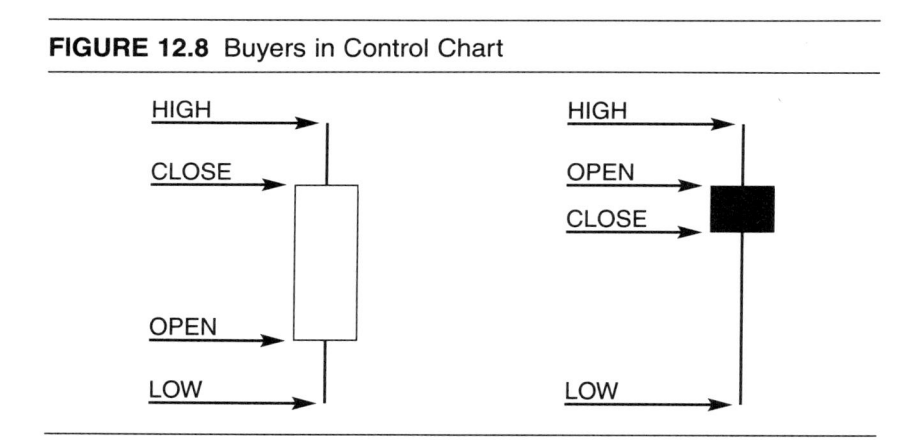

**FIGURE 12.8** Buyers in Control Chart

Another day started badly with a precipitous drop in price after the open. However, the buyers have come in and driven the price well up, off of the low for the day. *Can you see the buyers dominating?*

### Sellers in Control

On this day, the close is very near the low, showing no real buying pressure at the end of the day. The price rose after the open and was driven down quite sharply by aggressive sellers to close near the low for the day. *Can you see the difference when sellers control?*

**FIGURE 12.9** Sellers in Control Chart

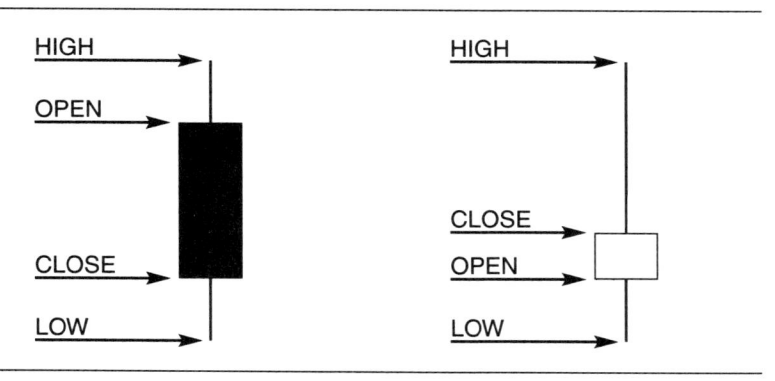

```
HIGH  →                    HIGH  →
OPEN  →   ┌─┐
          │█│              CLOSE →  ┌─┐
          │█│              OPEN  →  │ │
CLOSE →   │█│                       └─┘
          └─┘
LOW   →                    LOW   →
```

Another day started with a precipitous rise after the open. Even though the day still closed up, the sellers have come in and driven the price well down, off of the high for the day. *Can you see the sellers dominating?*

## Neither Side in Control

Notice there is no clear-cut direction here. It wouldn't matter if this stock closed up or down—neither side has the obvious upper hand.

**FIGURE 12.10** No One in Control Chart

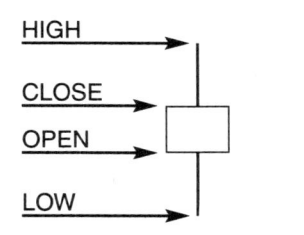

```
      HIGH  →
      CLOSE →  ┌─┐
      OPEN  →  │ │
               └─┘
      LOW   →
```

We will learn more about using Japanese candlesticks in Chapter 13.

## TRENDS

When prices move in one direction for an extended length of time, we call that a trend. If that direction reflects increasing prices, we call it an uptrend. You would see this on a chart as in Figure 12.11 as a succession of generally higher highs and higher lows. Demand is increasing, which means that the buyers are controlling the price movement.

**FIGURE 12.11** Uptrend Chart

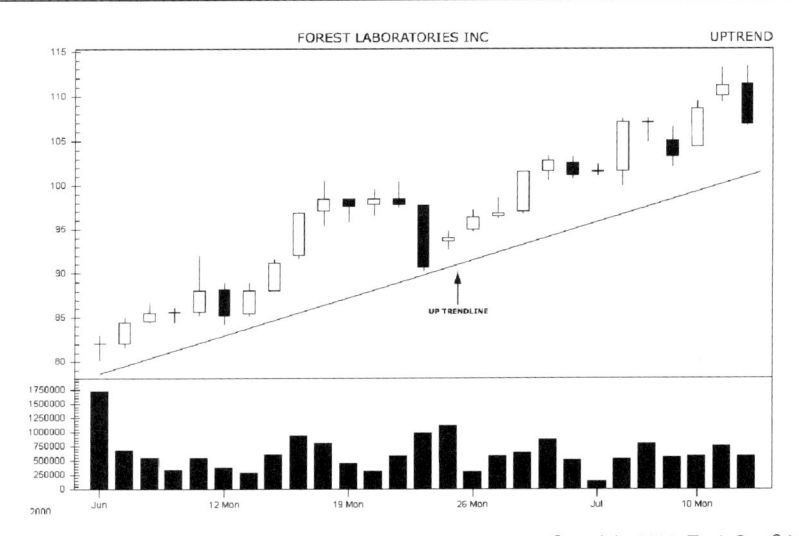

*Copyright 2000, TradeCast® Ltd.*

If the price direction reflects declining prices, we call it a downtrend. On the chart in Figure 12.12 this would appear to be a succession of generally lower highs and lower lows. Supply is increasing, which means that the sellers are controlling the price movement.

If the rate of change is relatively neutral, we call it a flat trend, or a range bound trend. Supply and demand are in balance, as shown in Figure 12.13. Neither the buyers nor the sellers are asserting themselves.

**FIGURE 12.12** Downtrend Chart

*Copyright 2000, TradeCast® Ltd.*

**FIGURE 12.13** Flat Trend (Range Bound Trend)

*Copyright 2000, TradeCast® Ltd.*

## SUPPORT AND RESISTANCE

Here comes a really important point. If you want consistent success in the market, you have a job to find out who is winning—the buyers or the sellers—and to trade accordingly. That's what charts are good for! One of the best ways to see who is winning the battle between buyers and sellers is at points of support and resistance. Support and resistance define natural boundaries to the price of a stock.

### Support

Where buyers are strong enough to keep prices from falling further, you find support. Remember, you don't care about the reasons why the buyers are buying. You just want to be able to observe the support and take advantage of the fact that they are doing it. Look at the chart in Figure 12.14 to see that every time the price declines to the support level, the buyers start buying and the price is prevented from falling further.

**FIGURE 12.14** Support Chart

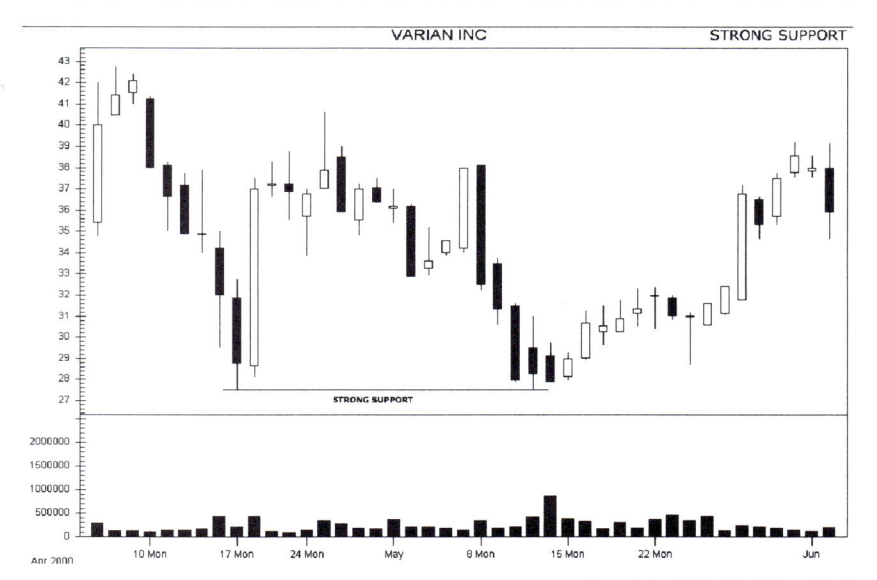

*Copyright 2000, TradeCast® Ltd.*

## Resistance

Where sellers are strong enough to keep prices from rising further, you find resistance. Again, you don't care why the market or a stock is behaving this way, you just want to learn to trade this situation profitably. Look at the chart in Figure 12.15 to see that every time the price rises to the resistance level, the sellers start selling and the price is prevented from rising further.

**FIGURE 12.15** Resistance Chart

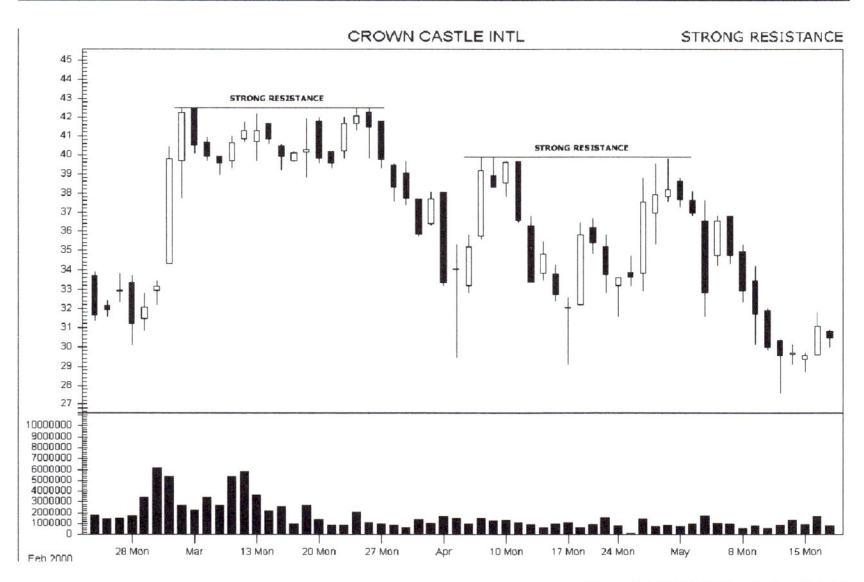

*Copyright 2000, TradeCast® Ltd.*

## SUPPORT AND RESISTANCE LINES

Drawing lines of support and resistance onto your charts can give you important visual information for making high-probability trades.

First, how do you draw these lines?

- *Support lines.* Within the period you have selected, start a line from the lowest low, draw it up and to the low point preceding the highest

high. The line should not pass through prices in between the two low points. This line shows the line of support for the trend.
- *Resistance lines.* Within the period you have selected, start a line from the highest high, draw it up and to the high point preceding the lowest low. The line should not pass through prices in between the two high points. This line shows the line of resistance for the trend.

Now that you know where support and resistance are, what do you do? Some of the easiest profits you will ever make come from buying when prices approach a support level and selling when prices approach a resistance level.

## THE END OF THE TREND

One of two things can happen when a trend comes to an end:

### Reversals

A trend can end in a reversal. The price can change direction and start a trend in the opposite direction from the previous trend. The strength shifts from the buyers to the sellers, or vise versa. Figure 12.16 shows a very clear and dramatic reversal.

### Consolidations

Another way that a trend can end is in consolidation. Rather than establishing a trend in the opposite direction, price movement "pauses" and prices remain relatively flat, as shown in Figure 12.17. During consolidation, the market is unwilling to establish a new direction. Neither the buyers nor the sellers are willing to step up and take control.

Where can prices move after they break out of consolidation? Prices can move in only two directions:

1. *Continuation.* Prices will continue in the direction they were moving prior to the consolidation, or
2. *Reversal.* Prices will move in the opposite direction.

The chart in Figure 12.17 shows these two possible breakouts from consolidation.

**FIGURE 12.16** Trend Reversal Chart

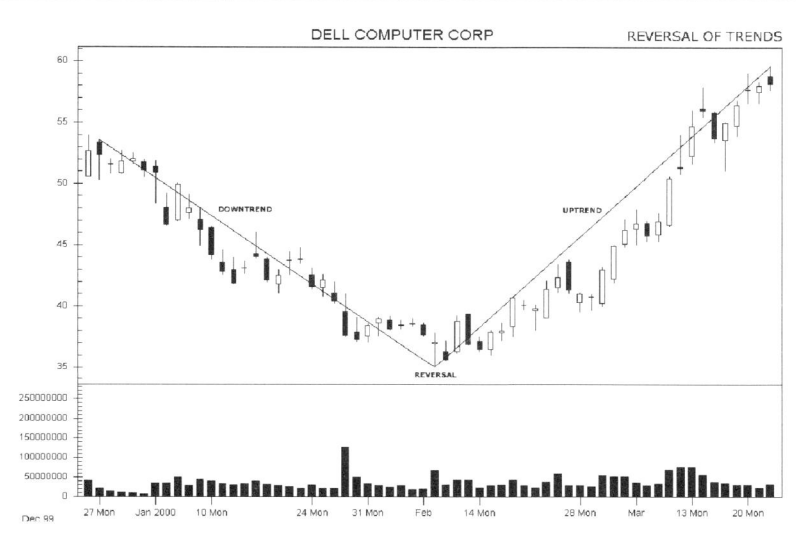

*Copyright 2000, TradeCast® Ltd.*

**FIGURE 12.17** Consolidation Chart

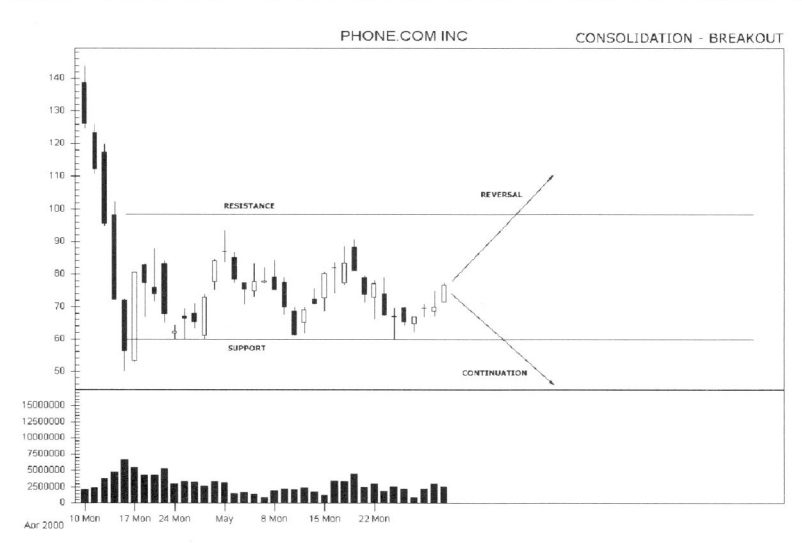

*Copyright 2000, TradeCast® Ltd.*

## BREAKOUTS

Trading against support and resistance sounds easy enough—just find those lines and trade your heart out. Except, there always comes a time when the price will break out of the support or resistance constraints. If you don't react to this change, you're toast!

Actually, there is a very sound trading strategy that says: Trade support and resistance. You will be right on every trade until the last one, when the breakout occurs. And if you know how to manage your stop loss (see Chapter 15), you really won't be toast—you will suffer a manageable loss.

What is really happening on a breakout? Take a look at the example in Figure 12.18. See how many times the price bumped up against the resistance level, only to fall back. Finally, for whatever reason (and we don't care what the reason is, do we?), the sellers were no longer willing to sell at that price. They—and their supply—disappeared.

**FIGURE 12.18** Breakout Chart

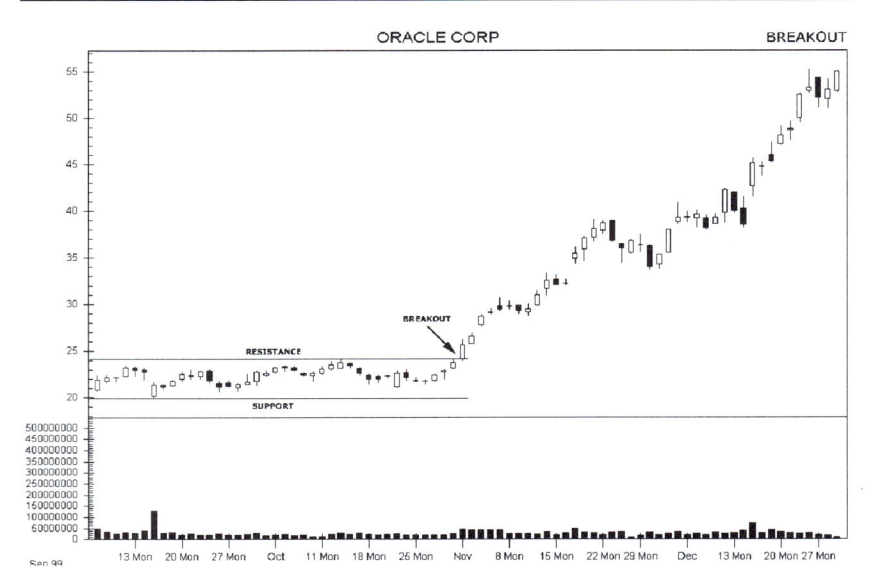

*Copyright 2000, TradeCast® Ltd.*

An entirely new pricing dynamic is now at work. Prices are free to rise. We are in uncharted territory. We don't know how far the prices will rise, so we have to find the new resistance level.

We also don't know how far the prices are likely to fall. But we don't have to look too hard to find the new support level. As shown in Figure 12.19, it is a reliable axiom that a punctured resistance level becomes the new support level.

**FIGURE 12.19** Resistance Chart

*Copyright 2000, TradeCast® Ltd.*

## TRENDLINES AND MOVING AVERAGES

Trendlines are an improvement over simple support and resistance lines. Trendlines help to identify trends and to show absolute points of support and resistance.

One of the most useful type of trendlines is the moving average, which will smooth the price series to make it easier to see the trend. Moving averages can be precisely drawn. Every chart software package

**FIGURE 12.20** 20-Day Moving Average Chart

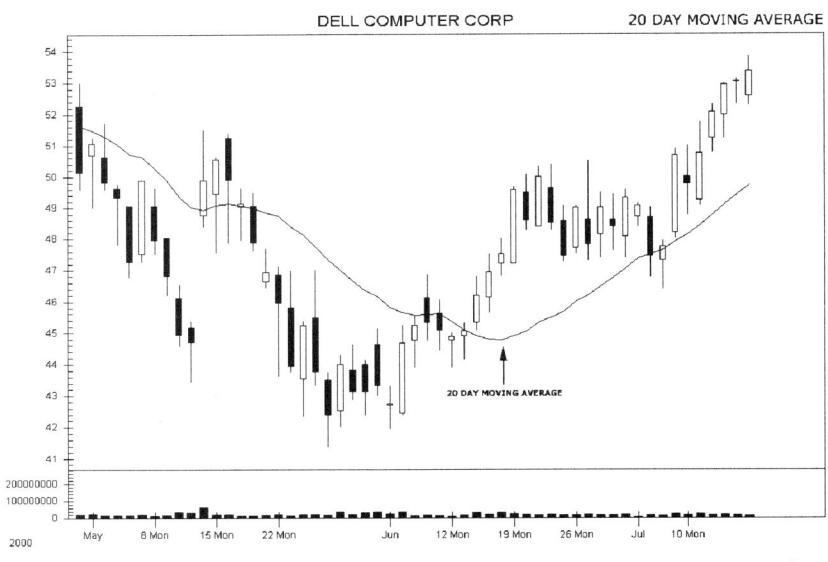

*Copyright 2000, TradeCast® Ltd.*

includes an automatic tool to draw moving averages. A 20-day moving average, as shown in Figure 12.20, is a series of datapoints calculated to be the average of the closing prices for each of the past 20 days.

In Figure 12.20, see how the 20-day moving average is superimposed over the Japanese candlestick chart. The moving average clearly reflects the trend while smoothing out the fluctuations in the data. The longer the period, the more the data will be "smoothed."

Use moving averages as you would support and resistance:

- If the current price is above the moving average, that is a bullish signal. In effect, buyers are driving the current price well above the trend.
- Conversely, if the current price is below the moving average, that is a bearish signal. Sellers are driving the current price well below the trend.

We also can use two or more moving averages on the same chart to look at the trend from two different time perspectives, say, 20 day and 40 day:

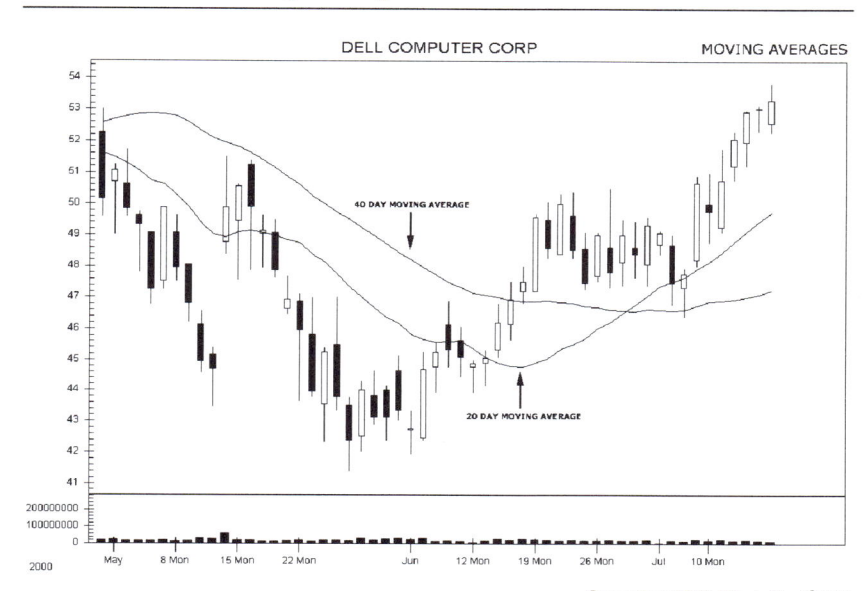

**FIGURE 12.21** Moving Averages Chart

*Copyright 2000, TradeCast® Ltd.*

- In an uptrend, the 20-day line should remain above the 40-day line. If the line crosses below the 40-day line, that proves that the trend is decelerating or reversing. That is a sell signal.
- In a downtrend, the 20-day line should remain below the 40-day line. If the line crosses above the 40-day line, that proves that the trend is decelerating or reversing. That is a buy signal. Can you see the buy signal in the next chart?

## VOLUME

What are the volume numbers telling us? Be careful that you don't jump to conclusions here because the answer to that question is not so intuitive. We never look at volume by itself; we look at it with associated price movement. The four associations are:

1. Above-average volume without strong price movement actually signals that the current move is coming to an end. Why? Because

the "other side" has taken control, fighting off further price movement despite the high volume.
2. Above-average volume with strong price movement in the direction of a trend indicates likelihood that the trend will continue. One side is in control and is moving aggressively. The bigger the price and volume, the farther the price will run.
3. Above-average volume with strong price movement following a breakout signals that further price movement in that direction is likely. One side is in control and is moving aggressively. The bigger the price and volume, the farther the price will run.
4. Below-average volume with limited price movement during periods of consolidation many times signals that the next move will be a continuation move.

That's a good start on overall understanding of charts. You probably have learned more than you realize. Now you can take your Japanese candlesticks to the next chapter where you will learn how to identify and how to trade proven, high-probability chart patterns. These patterns can become the basis for consistent profits!

# CHAPTER 13

# Step Four: Using Reliable Chart Setups

*"In the kingdom of the blind, the one-eyed man is King."*

ATTRIBUTED TO DAVE MACKIE

**A** stark fact of trading life is that there are millions of people making trades every day who do not possess market understanding, who cannot construct a trading plan, who can do little but wish, hope, and gamble, and who will not prevail in a contest against the prepared trader.

You are about to enter a place known only to a relative few, a place where education and reason triumph, a place where clarity of purpose abounds, a place where skills and experience mature into wisdom. The quote above creates such a perfect metaphor for us for we can never have perfect vision into the markets. The best we can hope for is one clear eye.

But in the markets, that is more than enough!

## PROVEN CHART PATTERNS DEFINED

It's one thing to read a chart. It is entirely another to be able to interpret and use that information wisely. The oldest form of interpreting charts is through pattern analysis that is based on the tendency of charts to repeat the same formations over and over again.

Over the years, through observation and back testing, analysts have identified and promulgated scores—if not hundreds—of chart patterns that produce known trading results.

What do we mean by "known trading results"? We mean that an analyst will study a particular, common chart pattern—say a "double top"—and may test that pattern back through years of data and on hundreds of different stocks to see what the profit and loss outcomes are each time that pattern is found. After extensive analysis, it can be said with certainty that the pattern will produce a winning trade 53.8 percent of the time.

On top of that, the analyst will be able to tell you two other pieces of information: (1) how much capital you need to risk to produce the desired results, and (2) how much profit (reward) you can expect from this pattern. As you will see, knowing your risk and reward points in a particular pattern will be vitally important to you!

Is that valuable information? Could you use information like that to improve your trading performance? Is it possible to get such information? Yes, yes, and yes!

## A PROCESS FOR TRADING SUCCESS

Let's lay out the steps of a logical trading process that can start producing for you immediately.

### Become Proficient at Trading Techniques

You must be able to enter and exit the trade efficiently. The earlier chapters of this book focused on: choosing a direct access broker, configuring your system and Internet access, developing self-awareness, learning market fundamentals, and understanding charts.

We are not trying to teach you everything—just the things you need to make money, starting right now.

### Learn to Recognize Chart Patterns

Memorize patterns that produce a known percentage of winning trades, and that give you proven risk and reward parameters. That's what you'll do in this chapter. Then, in Chapter 14 we will introduce you to a great way to find these proven patterns before each trading day.

## Use a Statistically Valid Trading Plan for Every Trade

Four elements are involved in developing a statistically valid trading plan:

1. *Determine risk and reward* before making the trade. In this chapter, we see how to use proven chart patterns to identify the action, entry point range, initial protective stop (which identifies your risk), and exit target (which estimates your reward).
2. *Use sound money management techniques* to determine the size of your position (the number of shares to trade) to protect your capital and to maximize profit. We cover this in Chapter 14.
3. *Manage the predefined risk.* You have defined your risk and set your stops. You now know where to exit if the trade is moving against you. Will you have the discipline to do it?
4. *Manage the predefined reward* with intelligent exit strategies. There are several successful exit strategies—from the conservative to the aggressive—in Chapter 14; we will explore them all.

## USING THE PROCESS

Once you learn to approach trading through this process you can put the mathematical odds in your favor. That's right, in *your* favor! With this process, you only use proven chart patterns that produce winning trades more than 50 percent of the time, that is, which risks $1 for every $2 in potential reward. You hold to these guidelines for each trade you make.

Here's the math:

|             | Percentage | (Risk)/Reward | NET  |
|-------------|------------|---------------|------|
| Winners     | 50%        | 2.00          | 1.00 |
| Losers      | 50%        | 1.00          | 0.50 |
| Expectation | 100%       |               | 0.50 |

If you will execute to these limits—don't "fudge" on them, you will return an average of $0.50 on every share of every trade you make.

You've heard all the arguments: There's no "system" that works forever, it's not possible to put the odds in your favor, there's no free lunch, and on and on. But that's nonsense; you can manage this process profitably.

This is serious stuff, so let's be crystal clear here. These are the rules you must follow:

- Every trade you make must be based on a chart pattern that has been back tested to show at least a 50 percent success rate. If one of the chart patterns you are trading does not return 50 percent winners, you stop using it and choose others that do.
- Every trade you make has a statistical risk/reward ratio of at least 1:2. If you find that you are risking too much, you can adjust your stops and trade stocks with a narrower spread or less volatility.
- Every trade you make applies sound money management techniques. If you are burning through your capital—*stop!* You can reduce your position size.
- Every trade you make manages risk ruthlessly . . . according to predetermined stops. If you are not executing at your stops, you can either start executing stops properly or quit trading! If you're not using stops, you're only gambling.
- Every trade you make manages reward through the application of intelligent exit strategies. If you find that your rewards are too small, you can revisit your exit strategies to adjust them for more profit.

All you have to do is hold firmly to your trading process. If you are not achieving the predicted results, the problem is not with the trading process, it is in your application of it. You can identify and change the things that are preventing you from sticking to these rules. You are in complete control of maximizing your profits.

Concentrate on the logic of the process—the math, the trading techniques, the valid plan—and you can be consistently profitable.

In Chapter 9 we defined confidence as the "expectation of a positive result." This is exactly what we are describing here. Chart patterns that return 50 percent winners and a 1:2 risk/reward ratio give you the "expectation of a positive result"—they give you confidence!

We'll give you even more reason to have confidence in the approach we outline here. Even if your chart patterns only produce winners 33 percent of the time—1 profitable trade in 4—you still would make money. Look at the math.

|   | Percentage | (Risk)/Reward | NET |
|---|---|---|---|
| Winners | 33.0% | 2.00 | 0.66 |
| Losers | 67.0% | 1.00 | 0.67 |
| Expectation | 100.0% |  | 0.01 |

So here is a very important point. You don't have to pick winners every time you trade. You can relax and forget about that kind of perfection. Instead, you need to become ruthless in your management of risk and reward!

## RELIABLE CHART SETUPS

This section will introduce you to several proven chart patterns.

## THE REVIVAL BUY

The Revival Buy is a continuation play. Do you recall what we said about "continuations" in the previous chapter? The stock has been in an uptrend but has been trading sideways for several days. We know that it will either reverse direction or continue in the uptrend. We are looking for a particular chart pattern that indicates that this stock will continue in the uptrend.

Look at Figure 13.1. What are you looking for on the chart? As we discuss each point, think about how logical all of this is:

- First, you want to see that the sellers have tried to drive this stock down. Before you want to take a long position you want to know that selling pressure has been exhausted—that there are no more sellers out there ready to drive the price down.

    So, for the day before the last trading day, you want to see that the stock closed down for the day—aggressively down—with the closing price to have been in the bottom 25 percent of the trading range. This tells us that the sellers were in control on that day.

    Look at the Japanese candlestick bar marked as 1 on the chart. This is the day before the last trading day. Can you see how the sellers controlled that day and drove the stock down hard?

**164**   THE SIXTH MARKET

**FIGURE 13.1**  Revival Buy

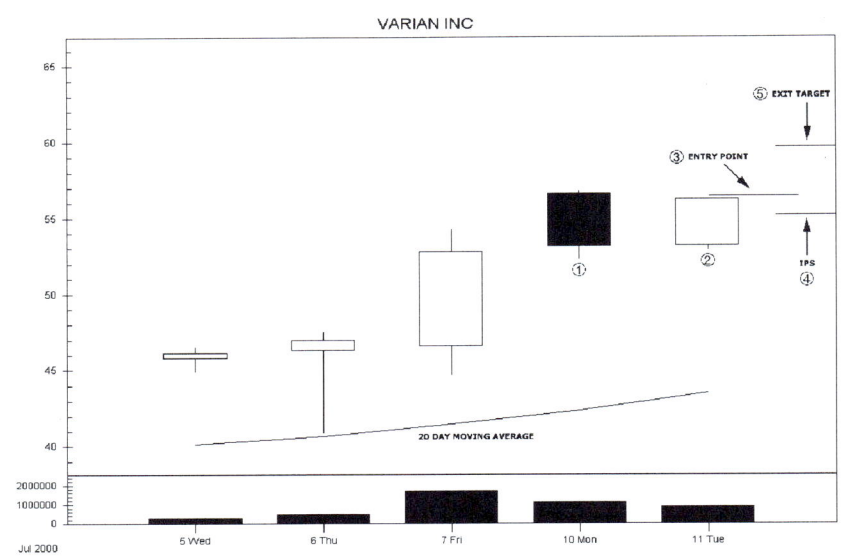

*VARIAN INC chart with Japanese candlesticks, showing points labeled ①, ②, ③ ENTRY POINT, ④ IPS, ⑤ EXIT TARGET, and a 20-day moving average line. Dates shown: Jul 2000, 5 Wed, 6 Thu, 7 Fri, 10 Mon, 11 Tue.*

*Copyright 2000, TradeCast® Ltd.*

- Second, you want to know that the buyers have reasserted themselves, that they have become active in the stock again and that there is evidence of strong buying interest in the stock.

  Look at the last trading day to be sure that the stock closed up for the day and that the closing price is in the top 25 percent of the trading range. That tells you that the buyers have driven the stock up strongly and have resisted any selling pressure late in the day. The buyers are back in control.

  Look at the Japanese candlestick bar marked as 2 on the chart on the last trading day. Can you see how the buyers took control and drove the stock back up hard?

- Third, you want to know that the stock is still in an uptrend. Why? Because when you take a position in a stock, you do not want to be bucking the trend.

  Look at the closing price on the last trading day to see that it is above the 20-day moving average. From the chart can you see that the close on the last trading day (see "↑") is above the 20-day moving average?

Is the psychology clear to you? The great tug-of-war between buyers and sellers is being played out right before your eyes in this setup. The sellers took firm control and drove the price down. Then the buyers stepped up, defined the bottom, and started driving the price back up strongly. When you see this pattern, you know that the buyers are poised to take the stock even higher. But will they? That's the big question for you as you get ready to trade the next day.

Here's where back testing comes in. From your back testing, you know that one more thing has to happen to make this trade a winner for you. You know that the buyers have to establish a new higher price to signal that they are willing to drive the price higher. That is market psychology at its most pure! The buyers have come back into control, but as a new day dawns, the battle begins again.

Will the buyers continue to assert themselves or will the sellers gain the upper hand? The answer is: *If* the buyers will step up and establish a new price above the highest price they were willing to pay yesterday, then and only then will you enter this trade.

You set an entry point that is ⅛ of a point higher than the high on the last trading day (see 3 on the chart). If the buyers will set this new, higher price, your back testing shows you that this trade will be profitable more than 50 percent of the time.

But there is more to do before you make the trade. Remember about managing your risk and your reward! In this trade, you set your initial protective stop (IPS) at 1 point below your entry point (see 4 on the chart).

Then, for this pattern, you set your exit target

- at a point either 3 points above the entry point, which helps you shoot for a risk/reward ration of 1:3, which exceeds your requirement; or
- at 50 percent of the average daily range above the entry point, whichever is greater (see 5 on the chart).

With those three prices set, you wait to see if the buyers will step up and set that new, higher price. Remember, never jump the gun. You do not have a proven trade set up until that price has been traded.

Now look at Figure 13.2 which shows what happened in this particular trade. The next day the stock opened right at your entry point and moved easily to your exit target, for a 3-point winner.

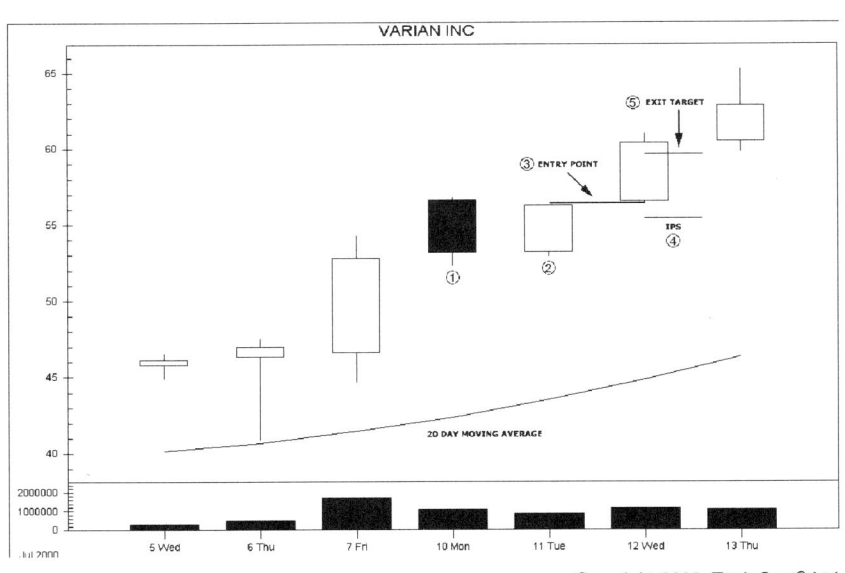

**FIGURE 13.2** Results of the Revival Buy

*Copyright 2000, TradeCast® Ltd.*

## THE REVIVAL SELL

Your second pattern is actually trading the same market psychology as the revival buy except that this setup alerts you to a possible short selling opportunity, as shown in Figure 13.3.

The criteria for the revival sell setup are just the reverse of the revival buy:

- For the day before the last trading day, the stock closed up for the day with the closing price in the top 25 percent of the trading range. The buyers had control, trying to drive the price higher. See 1 on the chart.
- For the last trading day, the stock closed down for the day. The closing price is in the bottom 25 percent of the trading range. The sellers have rejected the buyers and taken firm control, driving the price sharply lower. See 2 on the chart.
- For the last trading day, the closing price is below the 20-day simple moving average. You want to confirm that you are still in a downtrend.

**FIGURE 13.3** Revival Sell

TIME WARNER TELECOM INC

*Copyright 2000, TradeCast® Ltd.*

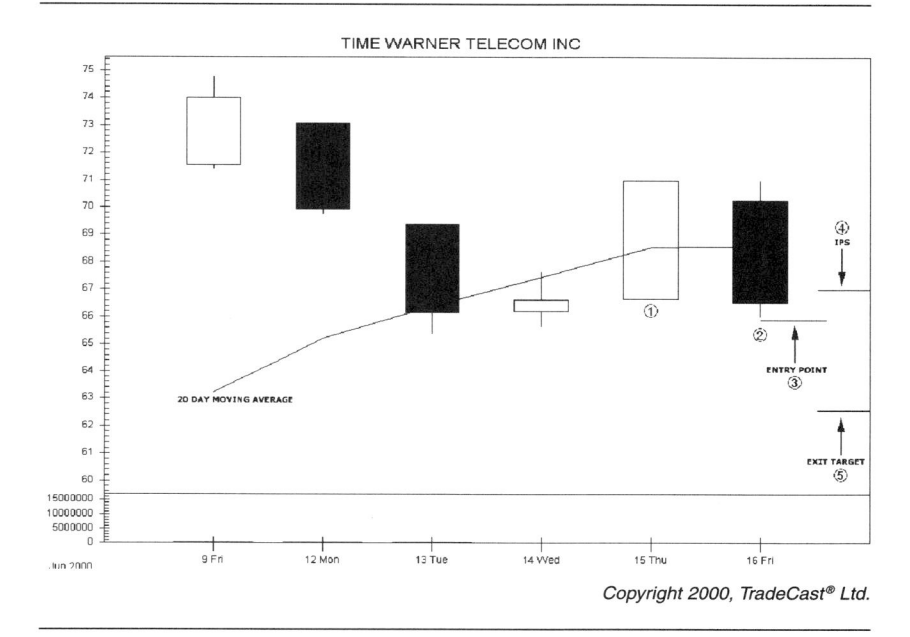

## How Do You Trade the Revival Sell?

- You set an entry point at ⅛ below the low of the last trading day (see 3 on the chart). This is to be certain that the old low has been taken out, which indicates that the sellers are ready and willing to move the stock lower. Remember to sell!
- You set your initial protective stop (IPS) 1 point above the entry point (see 4 on the chart). Remember, to get out of this trade you will buy shares back.
- You set your exit target at a point either 3 points below the entry point, or 50 percent of the average daily range below the entry point, whichever is greater (see 5 on the chart).

Then you wait to see how the battle unfolds.

See Figure 13.4 to track your results. The stock opened right at your IPS and began to immediately move lower. Once it traded at your entry price you executed your short sell.

The stock continued down without any meaningful pullback (as you know many shorts will do) until it reached your exit target. As you see

**168** THE SIXTH MARKET

**FIGURE 13.4** Results of the Revival Sell

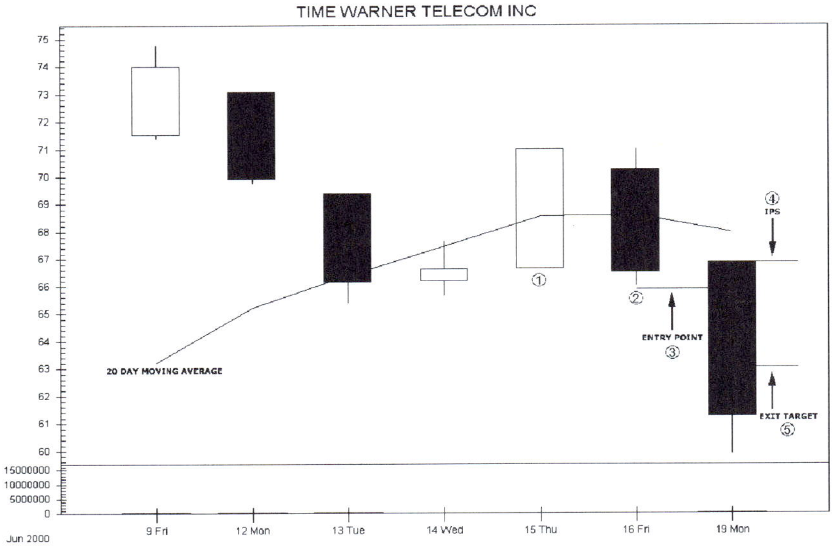

[Chart: TIME WARNER TELECOM INC, Jun 2000, showing candlesticks from 9 Fri to 19 Mon with 20 DAY MOVING AVERAGE, labels ①, ②, ENTRY POINT ③, IPS ④, EXIT TARGET ⑤. Copyright 2000, TradeCast® Ltd.]

in the figure, this stock continued to move downward after you exited the trade. Chapter 15 talks about other exit strategies that will allow you to capture more of this profit.

## THE WEDGE BUY

The wedge buy is a consolidation breakout opportunity. In this setup, the stock has been consolidating for several days. You are looking for a sign that it is ready to break out strongly, and you are looking for an indication as to which way it will break out!

Please refer to Figure 13.5 while you review the criteria for the wedge buy setup:

- For the last trading day (see 3 on figure), the closing price is above the 20-day moving average. This is your clue as to direction—you are expecting the price to break out to the upside.
- Confirm consolidation over the past three trading days:

**FIGURE 13.5** Wedge Buy

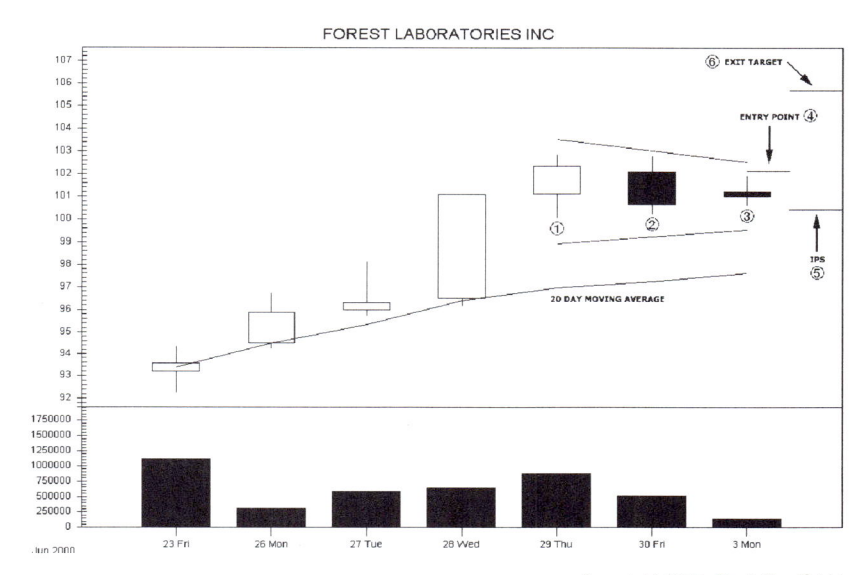

*FOREST LABORATORIES INC*

*Copyright 2000, TradeCast® Ltd.*

- Look to three days ago (see 1 on figure). It's high should be higher than the next two days, and its low should be lower than the next two days.
- Then look to two days ago (see 2 on figure). Its high should be higher than the last trading day and its low should be lower than the last trading day.
- Look to the last trading day (see 3 on figure). It should have the lowest high and the highest low of all three days. This is classic consolidation.

What is the market psychology behind this setup? First, you want the stock to still be in an uptrend, so you confirm a closing price above the 20-day moving average.

Then you want to see narrowing in the consolidation by confirming at least two "inner range" days. This just means that the range is constricting further and further each day. This shows you that neither buyers nor sellers are in control at this point. The consolidation is narrowing, which is always the prelude to a powerful breakout.

## How Do You Trade the Wedge Buy?

- You set an entry point at ⅛ above the high of the last trading day (see 4 on figure). This is to be certain that the old high has been taken out, which indicates that the buyers are ready and willing to move the stock higher.
- You set your initial protective stop (IPS) ⅛ below the last day's low (see 5 on figure). You know from back testing that there is support at that price, but you do not want to breach that level.

  If that is too big of a risk for you, you may choose to set your IPS ⅛ below the low for the current trading day. In either case, you set this IPS to give enough room to withstand one more "charge" by the sellers before the buyers take firm command.
- You set your exit target at a point either 3 points above the entry point, or 50 percent of the average daily range above the entry point, whichever is greater (see 6 on chart).

Then you wait to see if your entry point is reached. Once this stock has traded at that price, you send your order to buy.

Let's look at Figure 13.6 for the results of this trade. The price opened below our entry point and proceeded to trade even lower than our IPS (notice the wick below the main body of the candlestick). At that point, the buyers became active, driving the price up above the open to your entry point, at which point you entered the trade. Within about three hours, the stock had reached your exit target and you closed out the trade for a 3¾ point profit.

In Chapter 15, we discuss various exit strategies. One of these is to hold onto your position beyond your exit target when the stock shows strength. Had you done that in this case, you could have taken even more profit.

## THE WEDGE SELL

This is a consolidation breakout to the downside. Review Figure 13.7 to be sure you can identify the setup and the pricing points:

- For the last trading day (see 3 on figure) the closing price is below the 20-day moving average. This is your clue as to direction. You are expecting the price to break out to the downside.
- Confirm consolidation over the past three trading days:

13 / Step Four: Using Reliable Chart Setups   **171**

**FIGURE 13.6** Results of the Wedge Buy

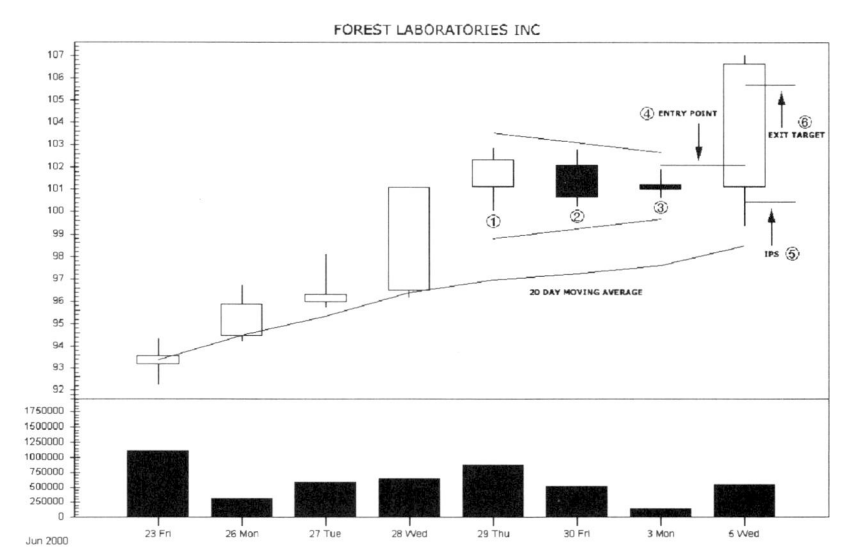

*Copyright 2000, TradeCast® Ltd.*

**FIGURE 13.7** Wedge Sell

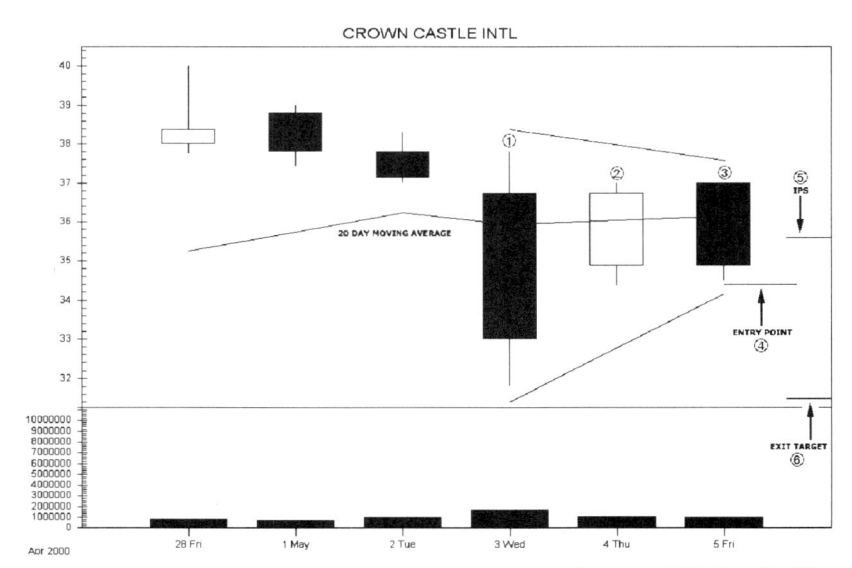

*Copyright 2000, TradeCast® Ltd.*

- Look to three days ago (see 1 on figure). Its high should be higher than the next two days and its low should be lower than the next two days.
- Then look to two days ago (see 2 on figure). Its high should be higher than the last trading day and its low should be lower than the last trading day.
- Look to the last trading day (see 3 on the figure). It should have the lowest high and the highest low of all three days. Again, this is classic consolidation.

### How Do You Trade the Wedge Sell?

- You set an entry point at ⅛ below the low of the last trading day (see 4 on figure). This is to be certain that the old low has been "taken out," which indicates that the sellers are ready and willing to move the stock lower.
- You set your initial protective stop (IPS) ⅛ above the last day's high (see 5 on figure) because you do not want to breach that resistance level.

  If that is too big of a risk for you, you may choose to set your IPS ⅛ above the high for the current trading day. In either case, you set this IPS to give enough room to withstand one more "charge" by the buyers before the sellers take firm command.
- You set your exit target at a point either 3 points below the entry point, or 50 percent of the average daily range below the entry point, whichever is greater (see 6 on figure).

Then you wait to see if your entry point is reached. Once this stock has traded at that price, you send your order to short sell.

Review Figure 13.8 for the results of the wedge sell. The trading day opened with this stock actually moving higher at the open, but it soon fell back to your entry point where you executed your short sell. The stock continued to move downward, although there was a small rebound near the end of the day. You held this position overnight.

The next day, the stock opened lower and moved sharply lower. You exited at your target price very early in the day for a 3-point gain. The stock actually moved another point lower, but you were already on to other trades.

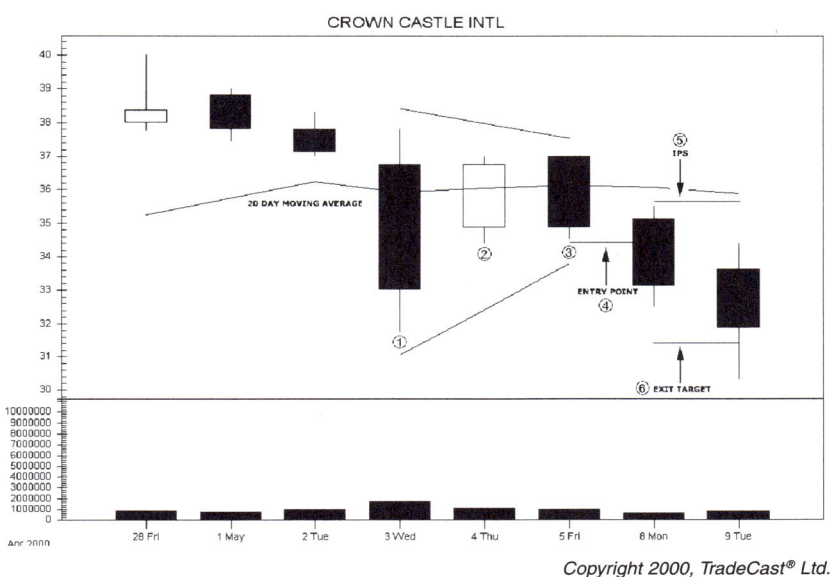

**FIGURE 13.8** Results of the Wedge Sell

*Copyright 2000, TradeCast® Ltd.*

## THE SMART BUY — REVERSAL

The smart buy is a reversal play. In this case, the stock has been falling. You are looking for a setup that tells you that this stock will reverse back to the upside as seen on Figure 13.9.

The criteria for the smart buy setup are:

- For at least the previous three trading days, you see consecutive lower highs and lower lows (see 1, 2, 3 on the figure).
- For at least the previous three trading days, the closing price each day is below or equal to the opening price (you can see that very easily by just looking for black bars).
- On the last trading day, you would like to see higher than average volume (see 4 on figure).

What is the market psychology behind this setup?

First, you want to see that the sellers have been firmly in command. For at least three days they have driven the stock down each day. After

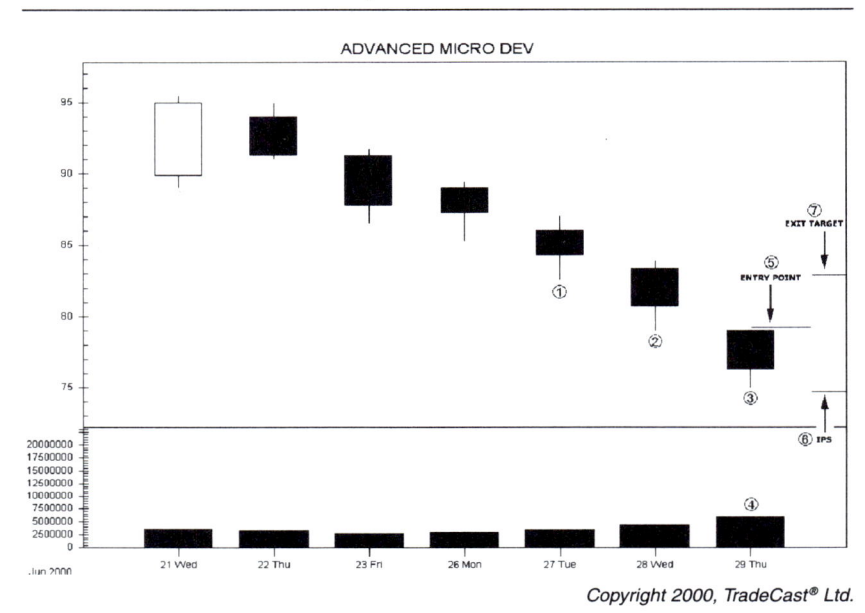

**FIGURE 13.9** The Smart Buy

three days of lower and lower prices, the buyers are poised to jump in to take advantage of these bargain prices. You want to be ready when the buyers bring their pressure to bear on this stock.

Then you want to see higher than average volume on the last trading day, which is a good indicator that a change of direction is at hand.

## How Do You Trade the Smart Buy?

- You set an entry point at ⅛ above the high of the last trading day (see 5 on chart). This is to be certain that the old high has been taken out, which indicates that the buyers are ready and willing to move the stock higher.
- You set your initial protective stop (IPS) ⅛ below the last day's close (see 6 on figure). If that is too big of a risk for you, you may choose to set your IPS ⅛ below the low for the current trading day. In either case, you set this IPS to give enough room to

withstand one more "charge" by the sellers before the buyers take firm command.
- You set your exit target at a point either 3 points above the entry point, or 50 percent of the average daily range above the entry point, whichever is greater (see 7 on figure).

See Figure 13.10 for the results of the smart buy, which shows the value of patience and staying with your plan.

The day opened well below your entry point. Don't worry, you simply wait for the entry point. It finally got there and you entered the trade. For awhile, it pulled back on you, going below your entry point. So you actually were holding a losing trade for part of the day. But it did not pull back to your IPS. You were patient throughout the day and held a slight gain in the position overnight. The next day, your position opened and moved strongly to your exit target, where you took a nice 3-point gain.

**FIGURE 13.10** Results of the Smart Buy

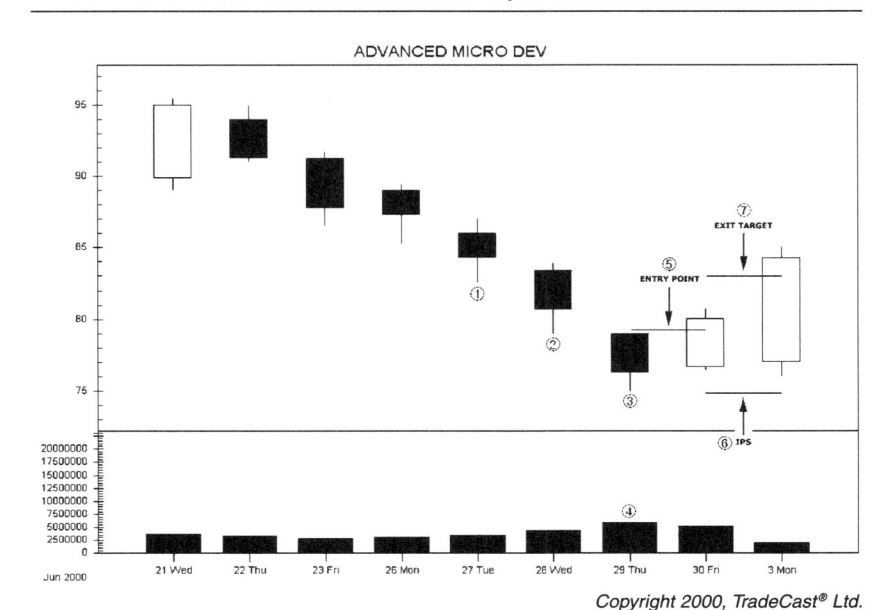

*Copyright 2000, TradeCast® Ltd.*

## THE SMART SELL

The smart sell is just the reverse of the smart buy, as you certainly have guessed by now. Look at Figure 13.11 to be sure that you can identify the setup requirements and the pricing points:

- Verify that the buyers have been in control for at least three days and that prices have been rising steadily during that time. That lets you know that a lot of these buyers may be ready to take some of their profits . . . in other words, to become sellers.
- Set your entry point, IPS, and exit target.

Then look at Figure 13.12 for your results. What a fun trade this was! The stock opened above your entry point and traded even higher for a short time. Then the sellers started to sell, driving the price sharply lower to your entry point, where you executed your short sale. You exited at your exit target for a gain of 4⅛ points. This is a situation where you are glad you exited where you did because buyers came back into the stock at the close to drive the price above your exit.

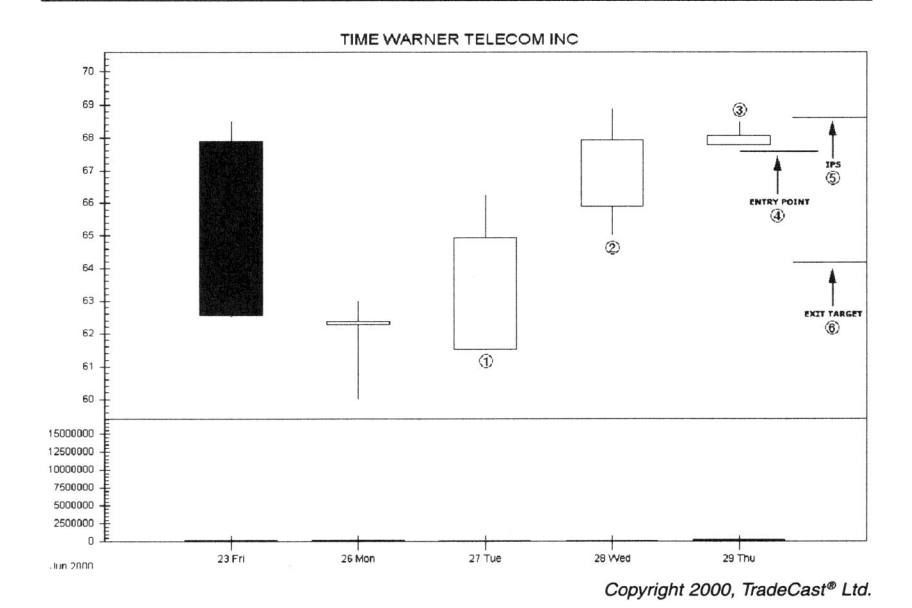

**FIGURE 13.11** The Smart Sell

*Copyright 2000, TradeCast® Ltd.*

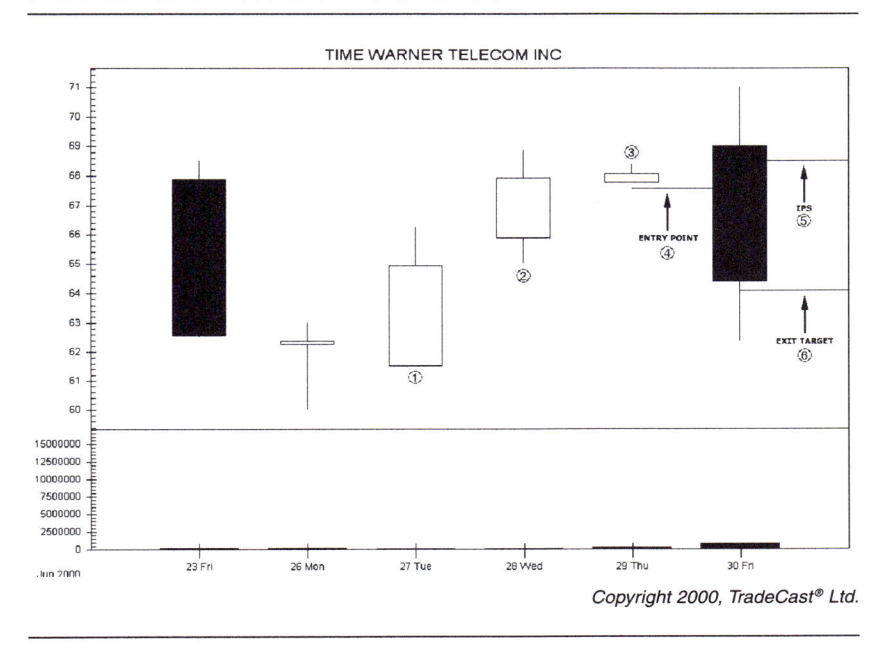

**FIGURE 13.12** Results of the Smart Sell

TIME WARNER TELECOM INC

*Copyright 2000, TradeCast® Ltd.*

## USING PROVEN CHART PATTERNS

If you only traded these patterns, you would have scores of trades to consider each day. Obviously, not all of these setups become trades because many of them will never "hit" the entry point, but you still would have the opportunity to make lots of trades—with excellent profit potential—each day. And, as you can now imagine, there are many more of these proven setups. You could literally learn about a new one every month for the rest of your life!

Here's what we want you to take away from this chapter:

- There is a trading process that can put the mathematical odds in your favor, using proven chart patterns and careful management of risk and reward.
- There really are proven chart patterns that you can learn to recognize and to trade against profitably.
- These chart patterns are easy to understand because they are exploiting basic market psychology.

- Knowing how to trade these patterns will improve your trading because they give you specific prices for entry, protective stop, and exit. As a result, you feel no confusion, no anxiety, and no room for doubts. You are the very picture of confidence and discipline!

In Chapter 14 we'll talk about how you can get the answer to the question: *What* to trade every day.

CHAPTER | 14

# More Step Four: This Education Is Fine, but I Really Want the Answer

> *"The great aim of education is not knowledge, but action."*
> HERBERT SPENCER

*In the past few chapters we have dealt with* How to trade. *We have shown you a simple, logical, and effective plan that you can put into effect immediately.*

*That still leaves the question of* What to trade *every day.*

*You have a life, a family, and other activities and responsibilities. There are more than 10,000 symbols on the NYSE, Nasdaq, and AMEX. How can you possibly find the time or the energy to ruin your eyesight reading chart screens for hours and hours late into the night? Every night?*

*Reread the opening quote. What good is all of this education if you aren't able to put it into action? If you aren't able to make some money with it?*

*Is there a secret?*

**Y**es, there is. You can't reasonably expect to find these opportunities by yourself. So you need help!

You can choose from hundreds of newsletters and advisory services that will alert you to trading opportunities. Some are good, some are real good, and many are useless. How do you know which is which?

Among the services we have previewed and found to be effective are: Pristine.com, eGoose.com, Tsignals.com, StreakingStocks.com, and TradeHard.com. Although their services vary, each does a good job of alerting you to potential trading opportunities each day.

As an example, lets look at *Digital Discipline Report*™, a daily advisory service offered by SixthMarket.com.

The *Digital Discipline Report* scans the entire NYSE, Nasdaq, and AMEX each night, searching for revival buy, smart buy, wedge buy, and others. The picks are delivered to you over the Internet each evening, featuring promising chart setups for the next day's trading. A service like this knows what good setups look like and helps make your work easier.

Each opportunity comes to you with a complete trading plan, including: symbol, action, entry price, slippage, initial protective stop, and exit target price.

Here is a sample from an actual report. Notice that the information is clear, concise, and easy to follow:

**FIGURE 14.1** Sample Trading Plan

| # | Symbol | Action | Entry Point | Slippage | IPS | Exit Target | Signal |
|---|--------|--------|-------------|----------|-----|-------------|--------|
| 1 | AKAM | Buy | 119 1/8 | 1/2 | 118 1/8 | 124 1/4 | Revival Bu |
| 2 | HWP | Buy | 125 1/8 | 1/2 | 124 1/8 | 128 1/8 | Revival Bu |
| 3 | ISLD | Buy | 49 3/8 | 1/2 | 48 3/8 | 52 3/8 | Revival Bu |
| 4 | ADBE | Sell | 124 5/8 | 1/2 | 126 5/8 | 116 5/8 | Smart Se |
| 5 | IBM | Sell | 108 1/2 | 1/2 | 109 1/2 | 105 1/2 | Revival Se |
| 6 | MER | Sell | 114 1/16 | 1/2 | 115 1/16 | 111 1/16 | Revival Se |

You should review more than one newsletter and advisory service, and use as many as you feel are useful. After all, you are looking for help in finding profitable trades, so subscribing to two or three services can help increase your chances for more successful trades. Be ruthlessly practical about making your choices, no matter what a service costs. Just one good trade can more than pay for a full year's subscription!

These services are among the best values in any trader's bag of tricks. However, always remember that ultimately *any* trade is your decision and your responsibility.

*So now you know how to trade and you will subscribe to a few advisory services to help you know what to trade. Now let's get to work building your own trading plan.*

CHAPTER | 15

# Step Five: Mastering Your Trading Plan

*"Your life can't go according to plan if you have no plan."*

RICK ENGEL

*"Take calculated risks. That is quite different from being rash."*

GEORGE S. PATTON

**E**arly in this book we asserted that trading actually is easy. The concepts are not hard. The skills can be learned. You can become a consistently profitable trader. By now we hope you agree that these observations are correct, and that you are well on your way to becoming that profitable trader.

But—hold on! You are like a fine, hand-crafted Swiss watch—a precision instrument ready to do its job to perfection, except . . . the mainspring is missing. And without that, you can't even tell what time it is. What's missing? Your commitment to using a trading plan for every trade you make. Let's stick that piece in there and start you ticking!

**D**istilled to its essence, a trade consists of just two steps: (1) the entry and (2) the exit. Sure, you have to manage the trade while the position is open, but we define that as part of the exit. From the second you enter a trade, you are in "exit mode."

## THE ENTRY: GETTING IN RIGHT

What does it take to "get in right"? Find a proven chart pattern, put together a solid, complete trading plan, and execute it.

We know about chart patterns, but what do we really mean by a solid, complete trading plan? We mean that you will never again make a trade—any trade—without having the following things solidly in mind.

### The Reason for the Trade

- If you are trading against chart patterns, the reason is a *revival buy* setup or a *wedge sell* setup.
- If you are not trading a chart pattern, the reason had better be just as well-articulated.
- You also have to use your judgment here. Just because some chart pattern tells you to buy QCOM at 120 doesn't mean that you *must* take that trade. Ask yourself:
  - Do I believe that the potential reward in this trade justifies the risk? Remember, you are shooting for a minimum reward that is three times your risk. Is that reasonable in this case?
  - Do I like the spread on this stock, or is it so large that I am effectively beyond my ISP when I get in?
  - Is the average trading range wide enough to give you enough upside potential on this trade? Why risk 2 points on a stock that only moves 1 point per day?
  - Is there enough volume in this stock to give you a good chance of getting back out of this trade when you are ready to exit? If you are in for 2,500 shares on a stock that only trades 46,000 shares a day, do you think you can exit quickly at the price you want?
  - Is there the potential for news or any other outside factor to affect this trade negatively? Do you really want to buy GM this morning when the results of their union negotiations are expected to be announced this afternoon?

### The Symbol

Hey! No kidding here. Some symbols are very close to others. If you mean to buy Microsoft, be sure you type in "MSFT." If you type in "MFST" you might be very unhappy!

## The Action

Do you plan to buy this stock or short sell it?

## Number of Shares

See the section on money management below. There is a method for the number of shares you pick and you need to follow that method for every trade.

## Entry Point

This is the price at which you intend to initiate this trade. It must be precise and chosen for a good reason.

## Slippage

This is how far you will chase the stock if you cannot get it at your exact entry price. For example, if your entry price to buy DELL is 48½ and your slippage is ⅝, you would be willing to pay as much as 49⅛ to get into this trade.

Your slippage may be set based on the spread in the particular stock, the average daily trading range of the stock, your risk parameters, or your knowledge about how this stock generally trades. In any event, slippage is a number, and you *will not* exceed this number.

## Initial Protective Stop (IPS)

This is where you will get out of this trade if it is moving against you. This is where you establish how much risk you intend to take in this trade. See the section on risk management below.

## Exit Target

This is only a target. See the section on exit strategies below.

What about the execution of the trade itself?

- This is where your new best friend—the direct access broker and its electronic trading platform—can really help. Use Nasdaq level II to help you with the timing of your order, anticipate when your strike prices will be hit, and get the "smart order logic" warmed up so you can be ready to jump in quickly and get the execution at the price you want.

  BUT don't ever actually get into your trade before your entry point has been executed and painted to the tape! There is a reason why you want that price to be established ahead of you, so wait for it.

- Take advantage of the three different kinds of orders:
  1. *To Enter a Trade.* Use a stop limit order to enter a trade at some point in the future according to your trading plan. For example: "Buy 1000 IBM 85 stop 85½ limit." You either get the price range you want or you pass on the trade.
  2. *To Exit a Bad Trade.* Use a stop order to get you out of a trade that is going against you at the price determined ahead of time by your trading plan. For example: "Sell 1000 IBM 84 stop." You do not want a limit on this order. If you hit your stop price, you want out of this trade at the best price you can get.
  3. *To Exit and Take Your Profit.* Use a stop order to get you out of a trade once your profit objective has been reached. The ability to issue and to manage stop orders is vital to trading with a high-probability trading plan.

## GAPS

What do you do if your stock has gapped beyond the entry point plus the slippage at the open?

First, don't do anything just yet. For certain do not go chasing it. Be patient. One of two things is at work. Either there is a real market reason for this gap or there is not.

Our observations have taught us that we should know if this gap is "real" about thirty minutes after the open. Here's what you do:

- *For a Buy*: After thirty minutes, set a new entry point ¹⁄₁₆ above the high for this day. Also, set a new ISP to be ¹⁄₁₆ below the low for the day. If, after 30 minutes, the stock then can make a new high, the strength shown by that gap is real.

- *For a Short Sell:* After thirty minutes, set a new entry point $\frac{1}{16}$ below the low for this day. Also, set a new ISP to be $\frac{1}{16}$ above the high for the day. If, after 30 minutes, the stock then can make a new low, the weakness shown by that gap is real.

## RISK MANAGEMENT

Assessing risk in your trade is not difficult. You know the entry point (plus slippage) and you know where you set your IPS. The difference is the risk. The problem is in managing risk. You must pull the trigger when your IPS is hit. You must not second-guess, you must not wish, you must not hope, you must not whine and cry. There will be hundreds or thousands of good trades in the future. Let this one go!

There are three things you must never do: Jump out of an airplane without a parachute, vacation in Chernobyl, or fail to execute at your IPS. All can be very fatal to your future!

## MONEY MANAGEMENT

Preserving your capital is more important than making a profit. Wow! Read that again because it is so important. Over the years, the authors have seen so many fine people destroy their financial dreams because they forgot that one message. They got into just one trade that turned against them, they wouldn't get out because "they just knew it would turn around," and they spiraled into the ground. Or they had a few losses in a row, decided to "double the bet," had a few more losses in a row, upped their ante again, and lost it all.

All you want to do is to preserve your capital so you can keep trading. That means sizing your positions in such a way that they are small enough that an extended series of losses will not "wipe you out." You also want them large enough that you realize material benefit from profitable trades.

The study of money management consumes the attention of many industry professionals. The subject can get quite complicated with intricate mathematical algorithms and time-consuming real-time capital allocation models. But we argue for simplicity. Here is a straightforward approach to money management that has worked for many:

- *Predetermine* the percentage of your capital that you are prepared to risk on any one trade. To do that, you need to make a reasonable assessment of how many losses in a row you are likely to sustain.

  For example: If you believe that you might expect to experience a worst case of 10 losses in a row, you might be willing to risk 2 percent of your total capital on every trade, or a maximum drawdown of 20 percent if you have those 10 losses in a row. Looking at the other side—you would still have 80 percent of your capital remaining.
- *Turn that percentage into a dollar amount.* For example: If you have $100,000 in trading capital, 2 percent would equal $2,000, which is your risk per trade.
- *Then determine your risk on this trade.* The difference in dollars per share between the entry point and the ISP.
- *Calculate the number of shares you can buy.* Divide risk-per-trade by risk-on-this-trade to see the number of shares you can trade. The following chart makes it very easy:

| Risk per Trade | Risk on This Trade | Number of Shares |
|---|---|---|
| $2,000 | $1.00 | 2,000 |
| $2,000 | $1.50 | 1,333 |
| $2,000 | $2.00 | 1,000 |
| $2,000 | $2.50 | 800 |
| $2,000 | $3.00 | 667 |

Remember that this chart shows the maximum number of shares you may trade to be within your personal money management guidelines. You also have to stay within your capital constraints. For example: If your risk on this trade is $1.50, the chart tells you that you can trade a maximum of 1,333 shares.

You then have to look at your buying power to be sure you have the capital to trade that many shares. For example: If you have $80,000 cash in your account, you may buy up to $160,000 worth of stock on margin. If the entry price on the stock you are watching is $150, you may only trade 1,066 shares ($160,000/$150).

## EXIT STRATEGIES

You've gotten into your trade like a pro. Now let's talk about how you manage this trade to its conclusion. Unlike the entry, which by design is a precise action at a specific price, the exit can be played several different ways, each of which has its advantages. This section will discuss the choices for your consideration. The choices are up to you, based on your risk perspective and personal preferences:

### IPS

If this trade is not going as planned and it hits your IPS, get out *now!* There's another good trade coming that needs your attention.

### Breakeven Stop

You're in the trade and it's moving your way—you even have a small profit in it already. Do you set a breakeven stop? A breakeven stop has the advantage of removing your risk. You will exit the trade if the price moves back to your breakeven. But be careful, if you do it too early you will get taken out of trades that would prove to be quite good.

### Partial Exit

There is an internal struggle in all of us. Should you sell now and take your profit, or hold on and hope for more profit? A popular notion among some good traders is to never sell your whole position at one time. Instead sell part when you have reached an acceptable profit level, hold the remaining part to see if you can reach a higher level. Just remember to tighten the stops on that remaining position. Don't let a winner turn into a loser.

### Trailing Stops

There are two widely used methods for setting trailing stops.

1. *Profit protection.* In this method, the trader calculates the profit in a trade and sets a stop to protect a portion of that profit. We have seen dozens of these systems. Here is one that is simple, yet has proven to be very effective:
    - Until you have a gain in the trade of $2 per share . . . you keep your stop at the IPS. This is to give the trade room to work.

- Once you have a gain of $2 per share or more, set a trailing stop at $2. In other words, if you have a gain of $4, you will risk $2 and protect $2. If you have a gain of $10, you will risk $2 and protect $8.
2. *Peg the lows.* In this method the trader sets a new trailing stop each day at the low from the previous day (or at the high if he or she has sold short). This method can create quite large risk, but has been proven to produce terrific profits in trades that are running your way.

## Other Exit Signals

- *Never hold a loser overnight—never hold a loser overnight—never hold a loser overnight.* Any questions about this one?
- *Weak (or strong) close.* Exit your position at the end of the day anytime the stock is poised to close in the bottom 25 percent of the trading range (for a long) or the top 25 percent of the trading range (for a short), which would signal that the other side is starting to gain control.
- *Gaps.* If you are holding your position overnight and it opens with a gap of ¾ of a point or more from yesterday's close, you should get out of your position if:
  - Long position: it is a gap down, the gap holds, and the stock goes on to make a new low after the first 30 minutes.
  - Short position: it is a gap up, the gap holds, and the stock goes on to make a new high after the first 30 minutes.
- *Time's Up.* When you enter your trade, you have a time target in mind, generally one to three days. If after four or five days, at the most, your position has not reached its profit objective, close the position. You cannot afford to keep your hard earned capital tied up in a nonproductive asset.

## PROVEN TRADING RULES

Every book, every seminar, every class, every videotape, every other form of teaching material you can think of, has a section devoted to "The Very Best Trading Rules Ever!"

Did you think we would be any different? Hey—but these really are good! Here they are:

- Create a trading plan based on proven chart setups.
- Identify risk and reward before you jump.
- Never trade without your plan—Entry, Stop Loss, Exit.
- Always take your stops.
- Think in probabilities—act in certainty.
- Never hold a loser overnight.
- Never risk more than a predetermined percentage of your capital on one trade.
- Use time of day to your advantage: look for reversal after the first 30 minutes of the day, and don't bet against the trend in the last hour of the day.
- Never add to a losing position.
- Avoid tips—even better idea: short them!
- Learn to sell short as often as you go long.
- Control what you can, manage what you cannot.
- Accept that you cannot know what will happen—react to what the market gives you.
- Identify your signal, act automatically, feel good about the trade!

Now isn't that much better? Don't you feel as if the last crucial pieces of the puzzle have been dropped into place? Don't you feel as if you really are ready to stand in there and trade with the big boys?

Don't get too carried away . . . your education is far from over. In Chapter 16 we'll talk about what you should do to continue to grow as a trader!

CHAPTER 16

# Step Six: I Don't Have the Willpower to Be Disciplined

*"When you believe in a thing, believe in it all the way—implicitly and unquestionably"*

WALT DISNEY

*All the pieces have come together. You have now acquired a set of skills, some valuable insights, and a body of trading knowledge. You are now close to knowing all you need to go into the market, to make trades, and to make them profitably.*

*But don't we come back to the one central issue that has dominated trading forever—discipline? It is entirely appropriate that we once again visit the concept of discipline. All you have learned about trading—all you will ever learn—is hostage to your ability to act automatically and without emotion in the face of what the market gives you.*

Trading success is contingent on more than just focusing on a trading process, learning profitable strategies, and sticking to your trading plan. Discipline is the key, but how do you get it?

It is a well-known fact that emotional traders are losing traders. An old floor-trading saw puts it this way: "Nervous money soon becomes someone else's money!" In our experience, the primary reason most traders fail is not because of strategy lapses or poor market timing.

They fail for the same reasons many new businesses of any kind fail: lack of capital and a poor analysis and understanding of the existing business environment.

The secret to success is to be a disciplined trader. For starters, you need more than simply meeting your broker's minimum account balance requirement. You must make sure you are adequately capitalized, which ultimately will allow you to become a disciplined trader and to think and act like one.

In addition, discipline requires that you are adequately prepared and that you learn the real-time realities of stock market trading. This book has been a good start in that direction.

Even if you want to be a part-time trader, remember the competition is full time and professional. You are going against seasoned market players who have no interest in bailing you out of bad trades except as it will affect them. Think of the competition as cruiserweight type A's with a special fondness for your miscalculations and your paycheck.

Scott Foster, president and CEO of Dominion Capital Management, a trading firm managing more than 350 million dollars, characterizes the competition this way:

> It has been obvious to me from the beginning that I'm competing with the best and the brightest in the world. I believe that the smartest people in the world are not curing cancer; they are in the financial markets, because that's where the money is! And if I am going to make a dollar, I have to pry it out of somebody else's hands. When you begin to look at trading that way, that there are two sides to the market at all times, you need to be certain about identifying what is your Edge. To be able to compete effectively against these traders and institutions, who possess unlimited financial resources and research capabilities, you need more than just a great trading plan. You need absolute discipline in everything you do.

The market has a unique way of constantly testing your discipline in the same way it relentlessly tests itself. Just as buyers and sellers continuously struggle to establish real value, the market has a knack for challenging the best prepared and most conscientious among us and showing utter disdain and wreaking humiliation on the ill-prepared, poorly researched, and undisciplined.

Bruce Johnson, a professional market maker, observed:

> The market just has a way of knowing what you are all about. It knows when you are really trying and needing to make money.

Ironically, when you are disciplined and don't need it, the market gives you the money. When you're pressing and looking for sure things, forget about it. It just doesn't work that way.

Pressured traders—like lazy or foolhardy ones—are never good traders. Their decisions are based on pie-in-the-sky thinking and unbridled emotions. Thoughtful logic or methodology is the essence of what is required to become a disciplined trader.

Self-awareness is the starting point to become disciplined. As well-known trader Mark Etzkorn advises:

> Start slowly, and put in the time and effort required of any entrepreneur attempting to launch a new business, expect your business to go through rough times initially, and prepare yourself psychologically and financially to survive this incubation period.

The same advice holds true for the experienced investor. Trading is a business requiring solid decisions with reasonable expectations within disciplined parameters.

So, is discipline just another term for "ultimate preparation"? Yes, we think this is very close to the core of the issue. Let's revisit the issue of discipline as discussed in Chapter 9:

To get and to keep the disciplined state of mind, we form an endless circle.

**FIGURE 16.1** Discipline Cycle

Knowledge → Confidence → Focus → Discipline → Great Results → (Confidence)

- Knowledge of our proven plan breeds confidence.
- Confidence in our plan gives us focus.
- Focus eliminates the distractions and makes it easy to remain disciplined to our plan.
- Discipline to our plan leads to great results.
- Great results give us more confidence.
- And on and on.

This is an endless chain. It is self-reinforcing and ultimately self-fulfilling.

Discipline is not some supreme test of willpower. Knowledge is the key to starting this positive chain of events. If you *know* your plan will work, why would you do anything else but stay disciplined to that plan? If you *know* your plan will work, discipline to your plan is easy!

*NOW does it all come together for you?*

*Do you now realize that you don't have to work at discipline . . . it will happen . . . if you just BELIEVE!*

## COMMITTING TO YOUR EDUCATION

Henry Ford said, "If money is your hope for independence you will never have it. The only real security is a reserve of knowledge, experience, and ability." That is what we have given you in this book: An entirely new approach to trading that is a simple, yet effective, process for consistently taking profits from the market.

We worked with you on your personal psychology. We covered certain key trading fundamentals. We showed you how to trade against specific chart patterns. We even showed you how to use advisory services to get a wealth of trading opportunities delivered to you each day. And we taught you to use a trading plan for every trade.

Most importantly, we showed you that discipline will happen easily if it is fueled by knowledge and a belief in your trading plan. With just this information, you can be a profitable trader.

So, does this mean you are finished learning? Do you now know everything there is to know about trading profitably? Of course not.

From this point forward, your education will be up to you—driven by your interests and guided by the educators and mentors you trust.

We hope we have whetted your appetite to learn more because no book can teach you everything. At this point, we have only opened that "one eye." It's up to you to carry your educational quest further.

If you need more information or clarification on a subject discussed in this book, please contact us directly for amplification. We will be glad to help:

- ken@sixthmarket.com
- bob@sixthmarket.com
- howard@sixthmarket.com

The three of us are totally engaged in education. We love to trade and we love to help others prosper as traders. Other services we offer are newsletters, seminars, online classes, CDs, videos, audiotapes, and books. Visit our Web sites to learn more:

- <www.sixthmarket.com>
- <www.invest2know.com>

Whatever you do, commit to a program of continual learning to assure your trading success. If you love to play bridge, you know that you can never learn enough—there's always room for improvement. If you play the piano, you know that you can never practice too much. If you are an artist, you know that there is always another technique—another perspective—for you to master. The same is true with trading.

There has not yet been the "perfect trader." In fact, we have not yet seen "the Tiger Woods of trading." Perhaps it will be you!

There is one great truth about trading: your upside is truly unlimited. The corollary to that great truth is: the only thing standing between you and your full potential is your education. Learn something new every day!

Reggie Leach, said, "Success is not the result of spontaneous combustion. You must set yourself on fire."

May this book be your match to light that fire.

We wish you success in all you do . . . but especially in the markets!!!

# Recommended Reading

Abell, Howard. 2000. *The Day Trader's Advantage: How to Move from One Winning Position to the Next.* Chicago: Dearborn.

Abell, Howard. 1999. *Digital Day Trading: How to Move from One Winning Stock Position to the Next.* Chicago: Dearborn.

Abell, Howard. 1999. *The Electronic Trading of Options.* Chicago: Dearborn.

Abell, Howard, and Koppel, Robert. 1999. *The Market Savvy Investor.* Chicago: Dearborn.

Barach, Roland. 1988. *Mindtraps: Mastering the Inner World of Investing.* Homewood, IL: Dow Jones–Irwin.

Baruch, Bernard M. 1957. *Baruch: My Own Story.* New York: Holt, Rinehart and Winston.

Davis, Rod. 1999. *What You Need to Know Before You Invest.* New York: Barron's.

Douglas, Mark. 1990. *The Disciplined Trader.* New York: New York Institute of Finance.

Eng, William F. 1993. *The Day Trader's Manual: Theory, Art, and Science of Profitable Short-Term Investing.* New York: John Wiley.

Eng, William F. 1990. *Trading Rules: Strategies for Success.* Chicago: Dearborn.

Friedfertig, Marc, and West, George. 1998. *The Electronic Day Trader.* New York: McGraw Hill.

Gold, Laura Maery, and Post, Dan. 1999. *J.K. Lasser's Invest Online.* New York: Macmillan.

Kiev, Ari, M.D. 1998. *Trading to Win.* New York: John Wiley.

Koppel, Robert. 1996. *The Intuitive Trader: Developing Your Inner Market Wisdom.* New York: John Wiley.

Koppel, Robert. 1997. *The Tao of Trading.* Chicago: Dearborn.

Koppel, Robert, and Abell, Howard. 1993. *The Innergame of Trading: Modeling the Psychology of the Top Traders.* New York: McGraw Hill.

Koppel, Robert, and Abell, Howard. 1994. *The Outer Game of Trading: Modeling the Trading Strategies of Today's Market Wizards.* New York: McGraw Hill.

Le Bon, Gustave. 1982. *The Crowd: A Study of the Popular Mind.* 2nd ed. Atlanta, Ga.: Cherokee.

Markman, Jon D. 1999. *Online Investing.* Redmond, WA: Microsoft Press.

O'Neil, William. 1995. *How to Make Money in Stocks.* New York: McGraw-Hill.

Rotella, Robert P. 1992. *The Elements of Successful Trading.* New York: New York Institute of Finance.

Schwager, Jack D. 1999. *Getting Started in Technical Analysis.* New York: John Wiley.

Schwager, Jack D. 1989. *Market Wizards: Interviews with Top Traders.* New York: New York Institute of Finance.

Schwager, Jack D. 1992. *The New Market Wizards: Conversations with America's Top Traders.* New York: Harper Business.

Schwartz, Martin. 1998. *Pit Bull: Lessons from Wall Street's Champion Trader.* New York: Harper Business.

Sperandeo, Victor, with Brown, T. Sullivan. 1991. *Trader Vic—Methods of a Wall Street Master.* New York: John Wiley and Sons.

Tharp, Van K. 1999. *Trade Your Way to Financial Freedom.* New York: McGraw-Hill.

# Glossary

**above the market** A sell order that is higher in price than the market's current price for that security.
**accredited investor** An individual who, under the SEC's Regulation D, has been proven knowledgeable about investing and who meets certain net worth and income tests. Accreditation is a requirement for certain limited partnership investments.
**accumulation** Refers to an addition to a trader's original market position; buying over a period of time, to avoid making a single, substantial purchase that might drive up the market price; or more generally, any buying. Opposite of drawdown.
**American Stock Exchange (AMEX)** The second-largest stock exchange in the United States, after the NYSE. Stocks and bonds traded on the AMEX tend to be those of smaller companies than on the NYSE. Some index options and interest rate options trading also occurs on the AMEX. Also called the Curb.
**analyst** A person with expertise in evaluating financial investments; one who performs investment research and makes recommendations to institutional and retail investors to buy, sell, or hold; most analysts specialize in a single industry or business sector.
**annual report** Yearly record of a publicly held company's financial condition. It includes a description of the firm's operations, plus its balance sheet

and income statement. SEC rules require that it be distributed to all shareholders. A more detailed version is called a 10-K.

**arbitrage** The simultaneous purchase and sale of two different—but closely related—securities to take advantage of a disparity in their prices. Profiting from disparities in the price of equivalent securities, commodities, or currencies when they are simultaneously traded on more than one market. Buying stock in a company that is the target of a merger or takeover when such action will cause the price of the stock to rise. No arbitrage opportunities would exist in a perfectly efficient market.

**ascending tops** A chart that shows that the price of a security over a period of time has had consecutive peaks, each higher than the previous one. Such a chart may indicate to investors that an upward trend may be expected to continue.

**ask** The current price for which a security may be bought, as in the OTC market.

**auction market** The system of buying and selling securities through exchange brokers with buyers and sellers competing against one another to get the best prices. The NYSE is the prime example. In an auction market, trades are not negotiated as they are in an over-the-counter market. Exchanges like the NYSE and the CBOE are auction markets with the actual trading floors, pits, open outcry, and hand signals. These markets do not guarantee the best price in or out because there never is a true "best price."

**average directional movement (ADX)** An indicator that measures how much a market is trending. Both bullish and bearish trends are shown by positive movement in the ADX.

**average true range** The average, over the last *"x"* days, of the true range which is the largest of the following: (1) today's high minus today's low; (2) today's high minus yesterday's close; or (3) today's low minus yesterday's close.

**away from market** A limit order bid which is lower, or the offer price is higher, than the stock's current market price.

**back office** Brokerage house clerical operations that support, but do not include, the trading of stocks and other securities. Includes all written confirmation and settlement of trades, recordkeeping, and regulatory compliance.

**back testing** The process of optimizing a trading strategy using historical data and then seeing whether it has predictive validity on current data.

**bear** An investor who believes a stock, a sector, or the overall market will decline (opposite of bull). Bears might sell securities short, hoping to make a profit by subsequently repurchasing at a lower price.

**bearish** An attitude carried by traders who believe prices are headed lower, whether pertaining to a particular stock or the market in general.

**bear market** A bear market is a prolonged period of falling stock prices, usually by 20 percent or more.

**beige book** Report on current economic conditions, published by the Federal Reserve Board eight times a year.

**bellwether** A stock or bond that is widely believed to be an indicator of the overall market's condition. *See also* blue chip.

**below the market** A bid that is lower than the highest bid for a specific security, commodity, or option.

**bias** The tendency to move in a particular direction. This can be market bias, but most of the biases discussed in this book are psychological biases.

**bid** The highest price any buyer is willing to pay for a given security at a given time (opposite of ask). Also, an offer of a specific amount of money in exchange for products and services, as in an auction. An indication by an investor, trader, or dealer, of a willingness to buy a security or commodity. Also called bid price. *See also* spread and quote.

**bid–ask spread** The difference between the best buying price and the best selling price for any given security.

**bidding up** The rising bid price for a security caused by increasing demand for the security.

**big board** *See* New York Stock Exchange.

**block trades** A large amount of securities being held or traded, typically at least 10,000 shares of a stock or $200,000 in bonds; transactions of a particular stock sold as a large unit.

**blue chip** Stock of a large, national company with a solid record of stable earnings and/or dividend growth and a reputation for high quality management and/or products. *See also* bellwether.

**bond** A debt instrument issued for a period of more than one year with the purpose of raising capital through borrowing. Federal, state, and local governments; corporations; and other institutions sell bonds. A bond is generally a promise to repay the principal and a specified interest on a specified date (maturity).

**book** A chronological record of a specialist's inventory of securities and orders that other exchange members have placed with the specialist. Also called specialist's book.

**breakout** The point when a security's market price moves out of its trend channel. A breakout indicates a rise in a security's price above a resistance level (commonly its previous high price) or a drop below a level of support (commonly the former lowest price). A breakout is taken to signify a new higher or lower trend and may be used by technical analysts as a buy or sell indicator.

**broadcast** To make available to the market the identity of a trader and his or her order as posted.

**broker** An individual or firm that acts as an intermediary between a buyer and seller, usually charging a commission. For securities and most other financial products, a license is required.

**brokerage** Used interchangeably with broker when referring to a firm rather than an individual. Also called brokerage house or brokerage firm.

**broker/dealer** Any individual or firm, other than a bank, which is in the business of buying and selling securities for itself and others. Called an agent or broker when buying securities and a principal or dealer when selling them. Broker/dealers must register with the SEC as well as with the states in which they conduct business.

**bull** A person who expects the stock market to rise or the economy to accelerate. An investor who believes that a particular security, sector, or the overall market is about to rise. (Opposite of bear.)

**bull market** A prolonged period of rising prices, usually by 20 percent or more. A market that is on a consistent upward trend. A long-term rise in security prices.

**bullish** An attitude by traders who think prices are headed higher, whether pertaining to a particular stock or the market in general.

**buy** A term used by traders to indicate that they are bullish on a particular stock or the market in general.

**buyout** Purchase of a controlling interest (or percent of shares) of a company's stock. A leveraged buyout is done with borrowed money.

**buying power** The total volume of open stock positions a trader may have at any one time. To calculate buying power, simply subtract the maintenance reserve from the cash equity in the account to find the excess maintenance. Excess maintenance is the amount of capital that is available for trading. Excess maintenance times two equals buying power.

**CAC 40** Index of 40 leading stocks traded on the Paris Stock Exchange.

**candlestick** Japanese candlesticks is an art form that has been passed down from the 1600s, when it was used to trade Japanese rice futures. The name *candlesticks* is used because the resulting chart holds what looks like a series of candles with wicks. Plotting the daily candlestick line requires the daily open, high, low, and closing prices. The thick part of the candlestick is known as the real body and represents the range between the open and close prices. The longer or shorter the real body, the more bearish or bullish the market, respectively, because the length of the real body represents the distance in number of points from the open to the close price. The thin lines protruding from either side of the candle are called shadows.

**capitalization** The amount of money in the underlying stock of a company.

**cash account** A brokerage account in which the customer is required by SEC Regulation T to pay the full amount due by the settlement date for securities purchased; buying on margin is not permitted. Also called special cash account. Some types of accounts, such as IRAs and custodian for minor accounts, must be cash accounts.

**channel** The area between two parallel lines that contains prices. These lines are drawn across the edges of congestion zones, leaving out extreme prices and reflecting a trader's speculation on support (the lower channel line) and resistance (the upper channel line). In day trading, the channel refers to the area between the intraday high and low. In charting, a price channel contains prices throughout a trend. There are three ways to draw channels: (1) parallel, (2) rounded, and (3) channels that connect lows (bear trend) or highs (bull trend).

**Chicago Board of Trade (CBOT)** An exchange where grain, gold, and U.S. Treasury Bond futures and options are traded.

**clearing house** An agency associated with an exchange, which settles trades and regulates delivery.

**closed trades** Positions that either have been liquidated or offset.

**commission** The fee paid to a broker to execute a trade, based on number of shares, bonds, options and/or their dollar value. Full service brokers offer advice and usually have a full staff of analysts who follow specific industries. Discount brokers simply execute a client's order and usually do not offer an opinion on a proposed purchase.

**commodity** A physical substance—such as food, grains, and metals—which is interchangeable with other products of the same type, and which investors buy or sell, usually through futures contracts. Or, more generally, a product that trades on a commodity exchange (this would also include foreign currencies and financial instruments and indexes).

**common stock** Securities representing equity ownership in a corporation, providing voting rights, and entitling the holder to a share of the company's success through dividends and/or capital appreciation. In the event of liquidation, common stock holders have rights to a company's assets only after bondholders, other debt holders, and preferred stock holders have been satisfied.

**confidence indicator** A measure of investors' faith in the economy and the securities market. A low or deteriorating level of confidence is considered by many technical analysts to be a bearish sign.

**confirmation** The written statement that follows any "trade" in the securities markets. Confirmation is issued immediately after a trade is executed. It spells out settlement date, terms, commission, etc.

**consolidation** A time of relative balance between supply and demand characterized by narrow price ranges—the opposite of volatility. Also known as a congestion period. A pause that allows participants in a market to reevaluate the market and sets the stage for the next price move.

**consumer price index (CPI)** An inflationary indicator that measures the change in the cost of a fixed group of products and services, including housing, electricity, food, and transportation. The CPI is published monthly by the Bureau of Labor Statistics and is the broadest gauge of costs and services. Also called cost-of-living index.

**contra broker** The broker handling the other side of a trade; e.g., when buying, the seller is the contra broker.

**correction** Any price reaction within the market leading to an adjustment by as much as one-third to two-thirds of the previous gain.

**cover** To repurchase a previously sold contract.

**crash** A precipitous drop in market prices or economic conditions.

**crossed market** When one broker's bid is higher than another's lowest offer, or vice versa. While crossed markets sometimes occur, the National Association of Securities Dealers Automated Quotations prohibits brokers from intentionally crossing the market.

**currency** Any form of money that is in public circulation.

**daily range** The difference between the high and low price during one trading day.

**DAX** A price-weighted index of the 100 most heavily traded stocks in the German market.

**day order** An order that is canceled if it is not executed on the day it is entered.

**day trader** Originally, an individual who would not take the exposure of an open position overnight. The term is now also used to refer to an active stock trader who holds positions for a very short time and makes several trades each day.

**dealer** An individual or entity, such as a securities firm, when it acts as a principal and stands ready to buy and sell for its own account. More generally, an individual or entity that buys and sells products and holds an inventory.

**dealer market** Exchanges like the Nasdaq are dealer or negotiated markets; they have no physical trading floor. Dealers post prices and execute orders for securities electronically. In theory, a dealer market should help an investor get the "best price." They afford day traders the ability to instantly identify and access the best market prices.

**depth of market** The number of shares of a security that can be bought or sold without causing an appreciable change in price.

**display rule** SEC regulation mandating that dealers must modify their quotes to represent the price and size of customer limit orders that would improve or equal their bid or offer. Requires market makers to publish immediately a bid or offer that reflects the price and full size of each customer limit order they hold that is priced better than their current quote.

**dividend** Distribution of a portion of a company's earnings, cash flow, or capital to shareholders, in cash or additional stock.

**Dow Jones Industrial Average (DJIA)** The most widely used indicator of the overall condition of the stock market, a price-weighted average of 30 actively traded blue chip NYSE stocks, primarily industrials. Also called the Dow.

**downgrade** A negative change in ratings for a security; two common examples are an analyst's downgrading a stock (such as from "buy" to "sell") and a credit bureau's downgrading of a bond. Opposite of upgrade.

**downside** The potential for loss for a given investment or activity.

**drawdown** The reduction in account equity as a result of a trade or series of trades. Opposite of accumulation.

**earnings per share (EPS)** The portion of a company's profit paid on each share of common stock. EPS is calculated after paying taxes and preferred shareholders and bondholders.

**earnings report** An official quarterly or annual financial document published by a public company, showing earnings, expenses, and net profit. An accounting of all of a company's income, expenses, profits, and loses. It is used as a measure of a company's fundamental soundness.

**electronic communication network (ECN)** A computer system that accepts buy and sell orders from users and tries to match those buy and sell orders whenever possible. ECNs are useful both as a place to send "lay off" limit orders and as a place to find "take out" liquidity. The Fifth Market.

**equities markets** Entities organized to facilitate the buying and selling of equity securities, such as NYSE, Nasdaq, AMEX, and the ECNs.

**equity** Ownership. The value of the common shareholders' equity in a company as listed on the balance sheet. Also, the value of one's trading account.

**exchange** The marketplace in which shares, options, and futures on stocks, bonds, commodities, and indexes are traded. Principal United States stock exchanges are: New York Stock Exchange (NYSE), American Stock Exchange (AMEX), and the National Association of Securities Dealers Automated Quotation (Nasdaq).

**execution** The process of completing an order to buy or sell securities. Once a trade is executed, it is reported by a confirmation report; settlement (payment and transfer of ownership) occurs in the United States between one (mutual funds) and five (stocks) days after an order is executed. Settlement times for exchange-listed stocks are in the process of being reduced to three days in the United States.

**exposure** The condition of being subjected to a source of risk.

**Fifth Market** The trading of Nasdaq stocks through ECNs instead of directly through Nasdaq.

**fill** An executed order; sometimes the term refers to the price at which an order is executed. A partial fill occurs when a buyer will not take all the stock offered or the seller does not have enough shares to fill a buyer's order.

**fill-or-kill** An order that instructs the floor broker to fill the entire order immediately or cancel the entire order—a partial fill is not acceptable.

**filled-at-next-level (FANL)** An event in which a trader's order is executed at a price level higher than the expected buy entry, or lower than the expected sell level. This occurs most often when a market order gets issued when stocks or markets are fast moving.

**financial instrument** A document containing some legal right or obligation having monetary value or recording a monetary transaction.

**Financial Times Stock Exchange Index (FTSE)** The United Kingdom equivalent of the United States S&P500 Index and the Australian All Ordinaries Index. The FTSE lists the 100 largest public companies traded on the London Stock Exchange. Usually referred to in the trade as "Footsie."

**First Market**  *See* Primary Market.

**floor broker**  A registered agent, working on exchange trading floors, who trades on behalf of clients.

**floor traders**  Employees of brokerage firms who work on exchange trading floors. Exchange members who trade only for their own accounts or for accounts in which he or she holds some financial interest.

**Fourth Market**  The direct trading of large blocks of securities between institutional investors through a computer network, such as Instinet, rather than on an exchange.

**fundamental analysis**  In equities markets, fundamental analysis attempts to determine the value of a particular company through analysis of the earnings, the management, and the relative data of that company.

**gap**  A significant price movement of a security or commodity between two trading sessions, such that there is no overlap in the trading ranges for the two days; or sometimes, such that the second day's opening price is outside the first day's trading range. A day in which the daily range is completely above the previous day's daily range. *See also* inside day.

**good-till-canceled order**  An order that is left in force until it is executed or canceled.

**Hang Seng**  A market-value weighted index of the stock prices of the 33 largest companies on the Hong Kong market.

**hedge**  An investment made in order to reduce the risk of adverse price movements in a security by taking an offsetting position in a related security, such as an option or short sale.

**hedge fund**  A fund usually used by wealthy individuals and institutions that is allowed to use aggressive strategies that are unavailable to mutual funds, including selling short, leveraging, program trading, swapping, arbitrage, and derivatives. Because they are restricted by law to fewer than 100 investors, the minimum investment is typically $1 million. The general partner (manager) usually receives performance-based compensation.

**holy grail system**  A mythical trading system that perfectly follows the market and is always right, producing large gains and zero drawdowns. No such system exists.

**index**  A benchmark against which financial or economic performance is measured, such as the S&P 500 or the Consumer Price Index.

**indicator**  A way of summarizing data in a meaningful way to help traders and investors make decisions.

**individual retirement account (IRA)**  A tax-deferred retirement account for an individual that permits individuals to set aside up to $2,000 per year, with earnings tax-deferred until withdrawals begin at age 59½ or later (or earlier, with a 10 percent penalty).

**initial public offering (IPO)** A company's first sale of stock to the public.

**inside day** A day in which the total range of prices falls between the range of prices of the prior day.

**inside market** The highest bid and the lowest ask prices made by Nasdaq market makers.

**institutional investor** Entity with large amounts to invest, such as investment companies, mutual funds, brokerages, insurance companies, pension funds, investment banks, and endowment funds. Institutional investors are constricted by fewer protective regulations because the SEC assumes they are more knowledgeable and better able to protect themselves.

**Institutional Networks Corporation (Instinet)** A computerized service that allows subscribers to display bid and ask quotes, and to execute transactions in the Fourth Market, bypassing brokers entirely.

**investing** Refers to a "buy and hold" strategy that many people follow. If you are in and out of positions frequently, or if you are willing to go both long and short, then you are trading, not investing.

**January effect** The tendency for securities prices to recover in January after tax-related selling is completed before year-end.

**level I** A computer subscription service that provides the highest and lowest price offers of securities traded through the Nasdaq.

**level II** A computer subscription service that provides the names of market makers and their bids and offers on securities traded through the Nasdaq.

**level III** A computer subscription service, available only to registered market makers, that allows market makers to revise their bids and offers on securities traded through the Nasdaq.

**liquidity** The ease and availability of trading in a particular stock. When the volume of trading is high, there usually is a lot of liquidity.

**listed** Instruments traded on a major exchange (NYSE or AMEX), as opposed to Nasdaq or over-the-counter.

**long** Owning a tradeable item in anticipation of a future price increase. Also see selling short.

**long bond** The 30-year U. S. Treasury bond. The most widely-traded bond and the benchmark against which all other bonds are measured.

**loss** A reduction in the value of an investment.

**margin** In stock trading, an account in which purchases of stock may be financed with borrowed money.

**margin call** A call from a broker to a customer demanding the deposit of cash or marginable securities to satisfy the SEC Regulation T requirements and the house maintenance requirement for the purchase or short sale of securities, or to cover adverse price movement.

**marked to market** A term used to describe the process of valuing open securities positions at the then-current price of the security.
**market** A public place where buyers and sellers make transactions, directly or through intermediaries.
**market capitalization** The sum of a corporation's long-term debt, stock, and retained earnings (also called invested capital) or, the market price of an entire company, calculated by multiplying the number of shares outstanding by the price per share (also called market cap).
**market maker** A broker, bank, or firm that continually makes a two-way price to buy or sell a security.
**market order** An instruction that informs your broker that you want to buy or sell a stock at the best possible price that currently can be obtained.
**market risk** The uncertainty of returns attributable to fluctuation of the entire market.
**market sentiment** Crowd psychology, typically a measurement of bullish or bearish attitudes among investors and traders.
**market value** The value of a company as determined by investors, obtained by multiplying the current price of company stock by the common shares outstanding.
**maturity** The date on which a debt is required to be repaid. See also bond.
**mircro cap** Securities with a market capitalization of less than $50 million.
**mid-cap** Securities with a market capitalization between $250 million and $1 billion.
**momentum** The perceived strength behind a price movement.
**momentum indicator** A market indicator that represents the difference in price now from some fixed time period in the past.
**money management** In trading, a term frequently used to describe the sizing of positions in such a way as to balance the needs of protecting capital and securing an attractive return.
**moving average** A method of measuring a trend that smoothes fluctuations in data. A moving average is calculated, for a period with $n$ values, as the sum of those values divided by $n$.
**mutual fund** An open-end investment company that pools investors' money to invest in a variety of stocks, bonds, or other securities. A mutual fund issues and redeems shares to meet demand, and the redemption value per share is the net asset value per share.
**National Association of Securities Dealers (NASD)** An organization of brokers and dealers who trade securities in the United States. Supervised by the SEC, the NASD regulates all over-the-counter brokers and dealers.
**National Association of Securities Dealers Automated Quotation (Nasdaq)** A national computer network through which NASD securities dealers execute and post transactions and record prices. Analogous to SuperDot.

**Nasdaq Composite Index** The Nasdaq Composite Index measures all Nasdaq domestic and non–United States based stocks listed on the Nasdaq. Today it includes more than 5,000 companies, more than most other stock market indexes, and is one of the most widely-followed and quoted major market indexes.

**NIKKEI index** Index of 225 leading stocks traded on the Tokyo Stock Exchange.

**New York Stock Exchange (NYSE)** This oldest and largest stock exchange in the United States is located on Wall Street in New York City. Responsible for setting policy, supervising member activities, listing securities, overseeing the transfer of member seats. Also called the Big Board.

**offer** An indication by an investor, trader, or dealer of a willingness to sell a security.

**open trades** Current trades that are still held active in the customer's account.

**option** The right, but not the obligation, to buy (call option) or sell (put option) an underlying asset at a fixed price, up to some specified date in the future.

**over-the-counter (OTC)** A security that is not traded on an exchange, usually due to an inability to meet listing requirements. For such securities, broker/dealers negotiate directly with one another over computer networks and by phone, and their activities are monitored by the NASD. Also called unlisted.

**plus-tick rule** *See* uptick rule.

**point** For stocks, $1.00 per share.

**preferencing** The attempt by a trader to direct a limit order (bid or offer) to a specific counterparty making a market in a security.

**Primary Market** The Primary Market (or First Market) is where the first buyer of a newly issued security buys that security. All subsequent trading of that security is done in the Secondary Market (or its derivatives, the Third Market, Fourth Market, Fifth Market, or Sixth Market).

**prediction** The attempt to make money by making trading decisions, employing analysts to predict prices. (Great traders make money by "cutting losses and letting profits run," which has nothing to do with prediction.) *See also* speculation.

**quote** The highest bid or lowest ask available on a security at any given time.

**range** The difference between the high and the low price during any given period.

**resistance** A price level at which rising prices have stopped rising and have either stabilized or started falling. The sellers are in control.

**retail investor** One who purchases securities for oneself, as opposed to the institutional investor who purchases for others. Also called individual investor or small investor.

**retracement** A price movement in the opposite direction of the previous trend.

**risk** The likelihood of loss or less-than-expected returns.

**Russell 2000** An index considered to be a benchmark of small cap stocks in the United States.

**secondary market** A market that provides for the purchase or sale of previously owned securities (not an IPO). Most securities trading is done in the secondary market.

**Securities and Exchange Commission (SEC)** The primary federal regulatory agency of the securities industry.

**Securities Industry Association (SIA)** The principal trade association and lobbying group for broker/dealers.

**Securities Investor Protection Corporation (SIPC)** A nonprofit membership corporation established by Congress that insures securities and cash in customer accounts up to $500,000—$100,000 of which may be in cash—against a brokerage bankruptcy.

**security** An investment instrument, other than an insurance policy or fixed annuity, issued by a corporation, government, or other organization, that offers evidence of debt or equity.

**SelectNet** Instituted in conjunction with SOES by the SEC, SelectNet is an electronic means of showing Nasdaq orders to all market makers. Order execution is entirely at the discretion of the market maker.

**selling short** Selling a security and then borrowing the security for delivery with the intent of replacing the security at a lower price. Short sales can be executed only through a brokerage margin account.

**short sale** *See* selling short.

**Sixth Market** The electronic trading of securities by the self-directed investor.

**size** The number of stock shares available at the bid and ask prices.

**small cap** Securities with a capitalization of less than $250 million.

**Small Order Execution System (SOES)** An NASD program through which over-the-counter orders for no more than 1,000 shares of a qualified issues can be automatically matched and executed to the best available price.

**special cash account** *See* cash account.

**specialist** A stock exchange member who serves to make a market for certain securities, maintaining an inventory of those securities and standing ready to buy and sell shares as necessary to maintain an orderly market for those shares.

**specialist's book** *See* book.

**speculation** Taking large risks, especially with respect to trying to predict the future; gambling, in the hopes of making quick, large gains. *See also* prediction.

**spread** The difference between the best bid and best offer of a given security.

**Standard & Poor's 500 Index (S&P 500)** A market-value weighted index of 500 blue-chip stocks, considered to be the benchmark of the overall United States stock market. Each stock is "capitalization weighted," ensuring that each company's influence on the index performance is directly proportional to its relative market value.

**stock** An instrument that signifies an ownership position—or equity—in a corporation, and represents a claim on its proportionate share in the corporation's assets and profits. *See also* equity.

**SuperDot** The NYSE's computerized trading and execution system. Analogous to Nasdaq.

**support** A price level at which falling prices have stopped falling and have either stabilized or started rising. The buyers are in control.

**swing trading** Trading, in the one- to five-day time horizon, designed to capture short-term moves in the market.

**symbol** A system of letters used to uniquely identify a stock or mutual fund. Symbols with up to three letters are used for listed stocks. Symbols with four letters are used for Nasdaq stocks. Symbols with five letters are used for Nasdaq stocks other than single issues of common stock. Symbols with five letters ending in "X" are used for mutual funds.

**technical analysis** A form of market analysis that studies supply and demand for securities based on price studies and trading volume in order to predict future trends.

**the Street** *See* Wall Street.

**Third Market** Over-the-counter trading of listed securities among institutional investors and broker/dealers for their own accounts, rather than as agents for investors.

**tick** The minimum fluctuation in price of a tradable item.

**ticker** A scrolling display of current or recent security prices and volume.

**trade** A transaction of a security or commodity.

**trading** Opening a position in the market, either long or short, with the expectation of either closing it out for profit, or cutting losses quickly if the trade does not work out.

**trading halt** The temporary suspension of trading in a Nasdaq security, usually for 30 minutes, while material news from the issuer is being disseminated over the news wires. A trading halt gives all investors equal opportunity to evaluate news and make buy, sell, or hold decisions.

**trading range** The difference between the high and low prices traded during a period of time.

**trading volume** *See* volume.

**transaction costs** Costs—such as commissions, exchange fees, and the spread—incurred when buying or selling assets.

**trend** The prevailing price movement.

**trend channel** *See* channel.

**trendline** A chart slope representing price movements, connecting the highest and lowest prices of a security. A line connecting either a series of highs or a series of lows is a trend. The trendline can represent support in an uptrend and resistance in a downtrend. Consolidations are marked by horizontal trendlines.

**upgrade** A positive change in ratings for a security. Two common examples are an analyst's upgrading a stock (such as from "sell" to "buy") and a credit bureau's upgrading of a bond.

**uptick** A security transaction made at a higher price than the previous transaction in the security.

**uptick rule** The SEC regulation that states that no short sale may be executed at a price below the price of the last sale. Also known as the plus-tick rule.

**volatility** A term that refers to the range of prices for the market or a security in a given time period. A highly volatile market or security has a wide range in daily prices, whereas a low volatility market or security has a narrow range of daily prices.

**volume** The number of shares traded during a given period, either for a security or for the entire exchange. Also called trading volume.

**Wall Street** The name for the financial district in New York City where the NYSE, AMEX, and many banks and brokerage firms are located. Sometimes used to refer to the investment community in general. Also called the Street.

# Index

## A

Actual size rule, 11, 21–22
Alerts, 62, 63
Analyst reports, 20
Anger, 102
Anxiety, 97–98
Archipelago, LLC (ARCA), 66, 115
Ask. *See* Offer
Attain (ATTN), 115
Auction market, 106, 107
Automated trading, 29
Automatic reaction, 92, 102

## B

Backing away, 22
Bandwidth, 17–18, 40–42
Belief system, 97
Bid, 11, 56, 109–11
Blind spot, 114
Board view screen, 58

Boston (BOSX), 127
BRASS Utility (BRUT), 115
Breakeven stop, 189
Breakouts, 154–55
    wedge buy, 168–70
    wedge sell, 170–73
Browser-based trading system, 52
B-Trade Services, LLC (BTRD), 115
Bulletproof, 95
Buttonwood Agreement, 4
Buyer in control chart, 146

## C

Cable connection, 41
Capital preservation, 95, 187–88
Certainty bias, 101
Chart pattern
    revival buy, 163–66
    revival sell, 166–68
    smart buy, 173–75
    smart sell, 176–77

Chart pattern, *continued*
    use of, 177–78
    wedge buy, 168–70, 171
    wedge sell, 170–73
Chicago Mercantile (CMSE), 127
Cincinnati (CINX), 127
Collusion, 22
Commission ratios, 68
Commitment, 93
Company information, 20
Computer
    hard drive, 44
    memory, 44
    monitor, 44–46
    processor, 16–17, 43–44
Conditional order logic, 62–64
Confidence
    definition of, 98
    knowledge and, 94, 103
    success characteristic, 92
    trading style and, 88
Confirmation, 40
Confusion, 102
Connection speed, 42
Consolidation
    breakouts, 168–73
    chart, 152–53
Continuations, 163
Control bias, 101
Customer service, 66
CyBer Corporation, 19

## D

Day order, 112
Day trader, 35–38, 90, 114
Denial, 102
Destructive self-talk, 94–95
Dial-up connection, 42
Diamonds, 121
*Digital Discipline Report,* 180
Direct access broker, 47–48
    real-time data, 40
    selection of, 50–52
    software trading system, 52
    trading tools, 52–65

Discipline
    personal, 99–104
    success characteristics, 92, 193–97
    trading style and, 88
Discipline cycle, 103, 195–96
Dow Jones Industrial Average (DJIA), 7
Down day chart, 145
Downtime, 66
Down trend chart, 148–49

## E

ECN Direct, 135
Edge, 95–96
Education, 71–73
Educational commitment, 196–97
eGoose.com, 180
Electronic communication network (ECN)
    access to, 65–66
    active, 115
    advantages, 13, 115
    definition, 9
    effect of, 27
    level II screen, 13
    market depth and, 11–13
    overview, 114–16
    purpose, 9
    trade execution time, 27
Electronic matching, 114
Electronic trader. *See* Online trader
Electronic trading platform, 19
    alert screens, 62, 63
    board view, 58
    conditional logic, 62–64
    data screen, 65
    exchange screen, 54–55
    open position screen, 64
    real-time charts, 57–59
    smart logic, 61–62
    stock screen, 52–55
    ticker screen, 56–57
    time and sales screen, 55–56
    top ten screen, 58–59
Emotional biases, 101–2
Emotional cycle, 100
Emotional detachment, 88

Enjoyment, 93
Entry point
    gaps, 186–87
    revival buy, 165
    revival sell, 167
    smart buy, 174
    smart sell, 176
    trading plan, 185
    wedge buy, 170
    wedge sell, 172
Equity markets, 5–14
E*Trade, 47
Exchange Alley, 72
Exchange information, 54–55
Exchanges, 21
Execution
    bid price, 56
    conditional order logic, 62–64
    delays, 48
    direct access, 51–52
    offer price, 56
    real-time, 40
Executioners, 27–28
Exit strategies, 188–90
Exit target, 94
    revival buy, 165
    revival sell, 167
    smart buy, 175
    smart sell, 176
    trading plan, 185–86
    wedge buy, 170
    wedge sell, 172
Exponential growth, 17

## F

Fears, 97–98
Fifth market, 9–14
Fill-or-kill order, 113
Financial consultants, 28
Financial services, 67
Flat day chart, 146
Flat trend chart, 148–49
Flexibility, 92
Floor brokers, 107
Fly on the Wall, 20
Focus, 92, 95, 103

Fourth market, 8–9
Fundamental analysis, 138
Fundamental data, 65

## G

Gaps, 186–87, 190
Gap up, 111
Goals, 91, 92
Going long, 118
Good-till-cancelled order, 113

## H

Hard drive, 44
Hesitation, 95

## I

Inaction, 102
Independence, 92
Index instruments, 121
Information
    availability, 19–21, 29
    proprietary, 20, 21
    real-time, 40
Initial protective stop (IPS)
    exit strategy, 189
    gaps, 186–87
    revival buy, 165
    revival sell, 167
    risk management and, 187
    smart buy, 174–75
    smart sell, 176
    trading plan, 185
    wedge buy, 170
    wedge sell, 172
Initial public offering (IPO), 6
Inside market, 11, 126
Instinet Corporation (INCA), 9, 66, 115, 134
Institutional investor, 8–9, 15, 28
Intelligent routing logic, 61–62
Internet
    connection speed, 42
    reliability, 17–19

Internet service provider (ISP), 18
    bandwidth, 40–42
    connection speed, 42
    customer service, 43
    price, 43
    redundancy, 42–43
    understanding, 41
Investment goals, 86–87, 91
Investor
    belief system, 22–23
    training programs, 29–31
Island ECN (ISLD), 27, 66, 115, 134
ISND connection, 41

## J–K

Japanese candlestick chart, 142–44
    buyers in control, 146
    down day, 145
    flat day, 145
    neutral control, 147
    sellers in control, 146–47
    up day, 144
Knowledge, 94

## L

Latency, 42
Law of the telecosm, 17–18
Level I screen, 53
Level II screen, 53–54, 127–36
    best price, 134
    clockwise movement, 132
    counter-clockwise movement, 132–33
    ECN, 13
    liquidity, 134
    1995, 10
    1997, 12
    rotation start, 131
    timing entry/exit, 133–34
    uptick, 121
Limit order, 111–12, 115
Line chart, 142
Liquidity, 115–16
    in fifth market, 11–13
    level II screen, 134
Long, 116
Long-term investment, 22
Long-term investor, 88–89
Loss, 94
    aversion to, 101–2
    healthy view of, 102

## M

Management, 93
Margin, 122
Market
    access, 15
    change in, 3–4
    forces, 4
    fourth, 8–9
    history, 5
    liquidity, 11–13
Market fundamentals
    ask, 109–11
    bid, 109–11
    ECNs, 114–16
    exchanges, 106–9
    margin, 122
    market makers, 113–14
    orders, 111–13, 115
    primary, 6
    professional, 22–23
    restructure, 27–28
    secondary, 6–8
    specialists, 113
    third, 8
Market maker
    actual size rule, 11
    level II screen, 10, 12, 13
    market depth, 12
    Nasdaq orders, 109
    overview, 113–14
    price disclosures, 21–22
    purpose of, 113
    SOES, 10
    tricks, 114
MarketXT (MKXT), 115
Mental attitude, 95–96, 98–99
Money management, 161, 187–88

Money managers, 28
Monitor, 44
    resolution, 46
    screen size, 45–46
    video card/cache, 46
Moore's law, 16–17
Motivation, 84–85, 91, 92
Moving averages, 155–57
Mutual funds, 28

## N

National Association of Securities Dealers (NASD), 21
    ECN definition, 9
    rule changes, 9
National Association of Securities Dealers Automated Quotation System (Nasdaq), 8–9
    ECN and, 13
    level II, 53–54, 127–36
    overview, 21, 108–9
    price quotes, 127–36
    SOES, 10
Neutral control chart, 147
Newsletters, 180–81
New York Stock Exchange (NYSE)
    ECN and, 13
    electronic orders, 107
    manual orders, 107
    overview, 106
    price movements, 113
    price quotes, 127
    regulation, 21
    Rule 390, 8, 13
    share volume milestones, 6–7
    SuperDot, 107, 113
    trade execution time, 27
Nex Trade (NTRD), 115

## O

Offer, 11, 109–11
Offer price, 56
Online broker
    commission rates, 68
    customer service, 66
    downtime, 66
    ECN access, 65–66
    financial services, 64, 67
    goals, 28–30
    network, 66
    selection process, 65–68
    service types, 66–67
    suitability, 67–68
    training, 67–68
Online trader, 3–4
    education of, 26, 30–31
    goals, 30–31
Open outcry, 106, 107
Open positions, 64
Order
    electronic matching, 114
    execution of, 134–36
    execution delays, 48
    handling, 49–50
    on Nasdaq, 108–9
    on NYSE, 107
    types of, 111–13, 186
Over-the-counter (OTC) market, 8, 108

## P

Pacific (PACF), 127
Partial exit, 189
Payment for order flow, 49–50
Peg the lows, 190
Pension funds, 28
Performance goals, 86
Personality, 90
Philadelphia (PHLX), 127
Pivot points, 89
Point-to-point connection, 41
Portability, 29
Positive mindset, 98–99
Post, 106, 107
Prepared trader, 35–38
Price
    ask, 109–11
    bid, 109–11
    disclosure, 21–22
    fixing, 22

Price, *continued*
    movement, 94, 113, 114, 139–41
    quotes, 126–27
    support, 11
Price chart, 119–20, 141–42
    breakouts, 154–55
    consolidations, 152–53
    Japanese candlestick, 142–47
    line, 142
    moving averages, 155–57
    pattern analysis, 159–78
    resistance, 151
    reversals, 152, 153
    support, 150
    trends, 148–49
Primary market, 6
Pristine.com, 180
Probabilities, 101
Profit, 94
Profit protection, 189–90
Proprietary information, 20, 21
ProTrader Securities, 37

## Q

Quotes
    availability, 20
    real-time, 40

## R

RAM, 44
Range bound trend, 148–49
Real-time charts, 57–59
Real-time data, 40
Redundancy, 42–43, 66
Regulations, 21–22
Regulators, 26–27
Resistance
    chart, 151
    lines, 152
Results, 86–87
Retail brokerage firms, 28
Revival buy, 163–66
Revival sell, 166–68
Reward management, 161
Risk management, 161, 187

Risk/reward, 161
Rule 390, 8, 13

## S

Secondary market, 6–8
Securities Exchange Commission
    (SEC), 21, 121
SelectNet Broadcast, 135
SelectNet Preference, 135
Self-awareness, 195
    anxiety, 97–98
    belief system, 97
    confidence, 98
    edge, 94–96
    investment goals, 86–87
    personal discipline, 99–104
    personal motivation, 84–85
    positive mindset, 98–99
    success characteristics, 92–94
Self-directed investor, 3–4, 22–23
Self regulating organization (SRO), 21
Seller in control chart, 146–47
Share
    number, 185
    value, 7
    volume, 6–7
Short, 116
Short sale, 36, 116–22
Short squeeze, 121–22
Signals, 95, 102
Skills, 86
Slippage, 185
Smart buy, 173–75
Small order execution system (SOES),
    10–11, 134–35
Smart sell, 176–77
Software trading system, 52
Spear, Leeds & Kellogg (REDI), 115
Specialist
    overview, 113
    post, 107, 108
Specialization, 5
Spiders, 121
Spread, 11, 109–11
State Securities Boards, 21
Stock performance analysis, 20

Stock screen
  level I, 53, 125–26
  Nasdaq level II, 53–54
  price quotes, 126–27
Stop limit order, 112–13, 186
Stop loss, 94
Stop order, 112, 186
StreakingStocks.com, 180
Strike Technologies (STRK), 115
Subscriptions, 180–81
Suitability, 26, 29, 67–68
SuperDot, 107, 113
Support chart, 150
Support lines, 151–52
Swing trader, 89
Symbol, 184

## T

TC2000, 20
Technical analysis, 138
Third market, 8
Tickers, 20, 56–57
Time and sales information, 55–56
Time target, 190
Top ten screen, 58–59
Townsend Analytics, 19
Trade
  direct access, 51–52
  execution delays, 48
  exit point, 94
  payment for order flow, 49–50
  reason for, 184
  software system, 52
  symbol, 184
  tools, 52–65
TradeCAST, 19, 61
Trader
  belief system, 97
  characteristics, 92–94
  competition, 194
  preparedness, 35–38
  stages, 137
TradeScout, 61
TradeStation, 20
Trading
  barriers to, 94–95
  beliefs, 94
  firm, 49–50
  goals, 86–87
  information needed for, 19–20, 22
  opportunities, 180–81
  patterns, 116, 117
  psychology of, 94
  rules, 99, 190–91
  skills, 26, 36–38
  steps, 76–80, 99
  style, 88–92
  success cycle, 4, 5
  tactics, 88, 91, 95
  theories, 72
  tools, 29
Trading plan, 102, 184–91
  sample, 180
  statistically valid, 161
Trailing stops, 189–90
Training, 67–68
Training programs, 29–31
Transaction costs, 29
Transaction volume, 29
Trendlines, 155–57
Trend reversal chart, 152, 153
Tsignals.com, 180

## U

Up day chart, 144
Uptick, 121
Up trend chart, 148

## V

Video card/cache, 46
Video monitor, 44–46
Volume, 157–58

## W

Wedge buy, 168–70, 171
Wedge sell, 170–73
Wireless connection, 42

## Z

Zacks, 20

# About the Authors

## KEN JOHNSON

Ken is recognized as a leader in the development of highly-effective educational programs for securities traders. A true pioneer in self-directed trading, he started trading in 1995, founded an independent broker/dealer in 1996, and became president of Cornerstone Securities in 1998.

At Cornerstone in 1999, he was responsible for 550 customers in 19 trading offices across the country, who executed more than 3.1 million trades for more than 2.4 billion shares. These traders generated net trading profits of more than $174 million. His innovative training efforts at Cornerstone helped to solidify its reputation as the home of the very best electronic traders in the country.

Ken, a successful entrepreneur since 1974, has founded, owned, and operated companies in securities brokerage, telecommunications, software development, and real estate development.

Ken has an MBA from Harvard and a B.A. in mathematics from the University of Texas. He is a licensed securities broker (Series 7, 24, and 63) and a licensed pilot with instrument and multiengine ratings.

## HOWARD ABELL

Howard Abell has been a successful trader of equities, futures, and options for more than 30 years. Howard began his trading career on Wall Street in 1968 before starting his own clearing firm, C.S.A., in 1973. C.S.A. was one of the leading trading firms in the Chicago markets.

Howard has more than two decades' experience as a floor trader and exchange member. In addition, he was a principal with Bob Koppel of a proprietary trading firm that trained its own in-house traders.

Howard is the author of *Digital Day Trading, The Day Trader's Advantage, Risk Reward, The Market Savvy Investor,* and *The Electronic Trading of Options.*

He is widely quoted in the financial media about strategies and tactics required for successful online trading. Howard's commitment to financial education goes back at least two decades.

## BOB KOPPEL

Bob Koppel heads the Innergame Division of Rand Financial Services, Inc. He is a former long-term member and professional market maker on the Chicago Mercantile Exchange.

Bob is the author of five books on the psychology of trading: *The Innergame of Trading; The Outer Game of Trading; Bulls, Bears and Millionaires; The Intuitive Trader; The Tao of Trading;* and *The Mentally Tough Online Trader.*

His books have been endorsed by the chairmen of the Chicago Board of Trade, the Chicago Mercantile Exchange, and the Chicago Board Options Exchange, and used widely to instruct professional traders. He holds advanced degrees both in philosophy and group behavior from Columbia University.

Bob was a principal of a proprietary trading company specializing in developing and capitalizing its own in-house discretionary traders. He codeveloped the International Trading Institute's online trading curricula with Howard Abell. He writes on investment for <onmoney.com>.